No Life

Military Wives in Canada

Deborah Harrison and Lucie Laliberté

James Lorimer & Company, Publishers
Toronto, 1994

James Lorimer & Company Ltd. acknowledges with thanks the support of the Canada Council, the Ontario Arts Council and the Ontario Publishing Centre in the development of writing and publishing in Canada.

Canadian Cataloguing in Publication Data

Harrison, Deborah, 1949-
    No life like it : military wives in Canada

Includes bibliographical references and index.
ISBN 1-55028-447-9 (bound) ISBN 1-55028-446-0 (pbk.)

1. Military spouses - Canada. 2. Canada - Armed Forces - Military life. I. Laliberté, Lucie.
II. Title.

U773.H37 1994   355.1'2'0971 C94-931905-8

James Lorimer & Company Ltd., Publishers
35 Britain Street
Toronto, Ontario M5A 1R7

Printed and bound in Canada

Contents

To Canada's Military Wives

Acknowledgements

First and foremost, we would like to thank the Social Sciences and Humanities Research Council of Canada for its financial support of the research on which this book was based (Award No. 882-91-0004). We would also like to thank Brock University for its contribution toward the transcription of interviews. Perhaps the most invisible — yet necessary — work that went into this book was done by the women who transcribed our interviews so competently: Lizzie Brievik, Wendy Carter, Janet Hastie, Heidi Klose, Addie Kobayashi, Arlene Longo, Terry Reid, and Joyce Samuels. Special thanks to Jenny Gurski for directing the transcribing process and to Jan Buchanan, Marianne de Carufel, and Kelly Payne for transcribing the interviews in French. Thanks also to Brock University for a sabbatical year in 1992–93, which enabled Deborah Harrison to construct the database and start the writing process; to Karen Bowder, Annie Relic, and Edie Williams at the Brock Library for the hours they spent tracking down references and photocopying; to Gloria Gallagher and Mary Pisiak at the Computer Centre for technical help; to Martina Gibbons in Accounts Payable for keeping track of our money; and to Deborah's students for their endurance and caring support.

Officials at National Defence Headquarters provided us with information, assistance, and permission to interview certain high-ranking officials. In particular, we acknowledge former Minister of Defence Hon. Kim Campbell, former Associate Minister of Defence Hon. Mary Collins, former Chief of Defence Staff Admiral J.R. Anderson, Assistant Deputy Minister (Personnel) LGen Paul Addy, LCol J.P. Bone, Rae-Ann Freeman, LCol Jim Jamieson, Peter Lufty, Deborah MacCulloch, LCol Rick McLellan, Capt Elizabeth Moar, and Lt Anne Rowe. We would also like to thank Ron Ensom and Dr. David Palframan of Children's Hospital of Eastern Ontario for their good advice.

Friends and colleagues put us up in their homes, organized inter-
views for us, read chapters and lent us support that was helpful and
heartwarming. We're sure to leave someone out, but a partial grati-
tude list includes Betty Alce, Ingrid Alesich, Mary Ballantyne, Joan
Barberis, Eunice Béchard, Malcolm Blincow, Joan Bond, Margaret
Christl, Susan Clark, June Corman, Ann Duffy, Margrit Eichler,
Cynthia Enloe, Gaila and Wayne Friars, Susan Gahrns, Dan Glenday,
Charles Gordon, Carolyne Gorlick, Alison Griffith, Terry Hancock,
Mary Anne and Bob Jablonski, Mike Johnson, Ronnie Leah, Patricia
Lefebour, Ann Manicom, Arlene McLaren, David Omand, Thérèse
Page, Sheila Pattison, Sim Posen, Jennifer Pothier, Joan Rayfield,
Ester Reiter, Stephen Richer, Mary Robertson, Janice Routledge,
Dianne Roy, Paul Sheppard, Stella Slade, Jim Stolzman, Jane Synge,
Peta Tancred, Leslie and Andy Taylor, Rod Tomlinson, Tony Tur-
rittin, Peggy Walden, Michelle Webber and Linda Williams. We
would also like to thank the staff at a number of military family
resource centres who arranged interviews for us, allowed us to use
their facilities, and treated us with wonderful kindness.

We owe a special debt of gratitude to Jim Lorimer for allowing
himself to be persuaded to take on this project. Diane Young, our
editor, has been truly delightful to work with. Our thanks are also
due to Jane Cowan, who copy-edited the manuscript, and Heather
MacLeod, who has worked hard to publicize it.

We can likely never repay our nearest and dearest. Deborah's
husband, Walter Schenkel, has done extra household jobs, read
countless drafts, counselled with patience and sensitivity, and taken
as vicarious an interest as could be expected of any supportive mor-
tal. Lucie's husband, Major Larry Richardson, has answered our
interminable requests for technical information, provided balanced
and valuable feedback, and willingly shouldered the entire domestic
burden when the project has taken Lucie away. Lucie's children —
Heather, Wayne, William, Ruth, and Kate Richardson — have endured Lucie's absences without complaint and have never stopped
believing that the final product will be worth it. Ruth Richardson is
to be especially commended for thinking up a brilliant title — even
if, in the end, we were not able to use it.

Above all, we thank our interviewees for their time and honesty.
And finally, Deborah would like to thank Lucie for introducing her
to a special world in which courage happens every day and the shared
sisterhood is genuine.

Introduction

In 1992–93, Canada spent 7 per cent of its budget — about $11.3 billion dollars — on defence.[1] This money financed Canada's aid-to-the-civil-power operations, search and rescue, external defence, membership in the North American Aerospace Defense Command (NORAD), membership in the North Atlantic Treaty Organization (NATO), and international peacekeeping activities.[2]

Such are the services that we, as taxpayers, receive for our military dollars. Some taxpayers support the present range of military services; others wish that certain military services were different; still others wish that we had no military at all. The role of the military continues to be controversial.

This book is not about the controversies surrounding the benefits of militarism. It is about its non-financial costs. Considering these costs of militarism means considering the qualitative ways in which having a military makes Canada a poorer, rather than richer, place to live.

In wartime, we associate deaths and economic devastation with militarism and, in peacetime, nuclear radiation casualties and the destruction of the environment.[3] Militarism also ties up money that many Canadians feel might more usefully be spent on social programs. These costs are considerable and should be debated more thoroughly than they have been thus far. However, this book is about certain other costs of militarism that have almost never been debated at all — the human costs to the people it affects most directly. Many of these people are military members. Even more of them are members' spouses and children. This book is specifically about what militarism costs military wives.[4]

For those civilian women who do not know any military wives or understand why their lives are significant, perhaps the best introduction is a "what if" visualization.

Supposing this is what your life is like now. You are married, you have two young children, and you have a stable job. Your marriage is tranquil, you share domestic and childcare responsibilities with your husband, and your family has put down roots in a pleasant place. Everything would change if you were to swap places with a military wife. You might suddenly find yourself living on a military base in a house whose size depended on your husband's rank. Your husband would go to work in a uniform. He would spend a lot of time away on exercises, leaving you alone to run the household. He would drink with his workmates and march in parades. Engaging in combat in "hostile" countries would be the highlight of his career. He would be more likely than other men to be an alcoholic or a batterer. To make sure he progressed in his career, you would be expected to do volunteer work on the base and/or entertain his workmates in your home. Your life would be based on his workplace, and your social identity would revolve around his rank. You — and your children — would be uprooted every three years to move to a different city — or country — and adjust to a new neighbourhood, school, set of friends, and low-paying job. You would be unlikely to accumulate much of a pension, and if your marriage broke up, you might spend your retirement years living on welfare.

What is the meaning of this situation for the women who live it? What is its importance to the military? What are its human and social consequences? This book begins the process of providing meaningful answers.

Historical Perspective

In history, military wives have emerged quite recently. England, for example, has maintained standing armies from about 1588,[5] but for a long time they were maintained as bachelor preserves. Unless they were prostitutes, women were viewed as a threat to military discipline and to military members' willingness to fight. Until the mid-nineteenth century, women had no recognized status in military camps, and even if they were legal wives, they were regarded as mere "camp followers" — women who tagged along with the camps, performing sexual and other unpaid services for the men.[6] Camp followers were always "on probation" in the military community: whenever commanders decided that their presence was counterproductive, they were evicted. The military's insistence on keeping women marginal to its enterprise, while at the same time exploiting their usefulness, persists to the present day.[7]

The Crimean War was fought in 1854–56; shortly afterwards, permission to marry was granted to about 6 per cent of army men.[8]

Gradually, the army came to recognize the benefits of marriage, although married members were not as legally obligated as civilian men to support their wives and children until at least 1900.[9] By the end of World War I, a "respectable family life" was considered to be an indispensable asset to a British fighting man's career,[10] although the British army's pay structure continued to be based on the assumption of bachelorhood until 1970.[11]

Recognition of American military wives occurred shortly after the turn of the century, but until World War II, only the officer ranks tended to be married.[12]

No books have yet been written about the camp follower stage in Canada. The Canadian army (from Confederation), navy (from 1910), and air force (from 1920) were basically militias until 1950, when Canada acquired "career" forces for the first time.[13]

There are currently about 46,000 military wives in Canada, about 20,000 former military wives, and perhaps 40,000 wives of members who are retired. Current military wives live on, or near, 41 Canadian military bases and stations. Or they live in the United States, England, or somewhere else in Europe because their husbands have been sent on an exchange or a NATO posting. Many wives also spent time living on, or near, one of Canada's two bases in Germany until these bases were closed in the mid-1990s.

Methodology

Between 1990 and 1993, we interviewed 112 current and former military wives in open-ended unstructured sessions that lasted between two and six hours. The interviews took place in a variety of locations in Ontario, Québec, New Brunswick, Nova Scotia, and Alberta. In 1991 we also conducted interviews at both of the then-operating Canadian bases in Germany. Although we generally used the snowball method of obtaining interviewees, we made sure that all ranks and elements[14] of the service were well represented. In some locations, the names of potential interviewees were provided to us by the base's Family Resource Centre staff. Although most of the interviews were conducted in English, several were conducted in French, and others switched back and forth from one language to the other. With one exception, our interviewees were Caucasian and ranged in age from 16 to 70.

Many of the interviews were emotional experiences. Some of the emotions were joyful. But some of our interviewees were also courageous enough to relive for our tape recorder harrowing portions of their lives. Several women began their interviews with a comment like: "I am going to have nightmares tonight as a result of talking about this, but it is worth it because I want people to know." The opportunity to tell their whole story was one that most interviewees appreciated, partly for personal reasons, partly for motives that were social. Many women expressed strong satisfaction with the goals of our project and told us it was "about time" that the real story of military wives "came out." Between booking their appointments with us and the days of their interviews, a number of women spent time thinking about their lives and greeted us in their living rooms with piles of notes. We were moved by this enthusiasm for our project and hope that our account will resonate with the most important aspects of our interviewees' lives.

Since these interviews were the most important part of our study, we have cited them extensively. We have treated them as confidential and done everything possible to keep them anonymous. We have changed all personal and family names; we have also changed place names, except in cases where doing so would be extremely mislead-ing. Soon after her interview, each interviewee was sent a copy of her interview transcript and reminded that she still had veto power.[15] In a number of cases we subsequently contacted interviewees, ex-plained how we were planning to use their stories, and asked them if they still felt comfortable.

Each interview was assigned a number, and our original intention was to identify the interview number of each quoted passage. But we soon realized that this practice would compromise anonymity. It would have been theoretically possible for a member of the military community to follow, say, Interview 100 through the whole book and, by piecing its bits together, to learn enough about Interview 100 to guess the speaker's identity. Since anonymity was more important to us than the appearance of scientific authenticity, we decided that we could not risk citing our interviews so precisely. Nevertheless, since it will be useful for the reader to know a husband's approximate rank and element, we have included these details whenever we have felt that we could do so safely.

What we wanted from our interviews was rich description. Almost every interview took the form of an oral history, which began with the wife's first military courtship, ended at the present, and paused frequently for elaboration along the way. Since our descriptive theme was military wives' work, interpreted very broadly, we often asked our interviewees to linger over a time period or activity. We frequently asked questions like: "Could you run us through a typical day?" or "What are all the things you do when your husband has been posted and you are getting ready to make the move?"

Since our purpose was to discover how wives are affected by militarism, we could not stop at the details of wives' work. We needed to understand the relationship of wives' work to the military organization: how wives' work contributes to the military, how the military makes sure that wives' work gets done, and what the overall place of wives' work is within the military's structures and goals.

For this reason, we did not interview just military wives. After completing and reflecting on our interviews, we ascended the military hierarchy, interviewing military members (both non-commissioned members and officers), Military Family Support Program personnel, social workers, doctors, padres, National Defence Headquarters administrators, and, finally, National Defence Headquarters generals. In addition, we interviewed a few adult and teenaged children of military members, male spouses of female members, and civilians who worked on military bases. A few of these people were also wives, and some of the interviews at family support centres and National Defence Headquarters were group sessions rather than confidential interviews with individuals. All in all, we conducted 47 interviews with individuals and groups of people who play significant non-wife roles in the military community.

In these latter interviews, our questions were guided by what the wives had told us about their work and the problems their work created. In most confidential interviews with military members, we used the same oral history approach we had used in our interviews with wives, thereby obtaining considerable insight into their work and what it meant to them. In the group sessions and with professionals and senior officers, our main focus was military policy: why the military believed it needed to organize members' (and wives') work in a particular way in order to remain "operationally effective." For example, wives are subjected to special pressures when members are away. We therefore asked members what their away-from-home taskings meant to their careers, and we asked senior officers and generals what away-from-home taskings accomplish for the Department of National Defence.

By the end of our interviews, we had learned a great deal about the military's organizational characteristics and about how they create work for — and rely upon — the work of wives. Accordingly, Chapter One and sections of Chapters Two through Six are exclusively about the military. These segments provide information that will enable the reader to insert the subsequent discussions of wives' work into the appropriate institutional contexts.

Our approach was influenced by the feminist sociological methodology known as *institutional ethnography*, which has been developed by Dorothy E. Smith. Institutional ethnography builds on Karl Marx's theory of alienation — his understanding that those who have been excluded from "the making of ideology, knowledge, and culture" find themselves caught up in systems that have power over, but do not reflect, their own lived experiences.[16] People who do not have very much power — that is to say, most of us — find that our everyday lives are structured by discourses we did not create. Women — who have been largely excluded from the production of knowledge, ideology, and culture — find that our experiences have been used as a mere resource, rather than as the genuine basis of most of the writing that has been done about us. Until recently, most writing done about women derived exclusively from Western men's ideologies and fantasies.

An institutional ethnography attempts to be different. First, it aims to discover women's real lived experiences — especially their work experiences — in order to make these experiences its intellectual starting point. This purpose is grounded in Marx's historical materialist method, examining humans' actual activities. Second, an institutional ethnography aims to understand how this work is embedded in social relations that, although not superficially visible, comprise a segment of the society's "relations of ruling."[17] Among other things, carrying out this task reveals how women's work, officially treated as insignificant, is essential to the perpetuation of these relations of ruling. It also builds on ethnomethodology's earlier insight that invisible, behind-the-scenes drudgery is responsible for most of what is displayed as spontaneously real at the public level.[18] As was the case in Hegel's parable of the master-slave relationship, women are excluded from the frontlines of most institutions, but it is largely their work that keeps these institutions going.

Most women have been excluded from the production of scientific knowledge. To begin from the standpoint of traditional sociology would therefore be to begin from a place outside of women's experience and to produce knowledge that reconfirmed the validity of social scientific categories that arose from the experiences of white Eurocentric males. In contrast, an institutional ethnography tries to work "for" women; it consciously attempts to "take their side."[19]

Like many feminist methods, institutional ethnography rejects the positivist assertion that there is a detached position, uncontaminated by experience, from which social phenomena can be scrutinized. Institutional ethnographers assert that since human beings are a part of what they observe, every observation is inevitably rooted in the observer's (or some other human being's) limited experience. Every investigation begins with particular assumptions, and these assumptions shape the investigation's results. Every investigation thus begins from a determinate place. No observer can avoid the responsibility of making a choice about where this place shall be. The institutional ethnographer's human choice is to begin her research from the standpoints of the actualities of her subjects' lives.

This epistemological stance is clearly relativistic. From it, one might be tempted to conclude that what the institutional ethnographer discovers is neither more nor less "true" than what is found by a male researcher using traditional methods: each perspective is equally valid. On the other hand, until recently women's perspectives have been so excluded from sociological research that institutional ethnographies should be valued for the enormous significance of the vacuums they are struggling to fill.

Institutional ethnography is an especially appropriate methodology for studying military wives. Its premise is that many persons who do a lot of work have very little social power. This notion certainly applies to a group of women of whom considerable unpaid work is expected but who have almost no control over how often they see their husbands, how long they live in one place, what kinds of jobs they have, how long their friendships last, how many disruptions their children experience, whether their accounts of battering are believed, or whether they will have enough money to live on after their working lives end. Military wives are also an excellent example of women whose lives have been harnessed to the requirements of a powerful institution. The military is self-contained as these institutions go and especially amenable to sociological study. It keeps itself isolated from civilians and exercises virtually undiluted influence over its members' and their families' lives. It represents a distinctive and clearly discernible existence.

The Gendered Division of Labour

Military wives can also contribute to the corpus of feminist theory. Their story comprises an important case study in the gendered division of labour and of how the gendered division of labour works to accomplish the objectives of powerful institutions. It also sheds light on the controversy surrounding the gendered division of labour.

In brief, the gendered division of labour has been theorized in the following four general ways:

Conservative Views: Conservative paradigms — especially biologism and functionalist sociology — do not view gender inequality as a problem and regard as "natural" the fact that women do far more housework, child care, and family tension management than men. Biologism argues that women are meant to do this kind of work because of their biological roles in giving birth to and lactating children.[20] Functionalist sociology, as personified by the late Talcott Parsons, argues that the family is a well-balanced "social system" largely because husbands and wives play complementary instrumental and expressive "sex roles."[21] Neither of these views is taken seriously by most sociologists in the 1990s.

Marxist Views: Marxists and Marxist feminists regard the gendered division of labour as a product of capitalist social organization and social relationships. Early contributions to this position implied that the needs of capital actually *determine* the gendered division of labour.[22] That is, capitalism accounts for the fact that men occupy a privileged place in the "public" sphere of paid labour, while women are relegated to the "private" sphere of unpaid household tasks.

It is clear that unpaid household labour is extremely functional to the capitalist system. A recent national estimate by Statistics Canada values this labour at $319 billion dollars a year.[23] This amount is less than what paid workers would receive for doing housework, and what paid workers would receive is in turn less than what housework would receive if it were remunerated according to its real contributions to capitalism. Unpaid housework prepares the next generation of workers for the capitalist workplace and restores the present generation after each workday — through food, sex, clothing care, and tension management — so that workers can return to the workplace refreshed the next day. If capitalist employers had to include the costs of live-in housekeepers, prostitutes, and nannies in their payments to workers in order to assure themselves a steady labour supply, corporate profits would be significantly lower.

Unlike conservative explanations, Marxist-Feminist explanations of the gendered division of labour view gender inequality as a problem. They often make the point that because housework is unpaid, women who do it are exploited by capitalism in a way that their husbands are not. Many Marxist feminists also show how women's assumption of primary responsibility for housework and child care severely handicaps them in the labour market.[24]

Dual-Systems Views: Although they do an excellent job of linking housework to capitalism, Marxist feminists fail to explain why it is women who are expected to do it. After all, individual men also benefit from their wives' unpaid work at home. According to many analysts, Marxist-Feminist explanations of the gendered division of labour have focused so much on the essentially gender-blind economic system of capitalism that they have ignored the process through which a separate system called *patriarchy* has legitimated the appropriation of women's labour by men and the relative exclusion of women from political power.[25] In their view, patriarchy and capitalism together, rather than capitalism alone, are responsible for the gendered division of labour.[26] Dual-systems feminists often cite historical evidence that patriarchy predated capitalism. Or they show how patriarchy operates in societies that are not, strictly speaking, capitalist. Or they attempt to answer the charges of Marxist feminists that patriarchy is too ahistorical to be useful as a concept.

In one of the more developed and inclusive versions of dual-systems theory, Sylvia Walby identifies what she considers to be six patriarchal *structures* (household production, paid work, the state, male violence, sexuality, and cultural institutions), two patriarchal *forms* (private and public), and two patriarchal *strategies* (exclusionary and segregationist). According to Walby, private patriarchy occurs in the father-daughter and husband-wife relationships of the household. It especially thrives when women are excluded from the public sphere. In contrast, public patriarchy originates largely in non-household patriarchal structures and uses strategies that are segregationist and/or subordinating. Walby argues that patriarchy in Western countries was largely private (and exclusionary) during the nineteenth century but that during the present century it has become more public (and segregationist/subordinating) as a result of the expansion of capitalism and the emancipatory (from the private sphere) gains of the First Wave feminists.[27] In making these arguments, Walby has attempted to link a flexible and historically sensitive notion of patriarchy with the unfolding of developments in capitalism. But, unlike Marxist feminists, she has not *subordinated* patriarchy to capitalism.

Later Marxist-Feminist Views: Not all Marxist feminists have been persuaded by dual-systems feminists of the need to develop a theory of patriarchy that accounts for the gendered division of labour in a sphere that is autonomous from capitalism. If most Marxist feminists no longer insist that capitalism *causes* the gendered division of labour, they still maintain that capitalism is historically associated with most manifestations of the gendered division of labour that we experience now. While they admit the existence of patriarchy, contemporary Marxist feminists do not believe that it is possible to isolate it from capitalism. They believe that patriarchy is always inseparable from the specific mode of production in which it finds itself. Marxist feminists are no longer preoccupied with connecting ideal-typical representations of the gendered division of labour with mechanized Marxist renditions of the market, production, and consumption. Instead, they try to link empirical instances of the gendered division of labour with institutions and relationships that can be associated historically with late capitalism. One of the most prominent advocates of this modified Marxist-Feminist approach is Dorothy E. Smith.[28]

This position makes fewer claims on behalf of capitalism than its earlier counterparts, and it is also more difficult to challenge. When we begin to look, we indeed find relatively few patriarchal phenomena that cannot be linked with some manifestation of contemporary capitalism. By making fewer claims on behalf of capitalism, this modified Marxist-Feminist stance also holds out more hope than its predecessors because it no longer implies that we need to dismantle the entire capitalist system in order to effect significant change.

Corporate Wives

Studies on how middle-class wives tend to be *incorporated* into their husbands' jobs presuppose the gendered division of labour and so do not contribute to the theoretical debates about it. They venture no sustained opinion on whether the gendered division of labour is functional, capitalist, patriarchal, or peculiar to certain organizations. Nevertheless, they provide some interesting empirical work that is relevant to military wives.

This literature maintains that certain male-dominated occupations — for example, corporate executive, military member, church minister, and politician — are structured on the expectation that the wives of incumbents will forego opportunities for their own careers in order to devote most of their time to providing support services to their husbands' work. Depending on the husband's occupation, these support services take such forms as entertaining, home visiting, mentoring other wives, attending public functions, doing volunteer work, displaying an exemplary family life, being amenable to frequent transfers, and taking complete care of the homefront so that the husband does not have to worry about it. Many middle-class women do not simply marry men, in other words; they are also expected to commit themselves to doing important parts of their husbands' jobs.[29]

Military Wives

What can the situation of military wives add to the foregoing discussions?

To say that the military community is gendered would be to state the very obvious. In Canada, 87 per cent of regular military members are male.[30] In all other militaries except Israel, the United States, and South Africa, the percentage of male members is even higher.[31] The vast majority of civilian spouses — worldwide — are therefore women.

In Canada, and undoubtedly elsewhere, military life is saturated with the taken-for-granted naturalness of the gendered division of labour. Chapter Two shows how members' frequent long absences presuppose their wives' willingness to assume 100 per cent of the couple's domestic work and childcare responsibilities during several months of the year. Wives are also expected to help members reintegrate into their families when they return home. Many military wives feel compelled to compensate for the destabilizing effects of members' absences by not seeking paid employment, thereby diminishing their future labour market bargaining power.

Chapter Four shows how frequent postings to new locations presuppose military wives' willingness to be continually doing the unpaid work of preparing for, unpacking after, and helping their children adjust to moves. The very fact of postings in itself kills most wives' chances of developing autonomous careers.

In Chapter Five, we see that wives' weak affiliations with the labour market create vacuums in their lives, which make them an ideal reserve army of cheap — and volunteer — "women's work" on military bases. The military takes full advantage of this situation. It also expects officers' wives to be active participants in the military's relentless social life and punishes those officers whose wives fail to comply.

The military is too old an institution to be treated as an epipheno-
menon of capitalism. Nevertheless, the contemporary military may
— for its own purposes — take advantage of capitalist organizational
forms. For example, just as from the bourgeoisie's (or manager's)
viewpoint, capitalism's class structure facilitates an ordered work
force, the military considers its ranking system to be essential to
combat discipline. This relationship between hierarchy and modern
work organization is normally considered to have originated with the
Industrial Revolution. However, the early industrialists actually may
have learned it from the military. As Gareth Morgan notes, Frederick
the Great, who ruled Prussia between 1740 and 1786, transformed
his military from an "unruly mob" into a disciplined machine that
was characterized by ranks, uniforms, rules, and specialized tasks.[32]
Many of Frederick's innovations are alleged to have been later
adopted by industrialists.

In effecting its own marked gendered division of labour, the military may also take advantage of the separation corporate capitalism
has effected between its public and private work spheres. In this
situation, the private unpaid work done by the homemaker is invisible from the standpoint of the capitalist marketplace and regarded
merely as a "personal service" that she performs for love.[33] Certainly,
military wives' unpaid domestic work, which escalates during absences and postings, their volunteer work on bases, and officers'
wives' endless social activities are treated by the military as private
gestures of support directed toward individual men. This fact is
something that the recently divorced military wife, now living on
social assistance, who spent her entire working life moving across
the country from one poorly paid job to another and accumulating
little or nothing in the way of her own pension, understands all too
well. Chapter Seven illustrates how specific military ideologies have
added to the effect of the normal capitalist public/private separation
to make the invisibility of military wives' domestic work even more
pronounced. Still, we should be aware that some authors have argued
that the separation between public and private spheres is not, strictly
speaking, a capitalist phenomenon. Instead, it may have predated
capitalism, and it may exist in certain contemporary societies for
reasons that are wholly religious.[34]

One spinoff of the public-private separation that *is* peculiar to
contemporary capitalism is the idea that through performing her
unpaid domestic tasks the middle-class wife invests in her own future
by investing in her husband's career. As she entertains her husband's

colleagues, advises her husband about the "people" aspects of his job, schools her children in proper deportment, and donates an appropriate amount of her time to charity work, the manager's wife feels personally rewarded as her husband achieves promotions, buys a larger home, and gains membership in more prestigious social circles. As Chapter Five shows, the military officer's wife is structured into an identical process. As a result of the military's segregation from civilian society, the many ways in which the military elicits her direct loyalty to its organization, and the fact that she has almost no opportunity to develop her own career, the officer's wife often invests in her husband's career even more intensely than would a civilian woman in comparable circumstances. The nature of military life also encourages non-commissioned members' wives to invest in their husbands' careers in ways that are not normally expected of non-managerial corporate wives.

In contemporary capitalist societies, the ways in which the military appropriates wives' labour thus roughly correspond with the ways in which civilian women find their work appropriated by their husbands and their husbands' employers. However, in the military instances, the impacts on wives are especially pronounced.

The ways in which the military excludes and subordinates wives fit into the Marxist-Feminist paradigm less readily. As Chapter One points out, male bonding is a very important feature of military culture. Its purpose is to facilitate unit cohesion, which, in turn, is considered indispensable to waging effective combat. Military male bonding cements itself largely by virtue of its ritual exclusion and derogation of women. Within the context of military male bonding, to be male is to be not female, which is to be valued positively.[35]

Even before the advent of capitalism, male bonding was an important aspect of military life. Varda Burstyn has attributed militarism's male bonding to a "masculine dominance" that she believes operates independently from capitalism.[36] The accuracy of Burstyn's observation depends on whether or not the nature of military male bonding has changed since pre-capitalist times.

Male bonding is not the only way in which the military endeavours to make itself exclusively masculine. According to Cynthia Enloe, the struggle of most national militaries to prevent women from playing combat roles has fundamentally comprised an effort to maintain the fiction that only "real men" are fit to fight.[37] In Sylvia Walby's terms, excluding women from combat has been a "segregationist" patriarchal strategy. Since combat bravery is a highly prized individual characteristic, excluding women from combat has also excluded them from sharing the honour that is bestowed upon individuals who wage wars successfully. Since in many countries only those persons who are fit to fight are considered fit to rule, excluding women from combat has additionally justified excluding them from positions of political power.[38]

The military is thus enormously gendered, both in the ways it appropriates women's unpaid labour and in the ways it excludes, subordinates, and segregates them. The ways in which the military is gendered are fuelled by, and also contribute to, the patriarchal elements of both the capitalist system and the political state. Appropriating women's labour is one of the military's ways of trying to keep itself exclusively masculine and to keep the social order revolving around the presumption of male pre-eminence.

A related military strategy, directed toward similar ends, is to cling to the conservative notion of a masculine-feminine polarity, as opposed to the liberal idea of a masculine-feminine continuum or the more recent postmodern view that "masculinity" and "femininity" are mere fabricated societal constructions. Keeping alive the masculine-feminine polarity notion realizes three important objectives. First, by claiming that women are fundamentally different from men, it justifies continuing the military's current behaviours of appropriating, excluding, subordinating, and segregating them. Second, as Cynthia Enloe has noted, the masculine-feminine polarity helps to justify the military's continued existence by keeping feminized victims set up as the idealized oppositional counterparts of the masculinized soldier-heroes who are supposedly needed to rescue them from danger.[39] Third, by reinforcing the masculine basis of military camaraderie, the masculine-feminine polarity solidifies unit cohesion and contributes to combat readiness.

In conclusion, military wives — and indeed women military members — can add to our understanding of the gendered division of labour, but they cannot settle the question of how it should be theorized. Certainly, male bonding, the attempt to exclude women from combat, and the idea of a masculine-feminine polarity are all features of the military that predate capitalism. Nevertheless, only a detailed feminist historical analysis could determine whether these features have changed in nature since the Industrial Revolution. Whether the military's present gendered division of labour is most attributable to capitalism, capitalism and patriarchy, or a patriarchal system that, while interacting with other institutions, remains fundamentally uniquely military is a question that has still to be answered.

Wherever the gendered division of labour comes from, the military utterly depends on it. Military wives place in bold relief the fact that all women are made extremely vulnerable by the expectation that they will do, largely by themselves, the invisible work that keeps social institutions going.

1

No Life Like It

It is an impressive sight from the road. Long white buildings perch astride rolling hills. Flags snap in the wind, and fierce cannon decorate the uneven landscape. Each barracks is named for a ship, and the ensemble collectively presides over a spectacular panorama of the Annapolis Valley.

The place is Canadian Forces Base Cornwallis, the training centre for English-speaking non-commissioned recruits to the military.[1] In 1992–93, 499 male and female recruits arrived at Cornwallis by bus.[2] After being processed through eight weeks of exercise, drill, attitudes, and hygiene, which culminated in a formidable obstacle course, most of them emerged as full-fledged privates (or, in the navy, able seamen), willing to serve the Canadian Forces for at least the 20 years it would take until they were eligible to retire with a full pension. Why did these young people enlist in the Forces? More importantly, why will most of them want to stay?

Why Recruits Enlist
Recruits enter the Forces for a variety of reasons. Some enlist because one or both of their parents did and provided a positive role model. Some recall their parents' remembrance of service in World War II as a time of close friendships and common purpose. Others enlist as a way of attempting to become closer to a military parent (usually the father) who was absent and/or remote during their childhood.

Still others enlist out of a fascination with machines, the glamour of certain military trades (e.g., fighter pilot), or an enjoyment of playing "war games" as a child that has continued into adulthood. As one male member puts it: "You can play cowboys and Indians (sic) until you're 55!"

Some recruits never enjoyed school and viewed the military as a respectable way to drop out.[3] Those in this category sometimes remember themselves as nonconformists or rebels who felt frustrated by the school's attempts to regiment them. They regarded joining the Forces as an instant promotion to adulthood, which would at the same time extricate them from a situation they found painful. For others, the painful situation was an unhappy home, from which the military offered a dignified exit that gave them money in the bank and the opportunity to move far away.

But most join the military for economic reasons. Some recruits come from families with many children whose parents are unable to pay for their education. Others join during a recession or because they can find no work in the field for which their education prepared them. Some, young and inexperienced when the recruiter came to their high school, remember thinking that the money they would be paid sounded phenomenal. Of the 2,567 applicants to the Canadian Forces in the summer of 1975, 51 per cent were unemployed, compared to only 7.5 per cent of the overall Canadian population.[4] The vast majority of economically motivated recruits come from the Maritime provinces, which have always offered relatively few viable employment options other than seasonal and/or factory work. While the Maritime provinces represent 10 per cent of the national population, they account for between 20 and 35 per cent of the Forces' annual intake.[5] Recruits from other parts of Canada often come from single-industry towns, which also offer only a narrow range of employment alternatives.

Economic need also motivates the decision to stay in the Forces. That is, one of the most important continuing powers the military wields over its members is money. Certainly, when they are asked why their husbands have decided to remain in the Forces, most military wives cite financial security as the most compelling reason. And members themselves often agree. But most long-time members also admit that their loyalties are more intricate. Whatever their original motivations for joining, something positive begins to happen to most recruits during their eight long weeks at boot camp.

The Military Ethos

The military has a job to do, which, according to its strategists, is second to none. This judgment rests upon two assumptions, the first being "The Omnipresent Enemy." "The Omnipresent Enemy" assumes that "we" — the nation, the NATO alliance, or the developed world — have military enemies and we will always have military enemies and that it is inherent in human nature to make war. There are also enemies within our own borders, as the separatist and indigenous land claim movements have apparently demonstrated. There are even enemies amongst our allies, who, if undeterred by strong forces of our own, could some day turn on us. There are enemies in the "overcrowded world," who covet our ocean and Arctic space.[6] Potential enemies still lurk in Russia. For all these reasons, armed forces are absolutely essential to our social formation. In 1962, the Canadian military was 126,474 strong, but the end of the Cold War has entailed a significant downsizing. By the end of 1992, the total had been reduced to 80,651; by the middle of 1993, it was closer to 78,000; and the total projected for the end of 1993 was 75,000.[7] These developments reflect public opinion and recessionary economic pressures rather than any belief on the part of senior officers that Canada should no longer prepare for war. According to one general at National Defence Headquarters, Canadian "peaceniks" fail to appreciate the permanent inevitability of human armed aggression:

> They feel, you know, that you remove all these causes and it's all going to fall into place. I mean, this is absolute garbage! I mean, it's like sin! I don't know whether you're Christians, but the Lord got crucified to do away with sin. We've got thousands of priests and deacons out there — there's a lot of sin still going on! So if we think that by removing the priests we're not going to have any more sin, I think we're smoking opium! The same thing applies to the Armed Forces!

The second military assumption is that force is legitimate. Negotiations, this assumption states, are perennially fragile, perennially vulnerable to chaos and collapse. Human nature being what it is, nations, alliances, and governments often fail to bring others around to their own "correct" view. At these times, they need to order their militaries to kill — and be killed — to uphold the righteousness of their interests. Distasteful as we may find it, killing "works."

If we subscribe to these assumptions, Canada needs a continued strong military, and militarism is an essential service. Several specific principles follow from this judgment. The most important of them is combat readiness, the doctrine that at a moment's notice a given quantity of person- and equipment-power must be prepared to fight. Combat readiness, the military's keynote preoccupation, results from the successful convergence of a number of factors. According to one general, readiness fundamentally requires capability and time — capability meaning top-capacity equipment and members, time meaning the time necessary to produce these capacities.

Since no activity is more stressful than combat, training is the military's major job. To do its work effectively, the military must inculcate both technical skills and the motivation to engage in combat, perform it effectively, and endure it until its end. The technical parts of combat are the results of training — in the skills and methods themselves and in responses that become so thoroughly ingrained that they will be automatic in any circumstance. The ability to respond quickly is especially important. Members must always be prepared for combat. They are often awakened in the middle of the night and ordered to report to their work posts as practice enactments of the real thing. They are sent on exercises, courses, or six-month postings to places like Cyprus at a few hours' notice, a practice that often has more to do with operational psychology than with operational necessity.

Operational psychology is crucial. At a second's notice, members involved in combat need to be able to fuse technical skill, cool-headedness, instantaneous response, fierce loyalty to their comrades, and the willingness to do what is necessary to eradicate a physical threat. The wife of a fighter pilot recalls, from her vantage point, how combat training changed her husband:

> When he went from the training squadron he went through fighter weapons school, and that is when he became a killing machine. And when I first met Pete, I said to him one day, "Could you fly over a village and bomb?" 'Cause I'm kind of a peacenik. ... And he said to me, "No, I couldn't do that." And about midway through fighter weapons school, I noticed this wall — not towards me or towards anybody — but I noticed something changing. And he was becoming this fighting machine. And I don't know how they did it, but they did it. And I said to him, "Could you fly over a village and bomb?" He said, "If I was ordered to, yes." That cold and simple. And I went, "My God, what have I married?"

Because military members must continually brace themselves for the ultimate — the sacrifice of their lives — the combat readiness imperative requires that they be "tough." Part of the struggle of being military is that so much of military life is at loggerheads with the values most civilians cherish — civil liberties, freedom from violence, reverence for life and nature, freedom from authoritarianism, and clearly defined periods of relaxation.

Military people often feel misunderstood by civilians, and so they tend to stick together — a development that is not at all unintended. Combat readiness requires the military to control its members, and part of this control means keeping them — and, to a large extent, their families — segregated from civilian society and from its competing preoccupations and ideologies.[8]

Erving Goffman defines a "total institution" as "a place of residence and work where a large number of like-situated individuals, cut off from the wider society for an appreciable period of time, together lead an enclosed, formally administered round of life."[9] Military members are extremely mobile, leaving their posting in a particular location every two to four years to accept a new one elsewhere. At any given time, about 7 per cent of them are serving outside of Canada. Nevertheless, the military is a portable total institution that isolates its members from civilians wherever they move, isolates them from civilians *because* they move, and makes the military community in many ways sufficient unto itself. As is the case with other total institutions, isolation from civilians facilitates control.

For many of the eight weeks of basic training, recruits are forbidden to leave the training centre. As in the asylums described by Goffman, the recruit is forced to relinquish most of the props of his or her previous life — clothes, jewellery, long hair, friends, family, privacy — and replace them with what the military provides — haircut, uniform, army cots, dormitories, and the beginnings of a new identity. Canadian officer recruits theoretically can either attend one of two officer boot camps — Borden in Ontario or Chilliwack in B.C. But they are in fact sent to the camp farthest from their homes, so that during the short breaks in training they will be unlikely to be able to visit relatives or friends.

Basic training is the recruits' initiation into the total institution of the military and into the military's preoccupation with bringing and keeping its members under control. We typically think of control as a constraint on personal freedom that makes us miserable. Civilians especially imagine military control to be disagreeable, because the stereotyped images military life projects outward — uniforms, guns, death, and regimentation — have so little appeal. In reality, however, much of military control makes its members happy. It entails a combination of rewards and punishments that achieves its operational objectives and moulds its personnel into the kinds of loyal enthusiasts that corporation presidents envy. There are as many tasty concoctions in the mixture as unpleasant ones.

Conditioned Obedience

Success in combat requires a chain of command that works. Those giving the orders must make quick decisions and command the respect of the people under them. Those receiving the orders must obey them — fast — in situations where their immediate instinct would be to run. Perhaps the most important thrust of basic training, and of the first few years of service, is drilling into members the habit of instant, unquestioning obedience. The strategy of basic training is constant drill, accompanied by constant negative reinforcement, until the recruit is ready to crack. At this moment, the instructor injects something positive to encourage the recruit to keep trying. Deprived of approval for so long, he or she pounces on this morsel. The ensuing emotional roller coaster produces dependence on the instructor's strokes. The instructor takes on the character of a parent whom the child wants to please. He or she becomes the source of all reward and punishment, the passionately revered leader. According to one non-commissioned member:

> They make you feel dependent on it. Once you're in, they make you feel like you can't make it out there. ... "You do what we want and we'll do everything for you." That's the attitude. "You can't do anything for yourself." ... Well, after a while it's just like a child with a parent. You don't want to disappoint them, you're afraid to. You don't know what the consequences are going to be, so you do it. You do what you're told.

Obedience saves lives during combat. An order provided by a person in authority, and the automatic execution of that order, can pull a whole unit out of life-threatening jeopardy. As a navy member explains:

> In the Falklands, a ship got hit — got whacked. And the shock was so great, even though the guys weren't killed. I mean, you are talking maybe 600 or 900 pounds of explosives hit the ship — just picked the ship out of the water. And what they immediately did — they found later on — they took an executive officer — an engineer — and flew him over from the other ship,

'cause the guys were just in a daze. And then as soon as somebody got on there, started issuing orders, everybody immediately came back. And that's where the drill comes by, okay? "Somebody is in charge — I am going to be all right."

Linked to obedience is hierarchy. For the same reason that obedience is crucial, military hierarchy is sacrosanct. Although enlightened supervisors will consult with the persons under them before making important decisions, the normal military flow is through the chain of command.[10] The most compelling rationale for hierarchy is knowledge. Since the commander of the mission is responsible for it, he or she must know every single relevant factor in order to exercise this responsibility optimally.

One of the worst sins a member can commit is passing information to someone outside the chain of command before people in the chain have learned about it. One non-commissioned member was disturbed late at night by other members making noise on military property that adjoined his backyard. Reacting like an annoyed civilian, he neglected to inform his own supervisor and went directly to the supervisor of the noisemakers. As a result, he was formally charged.

The commanding officer's need to know justifies his or her possession of an enormous amount of "pertinent information" about the individuals within the command. "Pertinent information" is interpreted so broadly that military doctors, social workers, and padres often violate the confidences entrusted to them.

The significance of the chain of command is one of the most strongly inculcated lessons of boot camp. Recruits who "mess up" in any way are terrorized about "what the sergeant will do." They learn to address their superior officers as "sir" wherever they see them, whether it be on base, at a house party, or at a shopping mall, and this habit remains with them until they reach the highest ranks. Even when they do not speak, they learn to salute superiors in uniform, wherever and whenever they encounter them. One practical reason for formal address arises from the requirements of combat. Officers find it easier to request "Corporal Bloggins" to lay down his life than they would to request it of Harry or Fred.

Higher military rank brings increased responsibilities. It also brings increased pay and exaggerated privileges, unrelated to operations, which seem bizarre to most civilians. "Messes," the places on bases where members eat, socialize, drink, and attend formal dinners, are rigidly segregated; even on the smallest stations there are three

— one for junior ranks, one for senior ranks and non-commissioned officers, and one for officers. Housing provided on bases is similar. Non-commissioned members and their families typically live in apartments or row housing, while senior officers occupy spacious detached homes with fireplaces. Rank also applies to medical care. Members who are sick are looked after by military medical personnel or by civilian personnel employed on contract. Spouses and children are under military care only at remote postings or outside Canada. At all MIR (Medical Inspection Room) facilities, sometimes regardless of the seriousness of their illnesses, high-ranking members (and, where applicable, their dependents) are permitted to jump queues in order to see medical staff. Civilian doctors who have worked in MIRs have been appalled at how the rank system operates in waiting rooms, and they have consequently found their working conditions difficult. In the words of one such doctor:

> Sometimes you'd be told "Oh so-so, he's a lieutenant colonel. He's coming over right now to be seen." And you know, I'm sure if he'd been a corporal he would have sat in the waiting room for a lot longer. And even with the dependents. All dependents were listed as W/LTC or W/Corporal or … Like everybody was wife of corporal, spouse of corporal, whatever.

Passing information up the chain of command is valued so highly in the military that the rewards for this behaviour sometimes threaten the stability of "unit cohesion," the well-known solidarity amongst peers that has its own operational rationale and that the military also encourages. According to many military members, those within the ranks who receive the fastest promotions are often the ones who spend the most time fraternizing with, drinking with, and feeding information to their immediate supervisors. One former non-commissioned member, who did not play this game, recollects:

> I would definitely say that if you're gonna go drinking with your sergeant or warrant officer or the guy who writes your PER[11] report, and you're gonna be buddy buddy with him, it's gonna be in your favour.

Members who were once supervisors admit that the information they received when members relaxed and unwound was highly prized and helped them to run their units more effectively. One former army officer remembers:

> When I really wanted to find out what was happening in the troop, especially if we were in the field, I'd go grab a couple cases of beer, gather everybody around, open up the beer, and go for it. I'd have one, stay sober, and they'd all get drunk and tell me everything that was wrong in the world, including what was wrong with me. And it was great, because I got more information that way. I really found out what was on their chest.

Linked with the violation of unit solidarity is the Code of Military Honour, which requires that members reveal secrets about their peers whenever supervisors ask them to.[12] Failure to do so is severely punished. This requirement again stems from the commanding officer's unquestioned need to know. It means that a member who confides in a friend risks having the confidence betrayed and that any member who is privy to a friend's revelation can suffer agonizing distress. After learning that her roommate was a lesbian, one member attempted to slash her wrists to avoid revealing what she knew to the authorities.[13]

In general terms, combat readiness demands such unquestioning loyalty that individual members have virtually no rights. Through "good behaviour" they are permitted to earn privileges that are often bestowed on the basis of whims. Military members do not belong to unions. Unions are anathema to military discipline, as is the entire principle of rank-and-file influence. There is no mechanism for collective dissent. Military members are not permitted to sign petitions complaining of unjust working conditions. If they do, they are considered guilty of mutiny. An individual who feels unfairly treated may register an after-the-fact protest called a *redress of grievance*. However, the appeal process is long and cumbersome and usually entails career costs, even though the regulations governing redress state otherwise. Since members are well aware of these costs, they seldom initiate proceedings. Every year, each member receives from the military a "merit rating" called a Personnel Evaluation Report (PER). These ratings are extremely important, especially because they are used by merit boards to decide on promotions. The member reads and signs the report, which has been prepared by his or her superior. Refusal to sign is a theoretical right and signals strong disagreement with the report's contents. In practice, most of those who threaten to refuse to sign are swiftly bullied into capitulating.

If drill and hierarchy inculcate the habits of obedience, the significance attached to the contents of the drills makes recruits realize that no matter how trivial a military job is, it needs to be done absolutely right. Among other skills, new recruits learn to take showers, clean weapons, make beds, shine boots, wash floors, pack lockers, shave fastidiously, dress wounds, and march in time — all according to military specification. Recruits who make a single mistake find their efforts ruthlessly torn apart and themselves mocked and humiliated in front of their platoon-mates. A minor infraction can result in the punishment of the whole platoon, a detail that deepens the transgressor's misery.

From the point of view of combat, the need to do things properly is as important as the need to obey and to follow the chain of command. If blowing up a particular bridge will keep the enemy from advancing, the task must be completed flawlessly. There will not be a second chance, and the lives of everyone in the unit will be at stake. Tearing apart recruits who do not make their beds properly lays the groundwork for producing Forces members who will not fail their units in times of stress.

An important aspect of recruit conditioning is the parade. To a civilian, a parade often seems like a mere spectacle carried out for children and patriots. But its real purpose is to teach concentration on tasks. When a Cornwallis drill instructor barks, "Move to the right in threes!" he points left at the same time, and then screams at the recruits who follow his hand. Concentrating means doing what the instructor actually says. To this effect, parade drills condition relentlessly. According to one military member, the soldier who stared down a First Nations leader during the Oka standoff was only using his boot camp parade skills:

> He stared down Lasagne because of parade training, not because of his superior intellect. He stared him down because he had been in a parade, and you don't move, you don't move, you don't move. And when Lasagne spit at him, he didn't move. That was parade training, that was conditioning, and he got his good press. Four or five of the kids didn't break, didn't hurt anybody, didn't hit anybody. Conditioning!

Performing flawlessly in the military means performing flawlessly under stress. New members are tested again and again on their abilities to perform difficult tasks competently while under physical or psychological duress. Punishments for making the most trivial mistakes are harsh. Some boot camp survivors report having been forced to go without water after exercising in extreme heat. And part of the boot camp instructor's general task is to find the weak spot in each recruit in order to exploit it ruthlessly. One former instructor summarizes:

> They'll pick a weakness in you one way or another. They'll find it somewhere. Some people are more concerned about their weaknesses than others, but everybody does have some sort of weakness or some fear. The instructor's job is to find it, capitalize on it, and apply as much pressure to that individual to see just how much he can take.

"A Bond So Thick It's Unbelievable"
But military life also has its rewards. While drill may inculcate the obedience and discipline essential to combat, it does not inculcate the willing spirit. The motivation to engage in combat — if necessary until death — arises from *unit cohesion*. The strong bonding and mutual commitment developed amongst members of a combat unit counteracts the anxiety of being in danger and provides its participants with an emotional high. Military members do not remain in combat for political ideologies or politicians. They do it for each other, for the others on their team, for their buddies. As one retired member explains it:

> A little private out in the trenches doesn't know beans all about why he is there, except he is there with his buddies and they will die for one another. It's as simple as that.

The unique structure of military life — its isolation from civilian life, its self-sufficiency, its distinct uniforms, traditions, rules, and values — facilitates a closeness and bonding amongst members during peacetime that only requires intensifying during war. In the words of one member:

> We are a society unto ourselves, and we do what we want. I don't have to go to a civilian doctor, dentist, lawyer or ... and

that's to make you look inward. You know what I am saying? Everything I need is in the Armed Forces; therefore I think of nothing outside. I mean, your thinking is nothing else. ... It's the way we do things, it's parades, it's the Mess. It's all done that way to make the bonding this close. The higher the risk job, the greater the call for the bonding.

Boot camp often provides members with their most intense — and remembered — military bonding. One member recalls:

You have a bond. You have a bond that's so thick that it is unbelievable! ... It's the pull, it's the team, the work as a team, the team spirit! I don't think that ever leaves a guy. That is exactly what basic training is supposed to do. It is supposed to weed out those who aren't willing to work that way. ... And that's the whole motivation, that when somebody says we want you to do something, then you'll do it. You'll do it because of the team, for the team, with the team, and because the team has the same focus.

Part of the solidarity of a boot camp platoon comes from doing things at the same time. Enduring the "gas chamber,"[14] the parades, the drills, and the duty of cleaning washrooms together itself enhances fellowship. During the first weeks of boot camp, interaction with people outside the platoon is discouraged, thus cementing the insiders' bonds. Meanwhile, the members of each platoon pull together as the platoons compete for awards. Receiving the commandant's pendant six weeks in a row for the cleanest barracks, for example, can result in a platoon being excused from the obstacle course. Punishing the entire platoon for one member's mistake likewise encourages solidarity, since the platoon will plot together afterwards to "get even." Meanwhile, eager to avoid more punishment, platoon members will vigorously police one another's conformity. The obstacle course is performed by platoons as well as by their individual members. Recruits who help their platoon-mates finish the course receive even more rewards at its end than those who run it well alone. Experiencing their fortunes rising and falling collectively increases the closeness of platoon members and also simulates the situation of combat, in which one member's false move — or act of heroism — reverberates on all.

In the years immediately following boot camp and trades training, those who are still single reside in barracks, while their married comrades often take up residence in PMQs (Permanent Married Quarters), which is base housing provided at market rent. The intensity of boot camp platoon life thus continues in diluted form as new members fit themselves into the military structure of maintaining combat cohesiveness by merging home with work. Members are generally encouraged to eat and drink in their messes and to spend their off-work time fraternizing and sharing information with peers and supervisors. But barracks occupants experience the merged existence most directly; the cramped conditions within their private quarters (between two and four to a room) literally squeeze them out into the common space. Companionship and cheap liquor, both always plentiful in military communities, provide incentive and stimulus. As one former non-commissioned member recalls:

> It was great, really. Because they had a live band. It was a very small club. They had a great big hip of beef or turkey or something. And you'd go and help yourself at night. The beers were ten cents a beer. A shot was 20 cents. You'd go up there, get a case of beer for a dollar twenty, take it unopened, put it under the table. And later on if you wanted a shot of rye, you'd take two beer, unopened, they'd give you a shot of whatever. … There was music there, there were pool tables, shuffle boards. And you'd go in after work and have a beer. And you'd socialize that way. Get out of the barracks.

The habit of unit esprit de corps inculcated at boot camp continues throughout the member's career. The platoon competitions staged at boot camp evolve into chronic good-natured rivalries between working units — as, in the army for example, between supply and transport. These rivalries do not impede the element's overall co-ordination, and they enable members to bond within contexts that are small enough to foster intimate comradeship. While members within units may have their differences, they have learned at boot camp about the indispensability of a united front. Members of units — and sometimes, in the army, whole regiments — normally stick up for one another and tolerate no criticism of members from persons outside. The united front often extends beyond the unit, regiment, or element to incorporate the whole armed forces. Retired members look back on this solidarity with wistfulness, as a once-cherished comfort that their lives no longer hold.

The united front within the unit is comprehensive and extends even to covering up and compensating for others' mistakes. This behaviour begins at boot camp where platoons, eager to win pennants, develop informal systems of spelling off or covering up for members who are tired or who have committed errors. Covering up for weaker members to enable the whole team to prosper is a behaviour that continues. Members' annual PER assessments are always partly based on their performances as team players, which includes fraternizing after hours and "supporting the Mess." Unit leaders develop feelings of responsibility and protectiveness toward those under them and will do small things to give them a break. For example, if army units are posted on exercises in a spot that is a short distance away from the PMQs, leaders will sometimes stand in for subordinates on guard duty and allow them to go home to their spouses for the night as long as they are back in time for the 4:00 a.m. reveille. Such gestures maintain everyone's spirits, forestall burnout, and keep up unit morale. The same kind of covering up is often extended to problem drinkers and wife batterers, however, to the detriment of their families.

Unit cohesion often means slavish conformity — being with the group even when one would rather be elsewhere. Conformity is the natural outcome of intense bonding and of the reward and punishment systems that are directed at teams. And conformity is the characteristic of young military adults that most stands out in comparison with their civilian counterparts. One university student who dated a military college cadet remembers going to the college Hallowe'en party and seeing at least ten cadets dressed up as Rambo. "Supporting the Mess" means being there during free time when some married members would rather be home. Newlywed members often experience a searing conflict of loyalties between the bonding behaviour military life demands — and expects — and the bonding that is meant to happen during the early stages of a marriage. While conformity is expected of members throughout their careers, the requirement hits them most conspicuously at boot camp, during their early years of service, and during important training courses. In the latter instances, even those who live on or close to the base where the course is held are expected to eat and sleep in barracks and return home to their families only on weekends.

The entire military career, however, is punctuated with social functions that every member must attend. Mess[15] dinners are especially important — and spouses are not invited.[16] Mess dinners are ritualized affairs at which the dress is extremely formal (a special outfit called a "mess kit"), the crystal and china are the best money can buy, the food is excellent, and the behaviour is highly stylized. Members are piped into the dining room in a particular order, sit at places assigned to them, are not allowed to leave the table, endure a number of ceremonial speeches and toasts, and pass the port in a specified direction without allowing it to touch the table.

Because it is most likely to encounter hand-to-hand combat, the army places the most emphasis on reinforcing unit bonding, team playing, supporting one's comrades right or wrong, and formal ritualistic traditions. The Canadian army contains several *regiments,* each of them specializing in a particular form of combat (for example, the Airborne Regiment or the Strathcona Horseguards), but each of them is also large enough to provide its own support services. Regiments — and, in the case of infantry, the sub-units within them called *battalions* — are like large families, which consider themselves responsible for their members' welfare. Battalion and regiment commanders know intimately all the persons who work under them. They know the names and backgrounds of their spouses, the names and ages of their children, their hat sizes, their shoe sizes, their important likes and dislikes, and their strengths and weaknesses on the job. This intimate knowledge has an important operational function, which relates back to the importance of information flow up the hierarchy. The leader of a group whose members might be faced with direct combat needs to have a good idea of how each of them would respond to the stress.

If infantry members run short of money, the battalion makes available an emergency fund. When members are away, the regiment assumes responsibility for their families and is available to the spouses (usually wives) to shovel snow, fix cars or toasters, provide entertainment, and babysit. Regimental members are extremely loyal and behave toward one another according to a strict morality code. One member was recently thrown out of a Canadian regiment for "stealing" the "property" of another member — his wife. Similarly, an army wife recalls being visited regularly by two of her husband's bachelor battalion-mates during her husband's six-month tour in Cyprus. On each visit, the young men politely asked if she needed anything — from the safe distance of the other side of her threshold.

Not once in the entire six months did they cede to her entreaties to step in for tea. The regimental code of keeping their hands off a unit-mate's "property" precluded their doing so.

While the army may be the most ritualized and closely knit of the military communities, the community spirit that envelops units and their families surpasses their civilian counterparts in all elements. Just as it is the unit's business to know its members, it is also its business to know what happens to them. When a member or someone in his or her family dies, the military family rallies around. The unit looks after funeral arrangements, provides limousines, flies relatives in on military planes, reroutes ships, and mobilizes women to donate food. When someone loses a family member, the military immediately flies him or her home. Even if it is someone in the member's spouse's family who has become ill or died, the military (with the member's permission) will try to accommodate the spouse on a flip.[17] When a member or someone in his or her family becomes sick or a member or member's wife has a baby, unit comrades will send flowers, visit, babysit, provide rides to the hospital, or take up a collection. Members who become terminally ill are often encouraged to report to work when they feel like it, and on these occasions workmates will go out of their way to help them feel useful. The "caring military community," often cherished by members and their families, is really a backup replica of the cohesive combat unit. At times like the Persian Gulf War, it can be revitalized quickly to supply needed support to spouses and children.

In similar fashion, the military often makes a special point of providing positive reinforcement for work well done. It has its own methods of assertiveness training that are designed to build its members up, to make them as strong as individuals as they are as members of teams. Some of these methods are as simple as public speaking lessons. The military also bolsters self-esteem more directly in the form of medals, awards, and ceremonies to celebrate members' promotions. A long-time member reports:

> Uniforms, medals, awards — that's self-esteem. We do it all the time. We hand out more things. Outward bound training? They invented that in World War II. What's that for? Self-esteem. I can accomplish. I can solve problems. That's what you are doing all the time. ... The whole system has got clear steps and stages. Boom, boom! It's very clear that you are advancing, getting better. You are achieving in the organization. We've got

it laid out better than the civil service, and the kid sees this. We make a fuss about your promotion, okay? The responsibilities we give you — we make a big deal out of it. And it works.

Independently of why it exists, of how its tentacles reach into all areas of military life, the bonding that occurs amongst members provides them with a sense of family belonging that within work organizations is likely inferior to none. How do people describe this belonging? For different members it means different things. For some, it means the simple pleasure of doing the same things as others at the same time. Present and former single members recall the camaraderie of their barracks days with nostalgia; it reminds them of the companionship of boarding school dormitories or university residences. Others speak of the camaraderie of field exercises or ship tours, when a group sleeps, eats, and completes tasks in harmonious unison. For these persons, being part of a gang whose members have everything in common provides psychological comfort. Often the gang is not place-specific but embraces the whole family of the Canadian military: an ethos, a philosophy, shared experiences and values that are not confined to a particular posting or group of people but that the member can be confident of encountering everywhere. While these sources of satisfaction enhance the military's control, they also provide the intrinsic benefit of in-group identity.

Military socialization is powerful, and for most members the military meets affiliation needs that it itself has taken care to create. But many recruits bring to the military an additional hunger originating in their past life, a life that failed to provide a stable family, a sense of rootedness, or perhaps a sufficient basis for a sturdy self-image. Some former "juvenile delinquents" have embraced the military with enthusiasm. Others brought a more existential hunger. It was a keenly felt desire to find a place, to end the uncertainties of a deeply experienced adolescent identity crisis. As one officer reflects:

So much of me is in the military that if I get out, within two weeks I'll be crying that I did it, because it's so much a part of me. I am a [senior officer]. I walk down the street. I have status. I meet people. I know where I stand. I'm part of a great big social club that is one big family. It isn't always a happy family. We're second-class citizens. But within our own family we have status. And that's hard to let go. ... It's a very comfortable world to be in, to know your place. I think most people go through their life trying to find out what their place is in the world. The military tells you.

"I never looked at it as a job after boot camp," another member summarizes. "It's a life."

It is surely a great paradox that the military mission, resting as it does on a faith in violence, requires a kind of love to propel it forward. Felt most intensely for the fellow members of the unit, this love spreads outward in diluted form to envelop everyone who wears the uniform, even the total stranger that one spots (and is saluted by) in the middle of a downtown street. It is a love nurtured by a common culture and the overt celebration of team spirit. Set apart from civilians, denied the opportunity to identify with a place, the military member grows, moves, and experiences a sense of belonging within the hothouse confines of an international cabal. The peacetime bonding that any effective military organization provides contributes immeasurably to its successes in war.

Conservatism and Intolerance

Apart from the many public debates about the military's future role, there are aspects of military culture that make Canada a worse, rather than a better, place to live, especially for some military members and the civilians closest to them.

The military objectives are control and mastery. Combat — the use of physical force to kill, maim, and destroy surrounding environments — is the ultimate mastery-motivated undertaking. It requires obedience, loyalty, adherence to hierarchy, and faultless accuracy under stress. Combat requires tight bonding among members of the unit, which is facilitated by members' intense feelings of personal identification with their "own" whether this "own" refers to unitmates or nation. Combat sets up a black/white antagonism between "own" and "other" that requires absolute loyalty and devotion toward own and completely reverse orientations toward other.

As an occupation, the military is therefore not conducive to political liberalism, open-mindedness, or tolerance. Its members are drawn inward rather than outward when they seek their spiritual reasons for being. Even senior military strategists and retired officers, who are a step removed from the immediate action, see themselves as preserving an order that is dear to them or creating order where there is presently chaos. Military work thus provides little incentive to be receptive to social change.

The artificially controlled environment of basic training, the geographical mobility, the social isolation and self-sufficiency of most bases, members' frequent absences from family life, the exclusive character of unit bonding, and the distinctive uniforms, jargon, traditions, and morality codes all ensure that the military community is largely closed. The military is well aware that without considerable segregation from civilian society it would not exercise sufficient control over its members to accomplish its objectives. Much of the military's conservatism stems from its fear of being contaminated by what it calls "civilianization" — the undue encroachment of civilian customs, values, and career expectations. Excessive civilianization, it is feared, would dilute the impact of what militarization has managed to achieve.

For example, insofar as those military members with a certain skill level are of a relatively high rank, it is impossible to replace those who leave with "imported" civilians who have comparable skills without bringing into positions of responsibility persons who have not been given proper military indoctrination.[18] The military therefore is afraid there will be shortages during healthy economic times, which are characterized by high attrition. In the United States, fear of shortages accompanied the government's change in the early 1970s from conscription to an all-volunteer force policy, and civilianization was the object of considerable study. Similarly, Canadian Forces' numbers dropped from 126,000 in 1962 to 82,000 in 1973 for reasons that military analysts partly attribute to the increased "civilianization" of Canadian values.[19] In both Canada and the United States, the military has also been apprehensive about the potential civilianization repercussions of such changes to their community as allowing women in combat roles and officially recognizing gays, lesbians, and common-law marriages.

The military is supposedly apolitical or politically neutral. Members are not permitted to engage in "political activities," which include campaigning for political parties, displaying political signs during election campaigns, or signing political petitions.[20] In fact, however, the military is conservative because it associates liberal and socialist values with civilianization. When asked to identify their own political leanings, military members invariably choose "conservative." In his classic study, *The Professional Soldier*, Morris Janowitz found that when asked to identify themselves as "conservative" or "liberal," 68 per cent of the 576 Pentagon staff officers he sampled in 1954 identified themselves as either "conservative" or "somewhat conservative."[21] Two decades later, Franklin Margiotta found that 64 per cent of 351 American air force generals identified themselves the same way.[22] In his opening remarks at a 1978 Canadian Forces regional social work conference called "The Child in the Military Family," Major J.C. Baril articulated what he believed to be the consensus view of Canadian military members, that they were persons who held "conservative values re achievement, work, family life, money, education, religion, laws, health, and patriotism." These conservative values included "strong family ties" and a patriarchal conception of the family in which the husband-father figure was "king of his castle."[23] Recently, it has become evident that a number of the Canadian military are members of right-wing extremist groups.[24] In short, the military's self-portrayal as apolitical is significantly inaccurate.

The military has always resisted changes in the composition of military personnel, or in military family structure, that would move toward greater liberalism. The recognition of women in combat roles (1989), common-law marriages (1991), and gays and lesbians (1992) have all occurred as a result of successful legal challenges under the Canadian Human Rights Act (combat) or the Charter of Rights and Freedoms (common law, gays/lesbians). None of these developments would have occurred otherwise. A 1987 survey of junior officers for the Canadian Forces Staff School publication *Perspectives* reported that 76 per cent of the respondents regarded a policy that would accept gays and lesbians into the Forces as "seriously wrong."[25] The military has tolerated the increased incidence of "working wives" in a similarly grudging manner. The Canadian government's commitment to pluralism, which protects (at least publicly) the language, cultural, and religious freedoms of a wide variety of groups, and the Canadian Human Rights Act, which is beginning to recognize the rights of more than one gender, race, sexual orientation, and type of family, are anathema to an organization that recognizes no rights and attaches privileges exclusively to rank. Cultural pluralism is also considered hostile to the objectives of the combat unit. In the words of one member:

> We had such a hassle over the Sikh coming in, because uniformity is the key. ... If you are not part of the team, you are not part of the team. It's nothing directed personally at you, it's just the way the unit operates — you are a part of us, or you don't exist. ... And when you go to boot camp — same uni-

form, same haircut, same routine, same style — you are part of it. The best is having the same colour, the same haircut, the same religion, the same colour of eyes, the same height, the same weight. Because everybody outside of that — we don't like difference.

The military stands by — and normally exercises — its right not to bend in any way to accommodate a member who has become unable to perform the work for which he or she was originally recruited. Those who become disabled are often released, even when their disabilities would not prevent them from remustering to other trades. The military's need for "perfect specimens," who are free to meet any kind of operational demand, overrides its obligation to assume responsibility for those who, after many years of service, have suddenly happened upon bad luck. This trend has become especially apparent during the recent downsizing.

Reflecting what he believed to be a general consensus about the characteristics of the population, Major Baril observed in 1978:

The military population is young of age. There are no older folks. The military population is generally healthy. There are no handicapped or chronically ill service people.[26]

If anything, this statement has recently become truer. Given the exacting nature of their work, the Forces maintain that they cannot function with less than optimal physical specimens. In practice, of course, some occupations accommodate infirmities more readily than others. If members become unable to perform their jobs, they are assigned a temporary medical category and reassigned to lighter work. After a few months without sufficient improvement, the medical category becomes permanent and the Forces have the right to move toward release. While this policy may seem heartless, the alternative — according to the military — would be a much smaller proportion of totally able personnel, who would have to be continually deployed and redeployed into the dangerous peacemaking missions overseas. In the words of a military doctor:

They say, "Well, I could still do something." Well, but the military system is not set up for that. I mean, we can't. If we keep that type of a process up, we are going to have an entire military, or a very large portion of the military, unable to go and respond as we are supposed to to taskings. I mean, can you imagine going through a sheet of paper and saying, "Okay, we are going to send three thousand people to Somalia." And you go through it, and you have to go through forty, fifty thousand people before you find people to fill that tasking. Well, those people go to Somalia, then they come back, then Yugoslavia appears. Well, guess who gets to go to Yugoslavia? It's the same people, where they are getting shot at. Then those people come back, and guess who gets to go to ___? The military has to have healthy members. It is an occupational requirement that we have to have a significant per cent.

Doctors who have worked in civilian and military environments report that in the military environment the pressure is much higher to get the member back to work after insufficient rest, whether the problem is a sprained ankle or the "flooding" memories suffered by survivors undergoing therapy for childhood incest. Downsizing has augmented that pressure, and there is far less latitude for disabled members to remuster than there was even a few years ago. Those who are not perfectly healthy often live in fear of being released. Doctors have difficulty treating them because they are understandably reticent about their symptoms. The military subjects some members to exhausting exercise regimens, dangling over them the threat of release if they fail to measure up. Until a few years ago, all members were forced to do a vigorous long distance run annually even if they had not had the opportunity to work up to it with prior training. Not surprisingly, some heart attacks resulted. As one long-time member perhaps aptly summarizes:

> The job of anybody who's placed in authority is to use people as a resource — to use you up, if you are in the Armed Forces, in the most efficient manner we can.

Military Women
Women's equality is an important casualty of the military's conservatism. The military views feminism as an especially threatening type of civilianization, consisting of a host of demands for special treatment, quota systems, and egalitarianism that, if allowed to flourish, would wreak havoc upon combat discipline. Feminism poses threats to an organization that is ordered, hierarchical, oriented toward preservation instead of change, and insistent that solidarity is

synonymous with identicalness. If allowed to choose, the military would not have women at all. To the extent that the military does permit women members to advance, it pressures them to do so on masculine terms. As one retired female officer puts it:

> I have found that if you want respect from male officers, then be one of them. Be an officer. The fact that you are a woman is not the issue here. Gender is not the issue. Don't expect special privileges, and you will be accepted.

The military keeps "creeping feminism" at a distance partly by perpetuating a male culture. Doing so is not difficult, given the patriarchal character of the larger society. The military nurtures a "male bonding" ethos that transcends rank, bridges the gap between members and non-members, and often ostracizes female members and wives. For example, a non-commissioned man recalls the camaraderie of a duck hunt he was privileged to participate in with his father-in-law (a senior officer) and a group of generals who were holidaying out in the bush. The husband of a female member recalls being the only spouse who was permitted to join Friday afternoon TGIF[27] celebrations at the small base where his wife was posted. A retired woman officer remembers the early days of her membership when, despite paying the same dues as men, women members were excluded from parts of their own mess. A former female navy reservist recalls that during the last evening of every ship tour the male crew members gathered together to watch stag movies.

Male bonding is also deliberately used to facilitate cohesiveness, especially during basic training. Just as recruits become members of one platoon at boot camp to the exclusion of every other platoon and become military to the exclusion of being civilian, male recruits start to become "real men" by proving that they are not "wimpy" women. Instructors encourage stereotypically masculine behaviours from recruits by using female-associated words to denigrate them. Women instructors of female platoons do it, too. As one recruit recalls:

> They'd just call you names and they'd swear at you. Fuck, slut, you slow lazy bitch. And oh, like anything you could think of, like stupid idiot, cunt, split-ass. Women — mostly women — talking to us. The senior NCO that I had, she wasn't so bad. But there were some there that were really harsh. ... It was terrifying.

A crucial subtext of basic training is the message: To be male is to be not female, which is to be valued positively. Basic training reinforces male objectification of women by using women as targets in weapons training films and assigning female names to bombs and guns. The control lever of a female-named fighter plane is called a joystick (slang for penis). A landmine designed to explode at groin level is called Bouncing Betty, a not-so-subtle reminder that a woman whom you do not subdue and objectify is likely to castrate you.[28] West Point male cadets participate in "pig pool" contests to reward the cadet who has managed to bring the fattest or ugliest woman to a dance.[29] Through its inculcated denigration of women, basic training provides male recruits with an important source of group identity and self-confidence. This source is not provided to female recruits and ensures that they will begin their military careers with a significant handicap.

Women have not been accepted into the Canadian Forces easily. Until 1970, married women were considered too civilianized to be reliable members, and women who married were released. Between 1970 and 1974, married women members were released as soon as it was discovered that they were pregnant. Women were not allowed into the combat trades until 1989. Today, women are still prohibited from serving on submarines, and women in the Forces still have a rough ride. Most male members admit that their female counterparts must try harder. And given the male character of military culture, those women who do succeed often become surrogate men who are as hard as "real" men on their less successful peers. Reflecting back on her training, a former West Point cadet notes:

> A woman who could make the runs, who could pitch a tent, who could fire a rifle well, who didn't snivel or cry, this woman would earn friendship and support. But if a woman was incompetent we would destroy her — even quicker than the men would — because she threatened all of us.[30]

The military environment may have acquired women, but it has not become receptive to feminism.

While military men have accommodated women in their workplaces and have sometimes truly bonded with them, the military in general has not changed its stance. Reflecting the way the military has conditioned them, most military men are fundamentally uncomfortable with women who step outside traditional gender roles — and their actions show it. A former female army reservist was barred from entering her chosen trade despite topping her class during summer training. A woman who was posted to the Airborne Regiment as a finance clerk was told on the first day by her commanding officer: "I don't want no fucking split-asses here." A female army member who had her PER on a course downgraded from "outstanding" to "average" was told that this situation "had to be," if she was to be prevented from scoring higher than the men. A female cadet at Royal Military College in Kingston who surpassed the male cadets at soccer was harassed so much that she became depressed, developed low grades, and was expelled. A recent survey of 4,055 members commissioned by the Department of National Defence found that at least one-third of its female respondents had been personally and/or sexually harassed.[31]

Some of this harassment is verbal ridicule. Other cases have been explicitly sexual. In a recent highly publicized American instance, (The Tailhook Affair), 26 women were sexually assaulted during a single military convention.[32] And a Canadian member reports the following about how she was told that her military career depended on "putting out":

> The Chief Warrant Officer was saying to me [at a party], "If you want to get ahead in the military, you'd better start drinking with the boys and associating with the boys." "What are you saying — have a fling?" He said, "You can use your own words, but you should get my meaning." And with me, like ordinarily I would have told him to pound salt, but where was I? ... I stood up and I was going to punch him out, and my warrant officer grabbed my hand and dragged me out of the room. He said, "You are upset now. Everyone's been drinking." ... He said, "He didn't mean it, and blah blah blah. Calm down," and all this. So the more I thought about it, the more I fumed. ... I said, "There is no need for this." A lot of women at that time too were getting that from a lot of the bosses: "If you want to get promoted, this is what it takes."

Members who have lodged formal complaints about sexual harassment have often been harassed further and have eventually lost their jobs.[33]

Fear that they will demand special treatment is at the root of many of the military's attitudes toward women. "Special treatment" is also a rhetorical device that the military uses to turn male members against female members and some groups of female members against others. The target of this tactic is always women. A former naval reservist reports that the women in her cohort were never allowed to take credit for their high ratings because of persistent rumours that their marks were inflated because they were women, because the instructor was sexually attracted to them, or because the instructions from command headquarters were that all the women must succeed. The fact that the male competitors believed these rumours made it more difficult. One childless female member, sent on three overseas tours in quick succession, was told by her male commanding officer that she was substituting for women with children, who were being given the special privilege of being allowed to stay home. As one might predict, she reacted angrily:

> I said, "I don't care." I said, "As far as I am concerned you can go right back up to the Major and tell him I am not doing it." I said, "There is no way. If they come down, order me to go, yes I'll go, but not without a fight, until the rest of the females in this unit at my rank have done at least one tour." Now if they can't go for medical reasons or whatever, like if they are pregnant, I can see it. But not because you've got kids!

In this instance, the "special treatment" rhetoric successfully inserted a wedge between women.

Another version of the same argument was used to attempt to keep women out of combat. Here it was asserted that women's special needs for privacy, the possibility of women being pregnant without knowing it, the possibility of women having their period, women's special responsibilities for their children, men's "natural" chivalry and the probability of them stopping to pick up a fallen female comrade all created extra problems in the field that proved that women could not be trusted to participate in combat equally. The military also tried to keep women out of combat by driving a wedge between female members and wives. To this end, the military circulated the (unfounded) rumour that wives of male members would be jealous of any women who were permitted to fight side-by-side with their husbands.

The military has recently claimed in the media that it has a "zero tolerance" policy toward personal and sexual harassment. But the military's negative attitude toward women is deeply embedded within its obsession with homogeneity, its methods of training, and its traditions of male camaraderie.

Social Problems

The military lifestyle is also conducive to social problems, the most important ones being alcoholism, wife battering, and the physical and sexual abuse of children.

At the 1978 "Child in the Canadian Military Family" conference, P.M. Hrabok described alcohol as one of the "consistently malignant facts of life" associated with the military environment. Figures cited by Hrabok indicated that 6.3 per cent of Canadian Forces members had been diagnosed as alcoholic, as compared with 4.0 per cent of the population nationally, meaning that the military alcoholism rate was about 50 per cent higher than the civilian rate. At one Canadian Forces base, 15.3 per cent of members reported that they considered themselves dangerous drinkers.[34] A number of studies of the American military have uncovered the same or higher incidence of self-reported alcoholism (or complaints about heavy drinking from spouses).[35]

One reason for the military's high alcoholism rate is the easy access to cheap alcohol on most bases, especially those overseas.[36] A related reason is the military's longstanding association of alcohol consumption with unit cohesion and military supervisors' traditionally positive PER assessments of members who "support the Mess."[37] Until recently, attendance at TGIF celebrations was actually compulsory. While the military is now attempting to cope with its alcohol problem and to encourage less alcohol consumption, most members still believe that units who drink together will bond more effectively. The pressure to drink thus remains strong. American research has also linked heavy drinking with members' frequent absences from their families[38] and with the isolation from friends and extended families they endure at remote and overseas postings.[39]

Wife abuse in the military community is also high. A recent Georgia study, which compared 30 army with 30 civilian couples, found that 23 per cent of the military wives reported being battered as opposed to only 3 per cent of the civilians.[40] The Adjutant[41] of one Canadian army unit recently speculated:

I think there are 93 married people [in the] unit. You could talk
to every one of the wives, and you would probably find a dozen
wives that have been beaten [in the last two months].

The recent report of the Canadian Panel on Violence against Women
singled out the military community as a special problem. The report
observed that violence against women in the military community —
members and wives alike — is attributable to the "overall culture"
of military life, which comprises "an atmosphere where violence
against women is tolerated and even fostered."[42]

Wife abuse, unlike alcoholism, can be kept hidden for a long time.
And military members and their spouses have even more reason than
civilians to fear the consequences of disclosure. Apart from the
tendency of many battered women to blame themselves, the military
perpetuates a "culture of fear" that keeps male members silent about
wife battering and motivates them to control their wives. As one
former officer's wife, who was battered, explains:

You wouldn't talk to anybody. I'm not sure I would have
anyway, but in the situation I was in I couldn't. You couldn't
in the corporate world either.

One explanation of military men's propensity to batter is "cultural
spillover theory" or the idea that "cultural norms which favour violence for socially legitimate purposes tend to be generalized to other
social contexts."[43] In other words, the legitimacy of violence inculcated by the military "spills over" into members' personal lives. A
more focused, and perhaps more plausible, variation of this theme is
that the military trades most associated with combat perpetuate a
subculture in which physical aggressiveness is positively valued. It
is thus from these trades that we can expect more wife abuse. Paul
Starr's research on subcultures in U.S. Reserve Officer Training
Corps university programs supports this view, as does Peter Neidig's
research on American marine drill instructors.[44] American research
has also found that combat veterans who suffer from Post-Traumatic
Stress Disorder tend to abuse their partners and to have learned (from
their combat experiences) to regard violence as a "viable" solution
to problems.[45]

According to a former military social worker, army combat units
especially take pride in their ability to produce "rough, tough, mean
sons of bitches," who drink, fight, screw, break things, and otherwise

show themselves to be the kinds of "real men" who can wage wars. He says:

> I can recall an army captain complaining over coffee one day at the Mess. He was concerned about the decrease in the number of chargeable incidents in the last several months. It's kind of like the guys aren't rough and tough and sharp any more. If they aren't drinking and screwing and fighting and getting into trouble and showing up on charges, there's something wrong.

His words are corroborated by disturbing reports of the Airborne Regiment's peacekeeping activities in Somalia, during which at least four Somali citizens were gratuitously killed, including a 16-year-old boy who was tortured and beaten to death. During the court martial of one of the boy's killers, the extent to which violent masculinity comprises the Airborne Regiment culture was revealed to the public for the first time.[46]

Pilots, especially fighter pilots, are also expected to be tough and daring. They are permitted to be extremely "disorderly" within the military community in order to keep themselves in fighting form. Smashing up the Mess is one such type of allowable pilot "fun." As one retired officer remembers about pilots:

> Occasionally they would have a squadron party or something in the Mess. And nobody was there except that squadron, which means it was all men, you know. And the next day, you would go into the Mess and it would be trashed, literally trashed. Everything broken, everything gone — everything.

Violence against spouses is another type. The battered wife of a pilot, who appealed to a colonel when her husband began throwing full beer bottles at her, was told: "So what's the big deal? They have to have a good time." And it was naval pilots who were the perpetrators in the Tailhook incident.

According to evidence reviewed by Anson Shupe and others, not only are military members batterers more often than civilian men, but also they are more likely to use weapons.[47] Military batterers are also often people who especially fear losing control. Some batterers may be obsessed with asserting control at home either because they feel oppressed by supervisors at work or because they are often absent from home and, threatened by their wives' ability to cope, feel a strong need to reassert their presence. As the wife of a non-commissioned army member summarizes: "They are not allowed to talk; they come home, and then everything comes out on us."

Apart from direct relationships between military conditioning and wife abuse, known or suspected, general research on wife abuse associates it with demographic characteristics that mirror the demographics of the military. As Gary Lee Bowen summarized it in 1983, wife abuse — like the military — is most strongly associated with youth (age 30 or younger) and newer marriages. Wife abuse is also associated with alcohol abuse, authoritarian husbands, stressful circumstances (such as frequent separations and moves), and social isolation, all of which are military lifestyle byproducts.[48]

Physical abuse of children is also a military problem. As early as 1975, the rate of child abuse in the American military was reputed to be five times the national average.[49] A Hawaiian study in the early 1980s found a greater tendency for military fathers to physically abuse their children than for members of a racially matched group of civilian fathers to do likewise.[50] In a recent interview with us, the Canadian military's Chief Social Worker estimated that child abuse accounts for twice as many referrals to his staff as wife battering.[51] There also appears to be a consensus that abusing parents (often — but not always — fathers) possess the same social attributes as many military parents: youth, geographical isolation, geographical mobility, social isolation, heavy alcohol consumption, crowded living conditions (true of some non-commissioned members), and the kind of "culture shock" that is associated with moves overseas.[52] Child abusers are often reputed to have been abused themselves as children,[53] which fits with the experience of some military members, and to be controlling and authoritarian by inclination or training.[54]

Male military members have also been found to abuse their children sexually. Anecdotes obtained during this study indicate that this problem may be significant. Nevertheless, the fact that so much sexual abuse remains hidden, especially in the military population, means that neither we nor anyone else can yet muster much evidence. At the moment, we can do little more than identify characteristics of abusive fathers and point out their similarities to characteristics of military members.

Women incest survivors often report that their fathers were controlling men who took pride in preaching conservative values.[55] In her article "Incest in the Military Family," Patricia Crigler identifies such a "tyrant" as a very typical abusive father. The tyrant is so afraid of admitting vulnerability that he can only express closeness through sex; his entire ego has been constructed around aggression.[56] Many military husbands and fathers fit the description of the tyrant. Because they exercise more control over their children than other fathers, tyrants are adept at keeping sexual and other forms of abuse secret.[57]

According to Crigler, other sexually abusive fathers are workplace introverts. The power these men exercise over their daughters is intended to compensate for the lack of ego support they receive on the job. Whereas the tyrant may be too successful at emulating the military macho ideal, the introvert may be too unsuccessful, and his suffering may be compounded by the military rank system.

Sexually abusive fathers often suffer from social isolation and/or alcoholism, as is also true of many in the military. Indeed, as in the case of wife battering, drunkenness can serve as an excuse for ignoring a terrible act that might otherwise need to be acknowledged openly.[58]

Finally, professionals who work with male sexual abusers report that many of them were sexually abused as children.[59] As we have hinted throughout this chapter, some (although certainly not the majority of) military members had dysfunctional childhoods, and for this reason they embraced the ready-made structure and identity that military life provides. Some of their dysfunctional childhoods included incidents of sexual abuse.

In summary, the military takes the aspirations of the economically marginalized (and others) and channels them into an identity of substance, which provides solidarity, belonging, and a sense of common purpose. In return for this identity, recruits relinquish control over their lives in order to be reconstructed for combat readiness. Of necessity, military control is internally totalitarian. The military organization nurtures strong bonding and feelings of identity within its ranks and relative hostility toward people outside. It wields its power from the top and crushes virtually all grassroots initiatives. Its members enjoy few rights.

The military equips its members to view with mistrust the concerns of any individuals or groups who are different, who even look as if they fail to share "our" mission. The military cultures of bonding, youth, isolation from civilians, authoritarianism, misogyny, and violence make members susceptible to such maladaptive behaviours as alcoholism, wife battering, and physical and sexual child abuse, behaviours that have a shattering impact upon the civilians around them.

The military provides positive perks for its active members and Canadians with an armed defence force. But what the military takes away from Canadians is significant, too. We will now turn to the deleterious impact of military life upon military members' wives.

2

Absences

A happily married navy member was deployed during the Persian Gulf crisis. While he was away, his wife developed a serious medical condition and required surgery. He was brought back for the surgery, and in the following months the couple's relationship deteriorated. He could feel nothing but anger toward his wife for having been the cause of his repatriation.

This story demonstrates the negative impact of military bonding on families. Absences from home are the major way that military bonding is cemented. This chapter is about military absences, the work they create for wives, and the military's efforts to contain the ensuing contradictions and problems.

Bonding Excludes Wives

While boot camp and similar peacetime experiences foster solidarity, they are superficial compared to the bonding during war. Intense bonding is considered the most necessary and pronounced part of combat because it holds out the greatest hope of saving lives. A navy member explains:

> You are conditioned — you are taught — that your commitment has to be total. Because it's war. And that's exactly it. [The member] should be thinking of nothing else — actually nothing else but fighting that ship — [otherwise] he's not going to come home.

Combat requires concentration, submission to military discipline, and complete suspension of civilian loyalties.

Less dramatic away-from-home military taskings include peacekeeping, aid-to-the-civil-power operations (e.g., the FLQ crisis, Oka, and natural disasters), training courses, and exercises. Leaving home is something every member does frequently, for anywhere from several days at a stretch to a whole year. From the base's perspective, these taskings represent incessant demands for personnel. In August 1991, an army officer reflected upon the preceding two years:

> We had to send a whole bunch of guys from Six Squadron to Iran-Iraq on seven days' notice at the end of the Iran-Iraq War. We then had to send about 250 to 300 people to Namibia for the UNTAG.[1] Then Lord Strathcona's Horse [Guard] went to Cyprus for six months and returned in the middle of March and was deployed on divisional manoeuvres in Wainwright and didn't return until July. So they were away nine months at a stretch from their families. After the Strathconas came back, we then had to send a whole bunch of people to Honduras. ... [Then] the Oka crisis came up, and we had about 50, 60 people that were sent out of here on no notice to Oka. After Oka we had the Gulf War. The first batch of five military policemen that were sent out of here into the Baghdad embassy left here on two hours' notice, and then we had to send 107 people, total, to the Gulf. In the middle of sending these 107 people to the Gulf, we had 600 members of Princess Patricia's Canadian Light Infantry depart for peacekeeping in Cyprus. ... We presently still have 48 people serving in Kuwait as second line detachment supporting one CER,[2] and the list will go on and on.

From the male member's perspective, continual taskings mean he spends relatively little time at home. A Québec-based non-commissioned member recollects the same period:

> I came here 5th May '89. I had one 7-working-day course in the fall in Bagotville. So I was coming back on weekends. After that they came back from the peacekeeping in Central America. I went six months — February till August '90. After I came back it was the Indian crisis. So I came back 3rd August, and 7th of August I was sent to St. Hubert till 10 October. After that I had a course in December, another ten working days in Bagotville, another one in June — seven working days. January '91 I spent two weeks in the field. Then in May we had a week exercise for tactical evaluation. After that I had five weeks in Gagetown (August '91). I came back for five days. Then I went for three and a half weeks to Europe.

Combat requires motivated members, who will concentrate zeal-ously, rather than dwelling on problems back home. Unit bonding produces and sustains members in this motivation. It should not have to develop from scratch during a crisis; like any well-functioning missile, it should be maintained at a standby state that can be brought up to par quickly.

One maintenance strategy is the field (or ocean) exercise. Like its real-life counterpart, this make-believe combat enactment gets mem-bers away from their homes for long periods, focused on a specific task, intensely bonded with their peers, and renewed in their military commitment.

A former army officer says:

When you're not out in the field, you're not doing your job. You're not doing the whole job. You're just sort of getting ready to do the job. Being out in the field and doing the job is where you get your greatest sense of satisfaction, because you find out if all the things that you've been trained to do are working.

A related — and more subtle — bonding maintenance strategy is the military's recognition that the domestic front must be managed. Civilian wives must never be allowed to forget that their husbands are military. And members themselves must stay primed for war. One effective way of managing the home front is to send members away on taskings frequently. Another way is pointedly to exclude spouses from after-hours base social functions. Keeping members socializing exclusively with one another accomplishes three things. It enhances the bonding necessary for combat; it habituates the member to other members' company; and it makes partings easier for the member's spouse by keeping him or her constantly conditioned to separations. Eighty-seven per cent of Canadian Forces members are male, and "male" is definitely the appropriate way to characterize military exclusive socializing.[3]

The most obvious example of exclusive socializing is the weekly TGIF celebration. This celebration often continues through until Saturday. TGIF used to be compulsory, but even in its present form it remains an important instrument of military bonding. As social occasions go, TGIF is spontaneous, and members find it hard to predict exactly how long they will stay. Their wives are consequently unable to predict whether or not they will be home for dinner, home drunk, or home at all.

A woman in this situation might be expected to call the Mess and ask her husband about his plans. But the military has discouraged this tactic by turning TGIF into a machismo test. According to military folklore, any man whose wife enters or telephones the Mess during TGIF is a "wimp" who cannot control her. A member whose wife does manage to get into the Mess is teased and ridiculed. Men consequently develop ways of ensuring that their wives will not come to (or telephone) the Mess, and they erect a united phalanx against wives who disobey. One officer's wife who used to try to telephone her husband recalls:

> I would be excited about going to Sears and finding a new rug or something, or set of crystal. And I'd call the Mess: "Could I speak to Roger, please?" Click. You know, you couldn't even do that. It was guys' night out and nobody interrupted. It was for the guys.

Being dismissed in this way is infuriating for wives, especially if they have small children, are living in remote locations, and/or are newly arrived and have few social outlets. Often it is not only Fridays that are off limits for wives at the Mess; it may be any time at all that members get together to drink. One air officer's wife was actually beaten by her husband for sending for him at the Mess when she was in labour.

Even mixed mess functions exclude wives in some ways, although less so now than 30 or 40 years ago. In the 1950s and 1960s, just as women members were excluded from parts of the Mess, wives were not allowed in the bar at all. They would be brought to dances by their husbands and left to chat amongst themselves while the men disappeared to drink. Even the Saturday night dance was fair game for military bonding. One former officer's wife, who was shy, used to lock herself in a washroom cubicle:

> We'd go to a dance, Bob would go into the bar, and I didn't know anybody. The room was dark and I knew some people, but they were dancing or they were doing whatever, and I was there alone. So I used to go into the women's washroom, stand on the toilet seat, and lock the door.

Eventually, teachers in the base schools, many of whom were women, were permitted to become paying members of the officers' mess and customers in the bar. Eventually and grudgingly, wives were allowed in the bar too.

Spouses are still excluded from formal mess dinners, although they are invited to separate occasions called Mixed Dining-Ins. The mixed dining-in itself provides space for military bonding during the hour between after-dinner speeches and the start of the dance, at which time spouses are sent away from the room for coffee and liqueurs while the members remain to enjoy port and cigars.

In general, the Mess's purpose is to facilitate military bonding without such counterproductive encumbrances as wives. Even on the afternoon that members of the Officers' Wives' Club decorate the Mess for Christmas, they may be asked to leave before happy hour starts. And wives who turn out to watch their husbands marching in a parade may be turned away from the after-parade reception.

Even husbands' and wives' mutual affection is a problem for the military because conjugal intimacy is a threat to combat bonding. Military rules prohibit PDAs ("public displays of affection") under any circumstances. But no rules prohibit members from viewing sex shows or watching the wives of other members take their clothes off, because the women in these instances can be represented as the sexual property of all.

From the military standpoint, civilian women might actually be more useful if they were the sexual property of all; as partners in monogamous marriages, they get in the way. They do not understand the military, have never bonded tightly with their co-workers, and are fickle enough to desert a man who is defending his country. While this conception of women is not held by every member, it does pervade the general military culture. It also legitimizes the extraordinary lengths to which the military will go to keep combat bonding uncontaminated by families. If women can be represented to male members as capricious, they will quickly thrust "problem girlfriends" aside to concentrate on the bonding at hand. Unaccompanied members serving overseas who receive worrying letters are often counselled by their supervisors to believe the worst. When the military has successfully resocialized a member about women, his wife or girlfriend sadly notices the difference. Reminiscing about the impact of basic training on her husband, a young army wife says:

When we were teenagers and dating, there seemed to be no
limit to what we could talk about, the hours we could spend
talking about it. And I think that he became a colder person in
some ways because of the training. He learned to distance
himself from me, from intimate discussion.

The gendered double standard about infidelity is taken for granted.
The same male bonding that encourages members to drop girlfriends
of questionable loyalty conspires to keep the secrets of male members who stray. In this connection, a male air element member remarks about courses and exercises:

Usually what goes on TD [Temporary Duty] goes on, and when
you're on TD it stays at TD. Like you don't mention it when
you get back.

His story is corroborated by female members. Members away on
group exercises usually adhere to the explicit rule that wives who
visit during the exercises are not permitted to attend unit social
functions or stay at the same hotel in order to ensure that they will
not carry tales back home.

The fact that wives are shut out of so much of their husbands'
lives gradually wears them down to accept the military's pre-eminence. Eventually, they learn to expect far less support from their
husbands than they would expect from civilian men.

Absences and Wives' Work

The military needs wives to be well-primed for members' absences
so that the required number of members will be more easily mobilized and that after each absence they will be more prepared for war.
The male member often anticipates his trips with pleasure, expecting
to learn a new skill, practise existing skills, see a new place, participate in gratifying bonding, and/or temporarily escape the responsibilities of home, all the while continuing to have his basic needs
catered to by others.

But his wife must repress her perspective because the military
mindset does not recognize it. From her standpoint, her husband is
simply gone, and she has been left with loneliness and extra work.

Her most significant extra work will likely be unrelieved child
care. Coping with small children is tiresome enough, even when

one's partner comes home every night. As an army officer's wife (and mother of three) reports:

> Steve is home at a quarter to 5. From 4:30 on, I find myself looking at the clock. If I can hold out 10 minutes, then Steve will be home, and I can give them to him. If he is 10 minutes late, it's no big deal to him. He gets yelled at when he comes home: "Where have you been? Why are you not home?" "It's only 5 to 5." "Well, it seems an awful long time from half past 4!"

When 5:00 comes and there is no one, tiresomeness can become living hell. Even school age children can be very demanding. When her husband was away, the worst part of one army wife's day was the after school/supper period when her four children competed for her attention:

> I used to hate supper time because there was nobody to divert any of their attention. ... I found that they all came in from school with their story of their day. And, you know, if there is somebody else to tell the story to or take turns telling it to people, or I find when Rick is home, I can always interrupt the story and say, "Wait and tell this to Daddy," and sort of gain a little peace. So there was none of that.

Often the wife coping alone gets no rest because two or more children are sick at the same time. One wife recalls:

> One started, and after that the other one followed. And Pierre was gone for three weeks. So if you have two, you get up in the middle of the night for one, and the other one is active during the day. So you end up for three weeks not getting that much sleep. And I was so tired that it took me a few months to recuperate from them being sick. ... When he got home it was sort of like, "These are your kids — take care of them." I was totally burned out.

Another problem is having to be the sole disciplinarian. Military members are away so often that they fall into the habit of failing to discipline even when they are home and come to play permanently (and enjoyably) the role of "Disneyland Dad." The result is chronic unpleasant work for their wives. One army officer offers this reason for being reluctant to discipline his children:

> The way I see it, if I'm away for two weeks or two months I don't want to come home and start being the disciplinarian when they haven't even seen me, let alone talked to me, or we haven't had a chance to spend any time together.

But both he and his wife admit that the getting-reacquainted process usually continues until his next trip. In his wife's words:

> I really don't think it's fair. The kids are getting older now — they resent it. They really resent my discipline a lot. Like me saying, "I want your room cleaned. I want the dishes done. I want your homework done." ... Lots of times if Ralph is there, he'll say "Well, you know, you'd better ask your mom." Like he can't make the decision to say yes or no. ... And I feel like I'm the bad one and he's the good one, and I think it's unfair. ... I don't think the kids could ever have a better father. Like he's a very loving, kind man. And he loves his children more than anything. But he wants to be the shining star.

Coping with children's emotions is another task. Much of this work involves the management of time, and there is no agreed-on way of doing it right. One army wife does not mark days off on a calendar and does not tell her children when their father is coming home, so that when he does arrive they will be delightedly surprised. But the widow of a military policeman pursued the opposite course: marking the days off and also drawing pictures on the calendar to save for Dad so that he could later "read" about what they had done each day.

Sometimes managing the children's emotions requires extraordinary measures. One air element member made the fatal mistake of coming home for a weekend in the middle of his long Junior Leader's course. His two-year-old daughter was so unhappy to have her father returned to her only to be snatched away again that she spent the rest of the course acting out. As a result, his wife made him promise never to come home for a weekend again. Another little girl, who went to a civilian school, was told by her classmates that daddies did not go away on courses and that her father's absence could only mean that her parents were getting a divorce. She was so upset that her mother had to fly her to the other end of the country so that she could be comforted by her father in person.

There is also the wife's own grief. Her husband's absence usually means that she has lost her partner — her daily companion, friend, lover, and confidant — and her children cannot occupy his place. She may now not have anyone close to share things with.

The member's early career is often the worst time, for it is the time when the military's socialization efforts are most intense. Basic training is usually followed by trades training and, sometimes not too long afterwards, a six-month overseas tour. The combination can be extremely hard on a new marriage. One army wife recalls being able to spend only ten minutes each week talking across the continent during her husband's 20-week trades training stint:

> He'd go to a telephone — I don't know where it was, a rec centre or something. I had the phone number there, so ... I would call there at nine o'clock on a Wednesday night his time. So that it would be twelve o'clock my time, so it'd be the cheap rate. And I had a little timer because, I mean, when he got in he was making $525 a month gross. So we didn't have much money. And I called once a week. And I put my little timer on and I talked ten minutes, because ten minutes was $4.30. And we'd talk back and forth — made all our major decisions back and forth.

But some wives with grown-up children claim that their loneliness is worse. A navy wife with teenaged daughters says:

> The teenagers are gone constantly, so when your husband is out to sea you are alone. You are by yourself. You don't have little kids to put to bed any more. So I find this is what is happening in my life now. My children are almost 17 and 13, so they don't need me as much as they needed me when they were younger. And I find that very hard, especially the weekends. They have their life too, and I'm not going to make them stay at home and keep me company.

Each wife finds a different moment in the weekly cycle most difficult. Some wives find evenings hardest, after the children have been put to bed and the house is empty. For others, the worst time is weekends, when most workplaces shut down, families look inward, and an adult without a partner can feel marginalized. The wife of a navy member says:

> Every time he's away I count weekends. I can get through the weeks, but the weekends are the hardest because weekends people are usually doing things with their family. And I've found that I'll say 13 weekends, 12 weekends — our count-down. That's how I get through it.

Still other wives find that they miss their husbands most when a crisis hits, when they are under stress, or when they are called upon to make a tough decision by themselves. An army officer's wife says:

> It's the lack of support, the lack of him not being there when I really need him. And sometimes that can be very important. I mean you can be married, and you can go three weeks without really needing him. I mean, he's there, but there hasn't been a situation where you really need to discuss something, or you really need to talk to him, or there's something really important. And sometimes he can be away for two months, and you can go through one and a half months without anything really coming up, and then suddenly something is there where it hits home that he's not around.

Dealing with loneliness takes work. Anyone who has one major area of their lives that has become unrewarding can become de-pressed. It can be unrewarding to run a household without a partner or to go to work each day and return to an empty house. The deployed member's wife must — and usually does — develop definite strate-gies for keeping her spirits bolstered through her rough times.

Despite these strategies, wives are often overcome by grief when their partners miss important events, such as the birth of a child. Wives always mention such an event with sadness, even long after the child is grown. Missing a birth happens frequently in the military, from whose perspective a birth is insignificant relative to the need to keep the member focused on his job. A non-commissioned navy officer shrugs the situation off as the couple's deserved punishment for bad planning:

Well it's considered important, but so what? You are out on a job, okay? Unless there's complications or some medical reason ... I would personally consider it bad planning.

Members who need a certain course for a promotion must take the course on schedule, regardless of family circumstances. Other members may be allowed to go home for their children's births, if the message gets to them in time and if sending them home is operationally convenient. When sending members home is awkward — such as when they are at sea — it is not done, except in the case of a serious medical complication. Sometimes non-commissioned members are ill-informed about current practice and miss a birth for no good military reason. The military perspective on childbirth seems to be that only the conception act counts. A former navy wife remembers:

My first awakening of what it was like being a military wife was when I was in labour for my son. I was so excited. Here I was, and I actually did get pregnant, and I was going to have my own baby. So I phoned my husband and said I was in labour, could he take me to the hospital? You know what he was told? "You have to be there for the laying of the keel, but you don't have to be there for the launching."

An army wife describes how it felt to be alone for the birth of her first child:

When I was pregnant with my first child, he was away most of the pregnancy. The last month, he was away the full month, and they told me they would have him back for the birth, and he wasn't there. I phoned and told them I was in labour — my water broke. And they couldn't get him down. He was in Wainwright, and they couldn't get him down. And so he never got back until the next evening to see the baby and me.

Against their will, wives are often forced to share the first joy of a birth with a neighbour, a stranger, or no one, or to adhere to the military chain of command and relay an impersonal phone message through a supervisor.

Just as the joy of a birth needs to be shared, so also does the pain of a family crisis. Another frequent bitter memory in the wife's repertoire is that her husband was not there the day it was discovered that a child was handicapped, seriously ill, or learning disabled, or that she had lost a parent or other close family member. She could not share her grief, and at the same time, she, alone, had to cope with the stress of interacting with professionals in unfamiliar and frightening circumstances. The mother of a learning disabled child remembers:

> She went to the Emily Stowe School at the Children's Centre. And so you go and you are invited in as a parent. You have your occupational therapist, you have your case worker, you have the teacher, you have the child psychologist. There is this big board, and you feel like you are on a trial going in there. I am in here all by myself; I don't have any support; I don't have anyone telling me that I am doing it right. And sitting there are these professionals telling me I shouldn't be doing this, I shouldn't be doing that. And most of them having no understanding at all of the military lifestyle.

Under some circumstances, the wife finds it especially demoralizing to be alone for weeks or months at a time. Parents or parents-in-law thus often find themselves opening their home to a military wife who has just had a caesarean section, lost a premature baby, or become ill shortly after a birth or who cannot cope with being stuck in a remote location for six months with only a two-year-old for company. Albeit in an indirect way, the military also organizes these parents' work. One wife of a navy member was released from hospital so soon after her caesarean section that she was not strong enough to lift her baby up from his crib. She wonders how she would have managed if she had not been staying with her mother:

> I walked over to his crib, but I couldn't lean over the crib and actually pick him up because my stomach muscles were [killing me], I was in so much pain. I crawled back to the bed, and I sat on the edge of the bed and put my hands on my head, and I started to cry. And my mom came and she said, "What's wrong?" And she picked up Matt, and she brought him over to me. She sat beside me, and I said, "I can't believe this. I am home and I have this child. I can't even get up to pick up my own baby." And, you know, I was cut from one side of my hip to the other — there was just no way I could pick him up. And

I thought, "What if they had sent me home and I didn't have you? What would I have done?"

Wives also need parental help when they become burned out. The wife of an air element member, who was alone with her children for five months, called her mother when she realized that if she did not receive help quickly she might harm them:

> I called my mother one time during the night and said: "Mom, come, because I'm gonna kill the kids." I couldn't do any more, I was just on the verge of being crazy. I felt that. And I said, "I don't have energy any more to take care of my kids." Mom said, "Okay are you able to wait until tomorrow? I'll go get the kids, and I'll keep them for as long as you need it." So she came over and stayed home for a week with me. And then after that, she took the kids home with her for two weeks.

As we will see in Chapter Four, postings often take wives far from their families and trusted friends. When emergencies happen under these circumstances, the consequences can be grim.

Family Reintegration

Numerous as they are when he is away, the military wife's problems do not end when her husband returns home. While he has been gone, he has been in another world. If he has been on a peacekeeping mission or in combat, he has been under considerable stress and looks forward to a haven of rest, good food, and sex. At the very least, he wants his family to be understanding if his mind should wander back to the deployment and expects them to make minimal demands. If he has been away on exercises or a course, he has been under less stress, but he has become rehabituated to a bachelor existence and has re-enveloped himself within military bonding. Whatever the nature of his absence, he will not reimmerse himself in the household quickly.

The military treats this situation as a collection of facts about which wives need to be "briefed." During her husband's absence, the wife may have been subjected to solo parenting, sick or unhappy children, crises, loneliness, perhaps a solitary childbirth. The last thing she needs is to be mobilized by the military to attend a post-deployment seminar that has been set up to enhance her "tolerance." In addition, her husband's re-entry has created new problems.

Children are a large part of them. Sometimes a child was not yet born or was at a much earlier stage of development when the husband left and is now an infant, larger baby, or older child to whom the member must reorient himself. It is normally his wife who plays the go-between and facilitates this process.

After weeks or months spent away from small children, some members also lose their ability to be charmed by them. Their wives must step in and mediate. As a non-commissioned army member's wife puts it:

> You know what it's like. You go somewhere, you visit, and you can see the people that aren't used to having kids around. Five minutes, and they've lost interest in them. And that's what the guys are like when they come home. Oh, it's all nice. Big hug and kiss to start off with. "Now I want to do the crossword puzzle. Go away!" … They are just not used to having to share themselves, because they've had two months on their own.

Sometimes, in contrast, the returning member does make his presence felt with the children, all too zealously laying down the law. Military discipline is, after all, what he has just experienced. Children, however, are always questioning because they are engaged in an intense developmental process. The member forgets that parent-child relations are different and tries to transplant military discipline into the home. His wife consequently copes with the fallout. The mother of a teenaged daughter reports:

> I try never to interfere at the time, but if I notice that he is being hard on her or maybe a little unfair, or maybe I feel that he is doing all the talking, and she's not getting to say anything back, then I'll sit him down afterwards and say, "Do you realize what happened during that little talk? Like nothing happened, other than the fact that you just pissed her off."

Sometimes the carryover of military discipline applies to the household in general: the member roars in and takes over, just as he was in charge out in the field. His wife, meanwhile, has managed the whole household by herself for several weeks or months and does not appreciate suddenly being treated like a nitwit. An air element member's wife says:

When they're gone you're the one who's responsible for everything. And then they come home, it's like you don't have a head
on your shoulder. You don't know what you're doing. Actually,
if I were talking for myself I would ask him, "When are you
leaving again?" Because he gets on my nerves.

Some wives become used to their independence while the member
is away and find it hard to "move over" and share domestic decisions
again when he comes home. Their difficulties are exacerbated by
husbands who are unable to shed their military demeanour or who
feel threatened by wives who managed well. It was suggested a few
times during our interviews that this situation might be a precipitating factor in wife battering.

Another reintegration problem for the wife is that the male-bonded
nature of military life, which competes with the bonding in the
family, is specifically antagonistic toward women and does not always diminish as soon as the member returns home. Far from being
a honeymoon, the homecoming can be an occasion for reminding the
wife that she is excluded from the most important area of her husband's life. A non-commissioned army member's wife says:

When the guys get together, they talk shop in the military.
Continual. On and on and on. Iran-Iraq stories. When he came
back, he was sick of these people he had spent five months with
and couldn't wait to get away from them. Well, they aren't
home two days, and these people he is sick of are coming over,
and they are exchanging pictures. "Remember when this happened?" "Remember, we did this?" You feel pretty excluded,
and they are quite close. Even if they have a function where
we'll have a barbecue with a bunch of the wives, the women
end up sitting and talking and the guys are in the living room
with their pictures and stories of Iran and Iraq. If they went on
an exercise for two months, stories about the exercise. It's
really hard.

The wife's hurt feelings are real, yet expressing them too much
may mar the celebration of homecoming. She may suddenly find
herself plunged into a struggle to keep her self-control. Added to her
resentment of her husband's readjustment difficulties are the wife's
accumulated resentments of what he missed when he was away.
There are a lot of feelings to repress, and she does not always

succeed. Yet she feels it is her job to recreate family harmony. An air element wife talks about how her jealousy of her husband's trips makes her feel guilt-ridden and conflicted:

> It's hard on a woman because you have to make the puzzle, you have to make your husband feel good, the kids feel good. And you have to be happy too. But you don't know how to make everybody happy — you're jealous. You cannot be happy when you're jealous of your husband.

An army officer's wife reports that the honeymoon period after her husband's re-entry is often followed by a "blow up," which she attributes to her repressed frustrations:

> The first couple of days they are back are, of course, wonderful. You have fantastic sex, it's brilliant, everyone's walking around with huge smiles on their face. And then it comes down, there's normally a huge fight. When I say a huge fight, there's normally a blow-out — a release of everything that's been building up for the last couple of weeks or months or whatever. ... I think the worst ones are when they come back from Cyprus.

Not every wife agrees that the first sex is fantastic. Sex right after an absence is often likened to sex with a stranger, something that a wife may consent to out of a sense of duty or repressed feelings rather than because she really wants it. As one army wife puts it:

> They are ready to jump into bed — slam, bam, thank you ma'am. Let's go have something to eat and then whatever. And it's like I'm getting into bed with a stranger. Here's this guy. He's been away for two months. All he wants to do is jump into bed. Well, no thank you! Please get to know me again first!

An air element member's wife who used to consent to "re-entry sex" reports that it made her feel terrible:

> You don't make love, you have sex. Period. That's it. You don't realize that really when you're in it, but after. Today I realize what I passed through, what I lived during that time. I didn't even love him when I made love with him. I had sex, that's it.

The day after, you wake up and start to live again together, but it's a lot different. It's hard to explain. He's a stranger.

One of the most important ways in which the member's return disrupts the couple's relationship is often at the time experienced as thrilling — the wife's gearing up and excited preparation for it. Navy wives, whose husbands are usually at sea for several months each year, are especially habituated to this gearing up, but it is at least somewhat part of the routine of all military wives. A navy wife says:

> You clean like mad for two or three days before they come home. Not that it's that dirty, but you get everything ready, and keep the house nice and spiffy, and make all their favourite foods, and get the kids ready and pack them up.

Standing on the jetty, waiting for the ship to come in, becoming more and more excited as it gets closer is the moment that navy wives describe with the most enthusiasm. As one of them puts it:

> You just can't wait for that ship to dock, so you can all run up. And you all stand there at the jetty waiting to see who can see their husbands and waving. The kids are all excited, howling to their fathers. It's really neat. "Daddy, I'm here, I'm here!"

Some wives claim that the highs of homecomings make up for the lows of separations and that the constant comings and goings make their marriages more exciting and romantic than they would have been if their husbands had been civilians. But wives also establish routines when their husbands are away, and they may find stopping everything to clean house and cook special foods tiring and disruptive. It is the husband's (i.e., the military's) schedule, rather than the wife's, to which the cleaning and cooking conform and around which the wife's gearing up efforts have been mobilized. When the member's return does not occur exactly when it was supposed to, the emotional letdown can be enormous. An army wife whose husband used to come home for long weekends in the middle of courses urged him to discontinue the practice because whenever his trip was suddenly cancelled, she became depressed.

Although to some women the highs and lows of separations seem romantic, they detract even more from military wives' control over their lives. Many navy wives also believe that a relationship punctuated by so many absences can never be truly intimate because its parameters are unrealistic. One former navy wife feels that much of the glue that holds a relationship together is the day-to-day events that are missed if a relationship is confined within the artificial boundaries of honeymoons:

> You know, what contributes to a relationship is seeing each other through thick and through thin. And you look back and say, "Remember the time that so and so broke his leg? And we didn't have enough money to cover this, and how we got the money?" A lot of that gets lost, I think, because it is rather artificial. Our best times together were certainly when he had staff appointments, which would be occasionally between a ship, when he was ashore and we settled down.

A navy wife whose marriage was often rocky reports that she and her husband developed communication problems because of the unnaturally blissful romances they enjoyed during his periods ashore:

> I tried very, very hard to solve all the problems, so that when he came home there would be nothing for him to do but relax and just enjoy his time home. I suppose that did create a lack of communication, because we talked about his time on ship and we talked about generalities, but we never really talked about the problems with the kids or the money problems, because I had coped with them all. So he never really knew a lot of them existed. … It made me proud to be able to do my part while he was away. Get the car started in the morning, get the kids to school, so that he wouldn't have to worry about anything. That was my part, I think, and I felt really good at being able to do it well, especially when I saw some wives not coping, you know, doing bad things. I loved him madly. I wanted everything to be just perfect for him.

Responsibility without Control

Absences are only one of the more obvious ways in which the wife's life is organized by military requirements and she finds little space in which to pursue an existence of her own. The military *always* expects wives to provide "the stability" in the family, which means doing virtually all household, childcare, and family management tasks, so that the member can concentrate on combat readiness.

Wives are therefore discouraged from developing careers or from becoming absorbed in any other activity that would weaken their ability to support their husbands' work. A general at National Defence Headquarters states this expectation of wives explicitly and bemoans the fact that some contemporary wives are failing to live up to it:

If you're a mother, as a spouse, or a father looking after children, you basically add the stability to the milieu. Because [the member] can be called on very short notice to leave. I mean, everybody talks about day care. The problem is war doesn't happen only in a day — it happens on a 24-hour basis. And it can happen that: Are you on the standby company that's on one hour's notice to move? I mean, that sort of institution doesn't exist out there. The spouses, in the past, were essentially doing a lot of that. And, of course, as they've become more involved in the milieu, the workforce, and they've had more of their own careers, that's complicated this particular aspect.

Not surprisingly, male members are encouraged to adhere to the view that all household work should be done by wives. A non-commissioned member recollects the years his children were small:

She had a job as far as I was concerned, and her job was to look after those kids in that house. And if she wasn't going to do that, I certainly wasn't. I wasn't going to take on her responsibilities on top of my own. Maybe that was a little strong, but, on the other side, she never understood that as I was going up in rank, my responsibilities within the service were growing. Not only was I responsible for the machine, but in a lot of cases I was responsible all day long and all night long for seven other guys. I was responsible for their actions. I was responsible to the government for them, for their development as soldiers or technicians — and a lot of other things. And when I came home, the last thing I wanted to do was to be saddled with more responsibility — the responsibility for her and the kids, the way she seemed to want me to. And I refused to do it. I really did. I got my back up a couple of times and I thought, "Hey — this is your job."

A retired female officer recalls the situation from her perspective, expressing envy of the unpaid labour her male peers commanded at home:

> These guys had a great life! They were doing what they wanted to do. It was adventurous, and everything was going for them. And the wife was home looking after the house and doing their laundry and cleaning the house and cooking their meals and looking after the kids, and always in the bed at night. This is the impression I got. And I thought, "God — wouldn't it be great to be a man! They've got it all!" And nobody ever questioned it in those days.

Members who live in barracks without spouses are similarly expected to exempt themselves from housework in order to have as much non-work time as possible for socializing and bonding in the mess. Referring to her years in barracks, the same retired member shows that she understood this connection well:

> We had maids even to do our beds. I never had to make a bed when I was in quarters — never had to make a bed. The sheets were changed, everything was done, it was dusted. Never had to do a darned thing. This left us free to be in the Mess and do all those good things — you know, socialize.

Most wives internalize these military expectations and refrain from significant paid employment in order to compensate their children for the fact that their fathers spend so little time at home. As one army officer's wife says:

> George is away enough. I mean, they lose their father enough. I don't really want to bring up children where they only see their mother in the evenings and weekends, and they don't really see their father for a big chunk of time either.

Wives who do have paid employment often feel so stressed under the weight of total responsibility for their children that guilt compels them to give the employment up. One such army wife recalls:

> After a while I said, "I can't handle this." I felt guilty. I felt really guilty not being home. I missed things. If anything hap-

pened at school, some play or something, I was there. Brown-
ies, I was there. Scouts, I was there. Now I couldn't do these
things any more. It was hard ... because he wasn't there. He
was on exercises or something. ... [The children] never complained, and they seemed to get along quite well. It was me that
couldn't work it out, so I stopped.

The military realizes enormous benefits from women's unpaid domestic work.

The Happy Military Family

The military motivates its members to conform to its requirements.
The military also tries to motivate members' wives to play their
backup roles. Despite its apparently offhanded exploitation of wives'
unpaid labour, the military knows it needs to keep them toeing the
line. After all, wives who are too unhappy with their lot are likely to
distract members from combat readiness, convince them to leave the
military, or even discourage their children from forming the back-
bone of the next military generation. The military attempts to create
a genuine community — on each base, within each army regiment,
within each ship's mess or wardroom — that incorporates not only
military members but also the members of their families. The military also propagates a "we take care of our own" ethos. Over the
years, it has implemented many "family support" measures, whose
purpose has been to contribute to combat readiness by filling some
of the void for families that is created by members' absences.

Permanent Married Quarters (PMQs)

At any time, about 50 per cent of Canadian members live in Permanent Married Quarters (PMQs) on Canadian Forces bases. Most
single members live in barracks, and many married members live in
self-contained family dwellings — apartments, row houses, or detached houses, depending on rank, location, and family size. Contrary
to the typical public view that military housing is free, all members
who live in PMQs pay market rents. Military members move so
frequently that they often find base housing convenient. PMQs save
members the worry of having to buy and sell a house in each new
location and cushion them from much of the work involved in acclimatizing to a new place. At remote and overseas postings, PMQs
comprise the only possible housing and/or sure way of guaranteeing
a supply of neighbours who speak the same language. The incum-

bents of some officer command positions — for example, the base commander or commanding officer of a unit — who are expected to know their men and women thoroughly, are actually required to live in special PMQs, which are provided for them.

PMQs are more than convenient. They comprise one of the most important ways that wives are encircled within the military community and their loyalty to it is secured. When their husbands are away, the PMQ neighbourhood provides wives with an instant network of other women who are in the same boat, or have been, and who are a tremendous source of understanding support. Given the situation in which their husbands' absences place them, the PMQ community provides wives with a remedy that many of them regard as a life raft. A former member's wife recalls:

> We had a group of us. There was always a group. In the PMQs, you find that you have a coffee group in the morning. You do your housework and you meet. I would say there never was a morning that, even when I wasn't working, somebody didn't come and visit, or you went to visit somebody, which was really helpful. ... Nobody ever sort of said, "Go away — I don't want to listen." They all had the same problems. Their husbands were all away.

Relative to their civilian counterparts, PMQ women almost uniformly rally round when a new neighbour moves in. They also show solidarity in a crisis. When one wife injured her arm while her husband was away, some of her PMQ neighbours came to the rescue:

> They had this huge box of food. And I kind of looked at them and I said, "Hello." And they said, "Hi — word has it you were hurt." And I said, "Well, just a small problem with my wrist." "Well, you know, we feel really bad about it. And we know your husband's gone away for awhile, so we brought all this." And they walked in the door and proceeded to put all these baked goods and stuff down on the table. And then from that night on they all took turns coming to my house after the homemaker left, putting the girls in the tub and getting them into bed. And I just sort of sat back and drank my tea. I thought, "Okay, I have fallen into a gold mine."

Living in a PMQ neighbourhood gives wives the message that the military itself can administer the most effective antidotes for the vacuums it has created in their lives. Nor is this lesson lost on the children, who learn quickly that the military community provides the prime continuity for them. As one military teenager says:

All military kids have a bond. We know about how we have to move and what problems there are in moving, and that's one thing we have in common. If you go up to some military kid, and you are a military kid, and you say, "Hey, how's it going — I'm new here," they know exactly what's going on because they have been through the same thing. ... We definitely know we have one thing in common.

Another important antidote to husbands' absences furnished by the PMQ neighbourhood is a built-in social life, opportunities for community fun amongst families who know one another that are exceedingly rare in civilian society. Especially on small or remote bases, social events like winter carnivals or Klondike Days suspend normal working hours, throw residents of the base together, temporarily eliminate rank differences, and emphasize that despite differences of all kinds, the military is a close-knit "family." Even during the weeks when nothing special is happening, social relations on many bases are close. A wife at one small station reports:

Here ... we're so close. This is only a small base. There's only 65 PMQs. And if you don't see anybody all week, you'll see them up at the Mess [on Friday nights], or you'll see them at bingo or at a card game. Or at a dart game. You'll see them, and it's like a family.

At the root of the goodwill and support within PMQ communities is the common experience of being military, sharing the culture, lifestyle, and value system that set military members apart from civilians.

By providing the PMQ community as a place to live, socialize, and receive help, the military meets many of the needs of wives who have temporarily lost their husbands' companionship. Through PMQs, the military also attempts to extend to wives some of members' experiences of tightly knit unit bonding. The PMQ community channels wives' frustration and despair into a positive military context, thus preventing these negative emotions from translating into alienation from the military and/or closer affiliations with civilians. The community provides occasions for the cathartic releases of rage, which wives soon realize is shared by others. The fact that other women bear the same burdens paradoxically works to trivialize them and to deepen each woman's resolve to bear them in better spirit. As one army wife reports about her group of friends at one posting:

> We shit all over the lifestyle several times. And that was good for us to discuss it. It did us wonders. It helped us to realize that we are all in the same boat, and some days are worse than others. And if you're having a bad one, fine. "Come on over, have a cup of tea, put your feet up. I'll take your kids out for a walk and, you know, if you want to go out and roll around in a mud puddle for an hour, that's fine — do it. If you want just to have a nice quiet hour, I'll give it to you." And if I'm in that position, I'm not about to ask you for it, but if you offer I may well take you up on it.

Some wives become so appreciative of the extent to which fellow PMQ inhabitants can empathize with them, relative to neighbours who are civilians, that they never want to leave. An air element member's wife summarizes:

> I like this life. It suits my socialistic nature — my community background. I find it very cushioned. I know what to expect. I know what tomorrow will bring and the next day will bring. It's like going to summer camp and being there forever.

Family Support
While PMQ neighbourhoods are loose structures, within which communities seem to just "happen," other military overtures toward wives are more direct. While these measures are altruistic and compassionate on the surface, their main purpose is to safeguard the member's work performance. If his wife and children are well looked after while he is away, he will be less likely to worry, more likely to concentrate fully on his job.

Family support is not new to the military. Ever since wives have stopped being thought of as mere camp followers and their usefulness to the military has been recognized, efforts have been made to provide them with the conditions that will foster their unpaid work. Prior to the unification of army, navy, and air force in 1968, each had its own methods of supporting wives, and most of them still exist.

Perhaps the most intricately developed method has been the army's regimental system, mentioned briefly in the last chapter. Whenever a part of the regiment is deployed on exercises, peacekeeping missions, or actual wars, a rear party stays behind to look after the families. Rear party soldiers will fix broken appliances, put up storm windows, shovel snow, chauffeur, babysit, sponsor social functions, and provide as much information as possible about the progress of the mission, all in aid of making it easier for wives to cope on their own. A general at National Defence Headquarters explains:

> We have rear parties, which are normally made up of people who are unfit to go in the theatre. And they basically run what I would call a look-after-the-family package. What they'll do is run things like car maintenance programs for the spouses, they'll run activities to keep them informed, they'll make sure they know what's going on. All that sort of stuff. And get togethers, you know — morale boosters. I mean, after you've been stuck at home and your spouse has been away for four months and it's the middle of February, it gets rather depressing. And so there are activities and all that sort of stuff to look after them.

The general explains further that the rear party's purpose is to enable the deployed member to concentrate fully on his job:

> That's essential. And why? Because when you're in an operational theatre 5,000 miles away, the last thing you want your soldier or your sailor or your airperson doing [is] worrying, you know: "That leak that she wrote to me about in the water — is the basement flooded?" You know, he shouldn't have to worry about that stuff. What we're paying him for is to get out there and concentrate on his job. Because if he's not concentrating on his job, somebody else is going to die.

Analogous to rear parties in the army are ship crews and segments of combat air squadrons that play similar roles. A navy wife, for example, reports:

In Victoria when the ships go for any length of time, a nice package comes home from the Commanding Officer. It explains about the trip that they are going on and how long they will be gone, the ports of call. And they always have what they call a sister ship, a home ship that is not going to be gone during that time, so if you do have a problem you can call that number. And if your toaster breaks down and you don't have money to repair it or replace it, you can give them a call, and a lot of the guys on their free time will come up to the house and see if they can fix your toaster for you.

"Rear party" support is also provided by members' wives. Wives' willingness to do their part to lend support to other women is rewarded by their husbands' faster career advancement. The National Defence Headquarters general makes it clear that the main purpose of during-deployment social functions is to enable regimental wives to get acquainted so that if they need support while their husbands are away, they will feel comfortable calling on one other:

The corporals' wives are there. And if they're doing their job properly and they get to know each other, there isn't too much turbulence. And you get to know them on a first name basis by these little groups and associations that these good units and stations and bases are running. When she has a problem she won't be afraid to phone Mary whatever-her-name-is, who's the Master Warrant Officer['s wife] ... And she'll get all kinds of tips and counselling from them.

If the wives lean on one other, the military can relax. The role that a particular wife is expected to play in the support system largely depends on her husband's position. The Commanding Officer's — or, in the navy, the Executive Officer's — wife is expected to be the "mother hen," who brings the unit members' wives together during deployments, shares information about how the men are doing, checks on each wife individually, and gleans valuable information about members' families that she saves to tell her husband. A former army commanding officer's wife recalls a posting in Germany:

I'd have the women from his company in for tea whenever the men were away. I'd have all the women in as often as I could. When the men were away, you as a major — and farther up the ranks — you'd make sure that the families that were in your husband's company were taken care of as much as possible. A lot of them didn't have cars. I drove the car. So I'd go round, I'd see them, I would invite them to my place, have coffee. If they had any problems, was there any way I could help them?

And this navy fiancée's story about an end-of-year farewell function reflects the extent to which the Commanding (or Executive) Officer relies on his wife's detective work:

The ExO [Executive Officer] had something like twenty bouquets of flowers. And the guys that were all being posted that were there with their girlfriends, fiancées, or wives, he called each one of them up individually and he wished them well and where they were going. He had something to say about every single one of them. His wife had kept him real informed as to what everyone was doing. ... Like the ExO and the ExO's wife are very much the social people on the ship.

It is the CO's wife's job to help other wives solve their problems so that the problems will not become unmanageable and jeopardize the deployment. The CO's wife's work is considered so important in this regard that her word often carries enormous weight. An army officer observes:

You'd be surprised how fast things can get solved if the CO's wife decides it's a problem. And in some cases the CO's wife doesn't even have to let her husband know that it's a problem. All that has to happen is that somebody has to know that the CO's wife knows that this is a problem, and a lot of times those problems just disappear.

The former wife of an army CO agrees:

I'm positive a lot of problems got settled with me just mentioning it to the padre, mentioning it to a major at a cocktail party. I knew things were much better after that.

Unit socializing and wives' functions continue between deployments, largely so that the wives can learn to trust one another.

Wives' clubs on the base perform a similar integrative function. They are usually segregated by rank, like the messes, so that each base has three, respectively for junior ranks, senior ranks, and officers' wives. Sometimes, however, especially in the army and navy, wives' clubs are linked with particular regiments or ships. Their activities include fashion shows, Tupperware parties, cosmetic demonstrations, making cookbooks, and community benevolence work. The clubs' main purposes are to help wives feel more a part of the regimental (or officer/non-commissioned) community and to provide them with an additional support group. If a wives' club is attached to a regiment or ship, it is sometimes asked by a rear party to prevent a wife from demanding that her husband be sent home. The former president of an army wives' club recalls:

> There were a couple of instances where I was contacted through someone in Wainwright to speak to a few of the wives because they were upset and things weren't working well, and they wanted their husbands sent home. So we were sent to see if there was something we could do to make things a little easier for them.

In general, rear parties and wives' organizations are important bonding mechanisms that draw wives further into the military community and encourage them to look first to that community for help.

The Military Family Support Program (MFSP)

On 12 April 1991, the Department of National Defence implemented a national Military Family Support Program (MFSP), whose purpose was to supplement the existing regimental, squadron, and naval support systems. Each base and station was invited to apply to National Defence Headquarters (NDHQ) for start-up and ongoing funding[4] to develop a multi-service family resource centre that would respond to family needs as defined by the local base community. The resource centre's purpose would be to "institute family support within the CF (Canadian Forces) community as part of the CF way of life."[5] The centre's program areas would include outreach to new families, child care, family life enrichment, and crisis counselling. The need to involve civilian spouses in decisions that had ramifications for families was explicitly recognized. Indeed, only those applicants who promised a majority of civilian spouses on their centres' boards would be eligible for funding. By March 1993, 38 domestic bases and stations had received funding for centres, two similar centres in Germany had received funding, and an additional two (naval) centres, which did not meet the "civilian majority" requirement, were being funded from different sources.[6]

The implementation of the MFSP has been attributed to a number of factors, the most important one being the military's growing belief that strengthened family support enhances member retention and readiness.

The relationship between family support and readiness was first acknowledged south of the border, where military family research began to flourish in the late 1960s.[7] Three developments during the 1970s provided further impetus to this research. First, when the American military shifted from a conscript to a voluntary organization in 1973, it realized that married men — whose wives could influence them — would now comprise the majority of members. Second, analysts began to believe that the American military was becoming civilianized: that career military members were exchanging their former "institutional" (or "calling") orientation to their work for an "occupational" (or "employee") mentality that was making them less intrinsically committed to military life and more susceptible to being persuaded away from it by wives and competitive employers.[8] Third, wives all over American society were expecting to develop their own careers because of the declining buying power of the single-income family and the influence of the women's movement. Yet this expectation is invariably incompatible with leading a military life. Consequently, between 1979 and 1982, the American military initiated major new family support projects in its navy, marine, air force, and coast guard communities.[9] It also mobilized a formidable battery of positivistic social scientists to conduct studies and recommend the family policies that would be most likely to acquire — and safeguard — wives' loyalty to the military system. Between 1975 and 1985, American military family research output multiplied by ten.[10]

Put crudely, these studies have built upon the psychological insight that human beings' perceptions can be manipulated. Influential studies of military families conducted between 1949 and 1964 concluded that the military wife's attitude toward absences and postings was crucial to how well she and her children adjusted to them. A particular event would not be experienced as stressful, in other words, by people who had been conditioned to regard it as an "adventure" or "challenge."[11] Virtually all military family research be-

tween the 1970s and 1990s has therefore posed the implicit or explicit question: How can the military encourage wives to develop
positive attitudes toward military life?[12] The subsidiary — and prior
— question has been: In which areas is a wife's positive attitude
likely to have the most useful impact? Accordingly, the Army Family
Research Program (1986–91) and other similar multi-million dollar
initiatives have explored the relative importance of such hypothe-
sized predictors of retention and readiness as spousal support,
spousal perception of the military's commitment to families, spousal
integration in the military community, spousal knowledge of family
support resources, and spousal exposure to family support programs.[13] One recent army study has even constructed a dependent
variable, "spousal [combat] readiness," which includes the compo-
nents: preparedness to cope (prior to the deployment), behavioural
adaptability (after the deployment), emotional adaptability (after the
deployment), and physical fitness.[14]

While the societal impetuses for family support (e.g., wives'
changing career expectations) have been similar in Canada, the military impetuses have not. Unlike its American counterpart, the Canadian military has been a volunteer force ever since it became
professional, and the majority of its members have always been
married. In this sense, the 1970s did not mark a significant change.
Canadian research has also failed to corroborate the American experience of members shifting from "institutional" to "occupational"
values. According to Charles Cotton's 1981 study of the Canadian
army, most members have not lost their vocational ("calling") orientations to their military work, and they have remained intrinsically
committed to it.[15]

Perhaps for these reasons, the Canadian military did not begin to
consider the idea of system-wide family support until the late 1970s.
To this end, a landmark event was the 1977 regional social work
conference on the Canadian military family held at Canadian Forces
Base (CFB) Trenton. Participants at this conference were alerted to
the fact that the quality of recruits to the Canadian Forces was
diminishing, and that since the late 1960s retention had become a
problem.[16] Military sociologist Franklin Pinch also expressed alarm
about the negative impact of the women's movement on the traditional family and, by extension, on retention and readiness. He said:

> If husbands are won over to the idea of equal sharing and equal
> opportunity within the family situation, much of the support

that the Forces have expected on the part of military families will simply not be there.[17]

The conference was followed up by another one at CFB Trenton a year later on the Canadian military child. In 1983, the military commissioned a large-scale survey of families, in which 3,077 respondents, 25 per cent of them spouses, filled out long questionnaires about their attitudes to military life. The disturbing results included the following: 62 per cent of spouses believed that the Forces did *not* look after families; 66 per cent believed that they contributed more to the military than they received in return; and 49 per cent believed that the military did not appreciate them.[18]

Another precipitating incident happened at CFB Penhold in 1984, when a group of wives was forbidden to meet on their own base to discuss how they might lobby the military for a family dental plan, day care, pensions, and a safer traffic intersection. The military branded their behaviour "political activity." The wives promptly formed a national organization called Organization of Spouses of Military Members (OSOMM) and sued the Department of National Defence under the Freedom of Association and Equality sections of the Charter of Rights and Freedoms. As part of their suit, OSOMM claimed that wives' inability to make decisions on issues that affected their daily lives amounted to discrimination on the basis of sex and marital status. This incident received considerable notoriety in Parliament and the national media and focused negative public attention on the military's attitude toward wives.

Even without OSOMM, the military might have eventually done something to foster the impression among wives that the Forces cared about families. But OSOMM put the military on the defensive. A subsequent inquiry also revealed that the OSOMM wives' complaints reflected a dissatisfaction that was far more widespread.[19] Accordingly, in April 1987 the military launched a Family Support Program Project, a pilot precursor to the nationwide program initiated in 1991.

If the military needed a final push to get a family support program going, certainly the 1990–91 war in the Persian Gulf brought military families into the spotlight, and members of the public questioned whether the Department of National Defence was doing enough to support the families of the members who had been deployed. The Gulf War was undoubtedly the final precipitating event. Of course, a few bases had implemented their own family support programs during the 1980s.

Family resource centres provide families with information, companionship, recreational diversion, childcare relief, short-term loans, homemaker services, programs for children, day care, family life enrichment, assertiveness training, and counselling. Some centres also attempt to improve their base-community relations, for example, with outreach programs in the schools. An army wife explains how she volunteers at her base's babysitting service in order to get some relief from her own children:

> Tuesday afternoon I'll take them around [to Totminders] and see if they have got space, and very often, in fact, it's a bad day. If Totminders doesn't have space, then I'll stay and volunteer, and at least I'll have other grownups to talk to. Caitlin and Jason are occupied, and occasionally I can give my baby to somebody else to carry for a while if they are not too fed up. It's a break.

A woman who helped to set up her base's family resource centre summarizes what she (and the military) view as its purpose:

> This is essentially for the women, their break away from it, so that when they go back home they can face the situation and cope with it in a more amicable way, a more understanding way, without getting all riled and probably hurting their children, taking their frustration and anger out on the children, which for children is reflected in their school work, in their behaviour at school.

The idea that wives are susceptible to getting "riled" is quite common in military circles.

The present Director of Military Family Support (DMFS) describes his program as "classic community development," and, indeed, the new Canadian program appears — for the military — to be uniquely democratic. Its philosophy is one of community self-help, the idea that if members have a say in the design and management of their community, they will be more empowered and have a greater stake in its success.[20] A recent internal military statement boasts that:

The MFSP is a unique program. In no other country or military force is family support organized in a manner that provides the families with ownership.[21]

The program's stipulation that most members of each base's family support board must be civilian spouses seems to demonstrate that the program's purpose is to empower wives. However, as the historical background of family support programs makes clear, their purposes are in fact to *control* wives in the interests of retention and readiness. It is therefore interesting to speculate on why the MFSP did not simply replicate the relatively paternalistic American approach to providing family support services. The members of OSOMM believe that the Department of National Defence chose the community development model to undermine the "discrimination" claims of OSOMM's lawsuit.

One wife, who is a family support program board member, regards the military's community development rhetoric with scepticism. She says:

I think it can work really well, but I think the base — the military — has difficulty in recognizing the skills and the strength of the spouses — particularly the women. I think they are very threatened by women who know what they are doing and who know the business.

And, when we look closely at the program's design, we see that the military has not in fact relinquished significant power.

Although the idea of a majority of civilian spouses on boards was initially threatening to many base commanders, they need not have worried. Base commanders have the power to approve the composition of resource centre boards, which enables them to keep out spouses they view as "troublemakers." The idea that board members must be people who "can work with" base personnel is used to justify the base's control over their selection. An army officer describes how he controls the selection of the members of his base's board:

There's no reason that you can't find the personalities to make this thing work. I haven't had any difficulty finding the personalities but, mind you, I will be the first to admit that I went out and I recruited. I recruited the people that I wanted, that I knew that I could work with initially. And then after it was over, I took my base of volunteers, and I went to them and I said to people [I trusted], "Have you got somebody that wants to sit on this board, that you feel can sit on the board, that will get along with everybody else and has the same sort of personality that we have?" And the names came out.

The fact that even a minority of family support board members are military can also be intimidating to the members who are wives. One such wife says:

It's intimidating. It can't help but be, simply because they have positions. Most of the other members are usually wives, and very often their husbands are not officers. These are officers.

Finally, while family support boards technically have "ownership," the expectation that they will not make decisions autonomously from military command is espoused at every level from National Defence Headquarters down. Financially and otherwise, the program needs the military's co-operation to survive. As the executive director of one family resource centre puts it:

You can't operate on the base and be totally autonomous, because you are only operating because of the Base Commander's approval. ... Because without his support, we wouldn't have the facility that we have, we wouldn't have the supplies that we get. We wouldn't be able to use Accounting Services. ... If we didn't have the Base Commander's support, we wouldn't have anything. We couldn't operate.

Despite the family support program's democratic rhetoric, these factors combine to enable the military to retain control. Using the rationale of "professionalism," the military has also tried to recruit executive directors for the resource centres who have had no experience in the military community and who have therefore lacked the typical insider ability to elude organizational control subtly.[22]

But almost from the beginning, the military has encountered problems in its control ambitions, usually because some of the spouses who have been involved — either as staff or board members — have taken the community development rhetoric seriously and tried to make the program run in a way that has been responsive to the local community's desires. The military's reaction on these occasions has been severe. On at least one base, a civilian-dominated board was prohibited from appointing its own family resource centre executive director, and was ordered to appoint instead the candidate desired by the base commander. At a number of other bases, military-dominated boards have dismissed so-called "uppity" executive directors without cause. At least one of these firings was preceded by alleged sexual harassment, actions of constructive dismissal, and instances of board members bypassing the executive director to give orders directly to the staff.[23]

Since the family support program has been operating for only three years, the frequency of these events is disturbing. Rhetoric notwithstanding, they demonstrate the military's inherent inability to relinquish control. They also demonstrate the military's inability to contain the politically sensitive contradictions it generates.

Self-Reliance: Real and Mythical

Even if family support mechanisms worked perfectly, they could not compensate wives for all the labour, loneliness, and disappointments that befall them when their husbands are away.

This is where the self-reliance mythology comes in, the idea that military wives are especially self-reliant women who can handle anything life throws at them. At NDHQ, at every base and station, in almost every military wife's living room, the mythology — and ideal — of military wives' self-reliance is taken-for-granted conversational wisdom.

Military wives do indeed learn to be self-reliant; the assertion that they are self-reliant is therefore more real than a myth. But the assertion is made so frequently in military communities that it has acquired an existence of its own and the power to influence wives' behaviour. Because military wives are reputed to be self-reliant, they individually often feel they *have* to be, and it is this detail that is socially important. Hence, as well as being a natural attribute of the military wives' community, self-reliance operates as a social pressure.

The military needs wives to internalize the self-reliance requirement so it can concentrate on its deployments. This is true despite all the traditional and recent family support initiatives. An NDHQ general spells the situation out:

You cannot in the military marry somebody who, as they say in French, "a les deux pieds dans la même botte." I mean, if they can't drive a car, use a phone, sort out the insurance, everything else, they're going to find this life a disaster, because the other part of the family isn't going to be around to sort it out. I mean, when you're in your slit trench in Yugoslavia and she says, "I've just had an accident, what do I do?" I mean what the heck do you want *me* to do about this? So they have to be very very self-reliant. And if you are in the military and you don't have a self-reliant spouse, you have a problem.

The general speaks from a position of power. Wives who talk of the need for self-reliance usually do so from the more fatalistic standpoint that they have no alternative, that their husbands' absences are something they must accept. An army officer's wife says:

You come to a point when you just have to get on with it. I mean, you could spend the whole six months feeling sorry for yourself and getting nothing done. But you can't change it. So, more or less, I carry on.

Wives often internalize the self-reliance prescription so thoroughly that they engage in self-censorship to enable their husbands to concentrate to the utmost during courses and missions. Wives find themselves not divulging bad news, coping alone with financial problems, and not asking that their husbands be brought back for a childbirth or major surgery. They feel that if they behaved otherwise, they would be letting the military — and themselves — down.

By praising wives who are self-reliant, the military shapes the way wives view each other. The fact that the military community so visibly values wives' self-reliance sets up an implicit competition, encouraging endless friendly and not-so-friendly behind-the-scenes personal comparisons. Some wives use other women's more difficult predicaments to inspire them, while others allow some women's perceived deficiencies to boost them. An air element member's wife says:

I feel like I'm more on an even keel, where I see a lot of people tipping. And I feel better, because I can come, pat them on the shoulder, and say it's going to be all right.

Still other wives reflect the community standard by speaking in disappointment or anger about women who have fallen short. Speak-

ing of a woman who managed to prevent her husband from being
sent to Cyprus, an army officer's wife says:

> When the rumour came out, the message came, that the guys
> were going to Cyprus in the fall of '88, the wife went to Social
> Services and said, "If my husband goes to Cyprus, I will leave
> him." So he got a compassionate posting out of the regiment
> for a year. But in fact she was militia, so she knew about the
> military. She had no children. There were a lot of other wives
> that had more reasons for compassionate postings than she did.
> ... Like there was no reason. His career has gone totally down
> the tubes. ... He's not going anywhere. He's not going to be
> able to do anything, because he had no control over his wife.

A chaplain's wife summarizes:

> It's pointless to be a wife that complains about these things. It
> just isn't something that you want to do. It's no good for his
> career.

The pressure to be self-reliant is strong in the military community
because when it is successful, the military agenda is safe. A frequent
consequence of the self-reliance mythology is that wives become
afraid to speak about their difficulties to anyone.[24]

Military bonding requires absences, which in turn rely on wives'
flexibility, loyalty to the military, self-reliance, and unpaid work.
Military organization is intricately calculated to ensure that wives
exhibit the proper attitudes and that, no matter what it costs, the
military's work will get done.

3

The Gulf War

On 2 August 1990, Iraq invaded Kuwait. The United States responded immediately, and Canada followed close behind. During the next few months, American officials mobilized against Iraq the moral weight of the United Nations and the military might of 32 other countries.[1] The thrust of most coalition propaganda issued was that Saddam Hussein was a modern-day Hitler. Nevertheless, many charged that the U.S.'s real aim was to thwart Hussein's efforts to raise the price of Middle East oil, which, if successful, would have resulted in a lower standard of living in the United States.[2] The United States was also anxious to arise triumphant from the Vietnam War ruins and re-establish itself as the world's superior power.

On 6 August, the United Nations imposed stiff economic sanctions against Iraq, to which Canada added its official support four days later. On 24 August, 934 Canadian military members set sail from Halifax — 562 on the destroyers *Athabaskan* and *Terra Nova* and 372 on the supply ship *Protecteur* — to help enforce the sanctions. Their mission was called Operation Friction. On 9 October, 24 CF-18 fighter planes, staffed by "Desert Cats" — a composite of 416 Squadron from Cold Lake and 439 Squadron from the Baden-Soellingen Canadian base in Germany — were deployed to provide air cover for the ships from the "Canada Dry" camp in the desert at Qatar. A number of army members were also sent to Qatar, from several bases across Canada and from the Lahr and Baden-Soellingen Canadian bases in Germany. On 1 January 1991, the crew of the *Protecteur* was replaced by a crew that was normally deployed on the supply ship *Preserver*.

On 29 November, UN Security Council Resolution 678 imposed a deadline on Saddam Hussein, demanding that he withdraw from Kuwait by 15 January. Otherwise, his troops would be evicted by force. On 16 January 1991, despite several withdrawal offers conveyed by Iraq and France, "Operation Desert Storm" commenced and lasted for 43 days. On 16 January, immediately after receiving a

phone call from President George Bush, Prime Minister Brian Mul-
roney convened his cabinet and secured its endorsement of Canada's
full participation in Desert Storm. This decision authorized the Desert Cats to be involved in aggressive "first strike" action. It was
Canada's first combat experience since the Korean War of 1950–51
and the first combat that the present generation of military members
had seen.

Coalition fighter planes dropped 85,000 tons of non-nuclear
bombs on Iraq, or the equivalent of five Hiroshimas.[3] They caused
between 11,000 and 24,500 *immediate* civilian deaths.[4] They also
destroyed, or severely compromised, most of the infrastructures of
Iraq's nuclear capacity, aviation, communications, power generation,
sanitary water system, and food production, thus causing an estimated eventual 100,000 more deaths. The long-term environmental
and health damage caused by war-related nuclear contamination and
oil spills still continues in the Middle East and promises to be extensive and profound.[5]

The coalition's ground offensive was initiated in the early hours
of 24 February. On 27 February, Kuwait was recaptured, and within
24 hours President Bush ordered a ceasefire. For the moment, the
Persian Gulf War was over. A Canadian field hospital had barely
been erected when the ceasefire agreement was signed. By then,
about 2,400 Canadian military members had been deployed to the
Persian Gulf area.[6]

The Gulf War and the Military

The Gulf War demonstrated that military socialization in Canada
works well. During the 30-odd years Canada had not been involved
in international combat, courses, exercises, internal security, and
peacekeeping taskings had managed to supplement basic training to
produce and keep combat bonding primed amongst the members of
her Forces. Nevertheless, from the military's perspective, the Gulf
War happened at an opportune time. The Cold War was over, budget
cutbacks were proceeding, many members felt that they had lost their
purpose, and morale was at an all-time low.

So, when those members tasked to the Gulf found out who they
were, many were overjoyed. For the first time since they had joined
the Forces, they would be able to put their training into action. While
some sent to the Gulf (especially women with small children) viewed
their deployment as an unpleasant "job," many others were far more
positive. The wife of a fighter pilot who served in the Gulf compares

the members of her husband's squadron to puppies straining at a leash:

> Somehow or another, somebody found out. ... And these puppies were [asking] "Is it right? Is it true? Is it us?" And [the CO] was like, "I can't tell you." He was just as excited as everybody else. And it was like a party atmosphere, a festive atmosphere. Finally they were just sort of leaping at the leash, wanting to go, wanting to do it, and not at all afraid of what was ahead of them. It was really a sort of old fashioned esprit de corps where you send them off with marching bands and whistles.

Because the Gulf crisis was a combat situation, intense bonding occurred within the deployed units. For deployed navy officers, this bonding began even before the ships left port. For others, like the Desert Cat fighter pilots, bonding did not begin until they had reached their destination, at which time a pilot and co-pilot who had formerly been strangers found themselves living, working, and sleeping as a pair.

Given the bonding that already existed among squadron members, it would have been extremely difficult for a member who stayed behind while his or her squadron went to the Gulf. The husband of a deployed air element member (who is himself a member) says:

> Heather's name was on it from day one, and it was never even questioned that she was going to be taken off. I suppose maybe she could have got out of it. Like saying, "Listen I have a small child, my husband works, can I stay back?" It never even entered her mind to ask, "Can I stay back?" And I gave full support. I said, "Heather your squadron is going over, you are part of the squadron, you have been there since day one. To me you are committed — you have to go."

Some felt their calling as military members so keenly that even though they were not deployed to the Gulf, they wished they had been. This husband of a deployed female member was one of them:

> I sent a memo, saying "I want to go." ... I said, "I won't feel right if I sit here and don't try to go." ... I thought it was my duty. My fellow airmen were there in a war zone, war situation.

To me that's what I get paid for — I should be over there too.
And a lot of my people had that problem — they wanted to be
over there. This is what we train for day after day after day.
Now it's here — why can't we go over there? But our commitment was only so many people, and they wouldn't up that
commitment.

If this airman and his wife had both been deployed, their young child
would have had to have been left with grandparents. The difference
between feeling that as a military member one was compelled to fight
and viewing the Gulf deployment as a less important job than parenting is visible in his description of how angry his wife would have
been if his efforts had worked:

I think she knew. She knew all the time that I wanted to be over
there. But she didn't know the steps that I went through to try
to get there until she got back. 'Cause it was something I didn't
tell her. ... Like I'd never have told her that I'd asked. She'd
have said, "What are you doing here? You have a child at home.
I left you there to look after our child." And to me, "Yes, you
did. But my duty is to serve my country, and my country is at
war 15,000 miles away, and that's where I belong." ... She just
wouldn't have understood why I would want to put myself in
the same situation she was in. She hadn't asked to go.

The Gulf Deployment and Wives' Work

As we have seen, the normal work burden of the deployed member's
wife is immense. The burden was much heavier during the Gulf War
for several reasons. First, the danger to the member was more real,
and the wife had more anxiety to manage. Second, the war was
prominently featured in the mass media, which meant that the wife
had to monitor her own and her children's exposure to these media
to keep their fears from skyrocketing. The involvement of the media
also meant wives had to deal continually with the possibility of
having their private raw emotions exposed to strangers. Third, the
duration of the war was indefinite, which escalated anxiety and made
it even more difficult than usual for the wife to exert control over
her future. Fourth, the wife had to manage the emotions she displayed
to her husband, who often had a different perspective from hers on
Canada's (and his own) rightful role in the conflict.

The wife's work usually began at the moment her husband told her he was going. All wives remember it vividly. Most of them remember it as a horrifying shock. One woman recollects:

> When I came home from work that day, he was lighting the wood stove downstairs in the rec room. I could tell by the look on his face that he had something to tell me, but I always think it is money or something like that — never think that there is a problem in the world except for money. And he said to me, "I have something to talk to you about." And we were talking about the Persian Gulf and all this stuff at the time. And I said, "What is it?" He said, "I'm going to the Gulf." And I said, "Yeah, okay." And I just walked away. I just thought he was joking with me. And I came down the stairs and said, "Now seriously hon, what do you want to talk about?" He said, "I'm going to the Persian Gulf, Mary. I have to go January the 1st." And I said, "No seriously now, hon, what are you talking about? Don't be ridiculous." ... I kept on saying, "Now don't be so foolish." Then all of a sudden it dawned on me that he wasn't lying to me. And I just broke down and I went hysterical.

The wife of a deployed air element member recalls:

> He came to work on January the 20th or something, or 22nd. It was a Friday, and he never comes to work, never comes to the hospital. He came to my work. I run the floor, so I had an office and I was talking to someone about a nurse ... and all of a sudden he knocked on the door. I thought to myself, "My God, somebody has died for sure," because he never comes. And he said, "They are sending me to the Gulf." And I ... honest to God, in all the times that we had been separated this was the one time it really took me by surprise. I didn't resent him going. I understood that. I just don't think I ever really got over the shock, because I never thought he would go. It never occurred to me that he would go. ... Anyway he had all his needles and stuff, and we had the weekend, and he left on Monday. I don't think I ever really got over that.

After absorbing the initial shock, wives found that their next task was to manage their emotions during the days and weeks until their husbands left. One wife recalls putting her own life completely on hold during this period, which only added to the emptiness she felt afterwards:

> It was really hard living together for that month. It was awful. Plus you know he's doing that because he's leaving. So that was really hard. And I put all my activities aside just to, you know, concentrate on him. I knew he was coming back, but you never know, eh? So all my activities, all my social things, I left aside, and spent all my month with him. Got his stuff. Saw his friends. Everything for him.

A woman who worked professionally with wives whose husbands had already been deployed spent Christmas waiting for her own husband to leave in January. She recalls how hard it was for her to keep reassuring the other wives:

> We had a very rotten Christmas, because all we kept on thinking about was this could be the last Christmas. And it's strange. I was still going out there telling these people not to worry, that their husbands were coming home and everything was going to be fine. But then I would come home and think that this could be the last Christmas.

Send-off day was another challenge. Send-offs ranged from quiet farewells at homes or airports to the nationally televised extravaganza that surrounded the departure of the ships from Halifax. The long-time wife of a navy member, who watched the ships sail off, says that it was the sight of the guns and weapons that brought the terror of the situation suddenly home to her:

> We were standing there, and when I saw the ship sail out with all the guns on it that had never been there before — all the weaponry — I think that's when it finally hit me. And I just. ... Well, I was glad for my son's big strong arms. I mean, he just sort of wrapped me. And it was really then. ... It was the not knowing. It was knowing that they were going into a situation that was totally different than anything that had ever happened before in our lifetime. And it was a sense of, you know, I didn't know if I was going to see him again. I was in a crowd of about 3,000, but I felt totally alone. ... I'd watched

the ship sail out many times and I'd hated to see them go. But I'd known they'd be back.

After send-off, the real work started. Managing emotions remained an important part of it. For understandable reasons, women with young children expended most of their energy on helping their children cope, while women who were fiancées, childless, or the mothers of grown children focused mostly on themselves. For the women in this latter group, what needed to be managed were their feelings of emptiness, purposelessness, and powerlessness, their sense of having nothing to do except wait.

The whole Gulf deployment was characterized by uncertainty, which demolished many wives' sense of having control over their lives. The fact that they did not know exactly when their husbands would return took on tremendous significance. A navy wife says:

I did count days. ... I started at number one and ended at 226. Usually I count reverse order. This time I counted up. There was no other way this time.

Some of the younger women who were not firmly established in work or childrearing reported that while the members were in the Gulf, they felt as if their lives had been indefinitely suspended. One navy officer's fiancée felt that she wasted a lot of time and could hardly concentrate on writing her nursing exams because her overwhelming focus was on writing letters and sending care packages:

I was writing my exams. My RNs. The second time. I couldn't concentrate. I was sure I'd flunk them again. And I said, "If I flunk them a second time I'll be so worked up the third time. Maybe he'll be arriving home, and I'll have to rewrite them again." He had seven weeks off when he got home. We had planned to go to Europe. So everything was kind of in the balance if I passed my exams. [And] was I going to move out, was I going to get an apartment now, or wait until he got back? It was like I couldn't make decisions. There were days I wouldn't get up til two o'clock. The days I didn't work I wouldn't get up til two, and then I'd stay up til two at night, watching the movies and watching CNN. I used to live by the TV and read the paper every day. On my days off, it was the weirdest existence. I spent all my time off writing letters and making care packages.

The fiancée of another navy officer was laid off from her job, but because she did not know when he would be returning (and they would be getting married and moving to another part of Canada), she could not mobilize herself to look for other work:

> He was supposed to be home in February, and he had all this leave, and we were going to go to Ottawa for a while, and then we were going to go out west. So I figured, "When he gets back I'll look for a job. I'm going to move back to Ottawa." Because that was where he was going to be posted. So [I thought] I'd go back home and look for a job. And then no, it's not February, it's March. Okay, well it's not March, now for sure he is coming home in April. So it was like up, down, up, down. It was very embarrassing trying to talk to people at work saying, "Margaret, what are you doing, you're supposed to be gone." "Well, I know, but now it's this date." ... So it was just contradictory all the time. I didn't go back to work. I could have worked something with the reserves, but I just drew unemployment insurance.

Even at this stage in their relationships, these fiancées were learning to be completely flexible about their lives.

Despite the media's focus on small children waving good-bye to their fathers and on young mothers coping alone, the women who did not have children at home may actually have become more depressed. A childless air element wife claims that the plight of mothers with children was so widely publicized that she felt reluctant to ask the community for help:

> We had a rough winter. We had lots of snow, so I shovelled and kept the house, made sure nothing would freeze and all that stuff, and it was rough. And I went through it by myself. I didn't ask for any help. ... I didn't have kids, I only had myself, so I said, "They have enough work with the rest of the people."

The fact that the Gulf War received so much publicity put burdens on wives that previous deployments had not. One of them was managing the fact that other people pitied them. One young wife grew so tired of the emotional stress that she occasionally wanted to run away. She says:

> Some days I said, "That's it — I'm running away! I've had enough! I don't want to be here any more! I want to go where no one knows me or no one says, 'Oh poor you, he's over in the Gulf, what are you doing? It must be so terrible for you.' " Just go away and be Jane Doe and start my life over again, and go out and have a great time. ... There was a period, like about two months, when I didn't send him any tapes at all, and he said, "Hey, what's going on, how come you're not writing me or anything?" I don't know — I just sort of shut down. Like I didn't want to do it. ... At first you want to sit down and tell him everything. And then you think, "Gosh, life's going on, what should I tell you sort of thing?" ... It's really hard. The closeness is not there when they have been away for a while.

At one level, maintaining their relationship was hard for a number of wives. Some of them deeply feared that their husbands would not come back. As a result, they became split in two: one part of them intensely hoping that their husbands would come back, the other part not daring to hope, believing it was realistic to begin to plan a new future and feeling guilty for doing so. Living both parts of themselves in sequence — first one, then the other, depending on moods and circumstances — was exhausting and destabilizing. One deployed member's wife says:

> I didn't think he was going to come home. And I didn't know what I wanted to do with my life. I didn't know where I wanted to go. I didn't want to go back to Vancouver. But did I want to settle in his hip pocket in Halifax? Did I want to strike out and start again somewhere? Did I even want to start again? Did I want a man in my life again? The answer was no to that. But, you know, it was like thoughts that you shouldn't be having when you're still married. And supposedly happily married.

Wives with growing children had different problems. Their main task was containment: trying to keep the children on an emotional even keel so that their fears would not become unmanageable. This work began when the deployment was disclosed and often did not end until after the member had returned home. Part of it involved repressing the wife's own fears in the hope that her children would not find out they were there. For this reason, at least one wife did not see her husband off:

> I didn't go to the airport. I figured it was going to be hard enough to say good-bye at the doorstep. A trip to the airport was too much, especially with the kids. And I figured the less of a routine we do this, and the more like a normal Daddy-is-going-sailing we make this, the easier it's going to be. So the girls said "Good-bye, Daddy" — da, da, da, da — and went to school. And when they came home, there were still a few, you know, and that evening still, but I figured I don't want to make a big deal about this, because the more I make of it the more upset she is going to be, or the other one is going to be. So they did pretty good with it.

Wives' containment work often included monitoring their children's exposure to the television. Although the war coverage was sanitized, relative to the coverage of the war in Vietnam, the footage of coalition prisoners and the constant sounds of alarms, bombs, and Scud missiles were not reassuring. Here the VCR came in handy; many women spent their Saturdays taping children's shows and the rest of the week doling out taped fare to prevent their children from tuning in live. In a few reverse cases, however, it was actually older children who stopped their mothers from tuning in. The mother of one teenager reports:

> Maxine said, "My daddy has to go. I am just going to say he's not going to get killed, and I am not watching the news." She did — she flatly refused to watch the news. And I would sit down once a day and watch the news and she'd start saying, "Let's forget it." … I just gave up, so we just didn't bother.

Influences on children from outside the home were harder to control than farewell scenes and TV, especially school and peer groups. One way that some mothers tried to control what happened at school was to alert teachers to their children's mood swings in the hopes that on these days the teachers would relax their vigilance. On at least one occasion, this kind of initiative worked, and a mother and teacher co-operated to make a child's day easier. According to the mother:

One day Cindy was having a hard time while Carl was in the Gulf. And I phoned up to the school and said, "She's really upset." And the secretary said, "Well, Mrs. Scott, all these children are upset." And I said, "Well, she didn't sleep well last night. I was just wondering if anything happens maybe you could give her an extra hug. And just be aware that something might happen." Well, so I guess when the secretary realized where it was coming from ... she told the teacher. The teacher kept Cindy in at recess and had Cindy do the boards and sort of become the special student. Well, Cindy came home at 4 o'clock and she goes, "Mrs. Webster kept me in today and I got to help her and I was the teacher's pet!" You know, she was just blown right up.

Even less easy to control were the thoughtless comments of children's peers. For wives struggling to keep a lid on the situation, this kind of event could be the last straw. A fighter pilot's wife broke down in front of a school principal after one student told her young daughter that her father was a murderer.

Often the experience of the war could not be contained, and the mothers had to cope with the consequences. Some children were constantly frightened that their fathers were going to die. One mother recalls:

They really believed that he was going to die. We had a lot of that to deal with. After he was gone, I was taking the kids home for Christmas and we were fat and happy and driving down the highway. And Shane just out of the blue turned to me and said, "Are you going to get married again if Dad dies?" And it was like whoa — instant tears in the eyes. And I just said, "Well, I don't want to think about that right now."

Children's school work also suffered, and some of them lost their year. Other children suffered severe traumas either just before or during the deployment, and the deployment exacerbated them. One child who had been sexually abused just prior to the war suffered a serious setback in her recovery. The mothers of these children coped with the fallout.

The Military's Containment Work

The military did everything it could to maintain public support for the war. In some ways, the most important part of this public was the serving members' families. They — especially the spouses — needed to be kept motivated to cope on their own. For an uncertain duration, they needed to believe that they possessed sufficient resources to manage all the negative emotions that the war would unleash and to handle each crisis as it arose. They also needed to continue to be willing to do all the extra work that the war created for them. If the spouses had either panicked or turned into peaceniks, they would have threatened deployed members' morale. They would also have conveyed these sentiments to the wider public and caused irreparable political harm. It was very much in the military's interest to retain the spouses' support.

The military had its work cut out for it. Throughout the lifetime of its present members, the Canadian Forces have staked their international reputation on peacekeeping. In addition, most of the current generation of members — with the support of their wives — originally joined the Forces for financial security, not because they intended to fight a war. For these reasons at least, not all military wives supported Canada's aggressive role in the Gulf conflict. One wife, whose husband was not part of it, says:

> I can't believe someone would say that it's their husband's job to go to the Gulf and get killed. I don't believe that. I mean, if he ever went to the war, I would just die. I couldn't handle it. I know he's in the military and may have to, but I think of the military as just being a job. Not as defending your country. It was just a job in '82 that he got because of a recession.

A non-commissioned navy officer has a frank answer for her:

> Too bad! This is the Canadian Armed Forces, and we act with the National Defence Act! We are going to fight a war here, and we are going to kill, and we are going to be killed and kill people, and we are a sledge hammer, and we haven't got time to get these ships mobilized and worry about whether somebody likes it or doesn't like it! ... I want my kids to come home, and I want the best guy sitting there, and I don't care if I have to take that spouse's husband! I just don't care! ... I don't care what he or she thinks, because I have no obligation to her! I

have obligations to these boys that are going in harm's way! She's not going in harm's way! Spouses are not going to open the door like they did in the Falkland Islands and find their friend bubbling in his fat because the ship has been hit by a missile. That's what we are talking about here! Let's not pretend that we are in some game here! I am in the war business, and until Canada decides to get rid of its army, I have only one obligation — to take care of my sailors!

His answer shows the phenomenal depth of combat bonding. It also bluntly reveals the military's attitude toward wives.

Another one of the military's problems was the fact that the public (and wives) could not be given complete information about the progress of the war, the role of the country's armed forces, and the exact distance of these forces from the heart of the hostilities. Apart from national security considerations, the situation often changes rapidly in a conflict, especially in a coalition context.

The story therefore changed about the position of the Canadian warships. First, it was announced that they would only go as far as the Gulf of Oman. Subsequently, Canadians learned that they would be moving much closer to the action, right into the Persian Gulf itself. The role of the Desert Cats fighter air squadron evolved, similarly, from merely providing cover for the warships to participating in the bombing raids over Baghdad.

The discrepancies among these accounts were frustrating for the deployed members' wives. For example, some navy wives believed the military had "known all along" that the ships would end up in the Persian Gulf and in the beginning had deliberately lied. Considerable effort was actually made to provide spouses with military information about new occurrences — especially negative ones — before they were revealed by the media as "news." But its need to withhold information frequently landed the military in difficulty. According to a navy wife:

They lied to us from the word Go. ... They showed us this map where the ships were going, and they said, "Our ships are only going to the Oman Canal." And, I mean, being a navy wife, or I should say military wife, when they tell you something, you know you don't believe them until they're there. Because they lie so much. The military lies so much to us — I find anyway. And then we went to another briefing and, "Oh, they're going further." Like they had told us the ships were never never up front. And they were. They lied the whole eight months.

Another navy wife says:

> The whole time the guys were gone, we were told nothing. We knew more from the news than we did from anything else. If we wanted to know something, we'd tune into the radio or the TV.

The military's efforts to contain and minimize such cynicism needed to be executed carefully. The military was quite fearful of possible "hysteria" from wives, especially wives of the members who had been sent to the Gulf from the two bases in Germany. According to a family support staffer at one of those bases, the military worked very hard:

> They bent over backwards — they really did. And the reason they did was because they didn't know. ... They were so worried that they were going to have mass hysteria amongst the women. They were going to have plane loads of people wanting to go home to Canada, you know, all that sort of thing. They did. They bent over backwards.

She continues:

> You see, our biggest fear was, after the war broke out, that there was going to be a death. And we knew that once that happened, if it happened, there was nothing that we were going to be able to do for any of these women. They were going to go berserk. I mean, as well they should, you know. I mean, there's no question on that. Our greatest fear was that no matter what we had in place to deal with it, there was not going to be enough to deal with that first death. It never happened.

On the bases in Germany, the military briefings to wives were frequent and thorough, and some genuine attempts were made to answer their questions. The staffer recalls:

> When we had our support group every Wednesday night or every Wednesday afternoon, there were at least three — either

the Base Commander or his right hand person, the Base Service Officer or his right hand person, the PR person (public relations), myself, or Kelly. There was no aspect that wasn't available to them. They were available. Then they would come, they would make a 15-minute statement to say there was news, or there wasn't news. Or women who had questions about certain things asked them. Then after the 15-minute session, the Base Commander would be here to answer questions or Commander Finch was here. Then they left if there was no discussion, and then the support part of the meeting carried on where the wives arranged to do things with each other or help each other out, or that sort of thing. I don't think there's a woman over here that can complain about lack of being involved.

Special family support services were erected at every affected base to keep wives calm during the Gulf crisis and to prevent them as much as possible from requesting that their husbands be repatriated. Efforts were made to make these services as comprehensive as possible. One family resource centre director recalls:

We did it on "tri-effort." There was one squadron, ourselves, and the padres. And we each took a certain aspect of that. The squadron developed home uses, like pet sitting, shovelling driveways, and things like that. So they took care of the physical needs, and we [Family Resource Centre] did a lot of the emotional needs and some physical needs, but mostly emotional. And Freda did an awful lot in the schools, helping the kids get through their feelings and their emotions. The rest of us just did the emotion bit and helped out with homemakers and babysitters and that type of thing. ... It was really a very combined effort of all the aspects on the base.

Purely social functions were considered excellent morale-boosters. Another family resource centre worker says:

We tried very much with our functions. We always had at least a couple a month that involved the children. Valentine's Day you'd have a Valentine's party, and a Hallowe'en party and Christmas parties. We went on sleigh rides. We had arts and crafts that we made to send over to the guys for Christmas time, with a Christmas tree. We had the kids involved in making cookies to send to dad. They were always involved one way or the other. We had functions where we would go to people's homes and play football and do videos. There were videos and pictures made galore on the Persian Gulf, and that always kept us busy too, so we tried to have two evenings a month where the wives would come together at a social where we could talk about what was going on.

The regimental rear party system operated as usual for deployed army members' wives, as did their equivalent organizations on ships. Even the deployed air squadrons organized rear parties, and each deployed member's wife was assigned a member of the rear party as a sponsor. In addition to their usual post-deployment arrangements, each of the three warships organized a special Operation Friction support group, which was co-led by a family support centre staffperson, a wife, and a co-ordinating committee. An effort was made to represent all ranks on the committee. The evening that the Operation Desert Storm offensive was initiated (16 January 1991) and the coalition planes began bombing Baghdad, each 416 air squadron rear party sponsor visited all of his assigned homes to make sure that none of the squadron wives spent the evening alone. On another occasion, the rear party provided a "drunk bus" and a male stripper for a squadron's wives' dinner party and authorized a special phone call through to Qatar so that each woman present could speak to her husband. In Halifax, a permanent phone number was set up which spouses could dial for news and messages.

Despite the impressive number of services it rendered, the military's main objectives were to get the wives networking with one another and to motivate them to take the steps they needed to take to learn to support themselves. Groups of women going out together was an important part of this networking. The fiancée of a deployed navy officer claims that these outings were very therapeutic:

It was good to get together and talk to them, because they were in the same situation as you. There you weren't pitied by everyone, because everyone was in the same situation. You always thought that you were in the worst spot, but there were others who were always worse off than you. ... We would call one another and say, "Listen, this is what is going on now," or "We're planning this night out for dinner — if you want to come you're more than welcome." Or we'd have people over to our homes just for a get-together, for a drink and get together and talk and that.

For at least one navy wife, these encounters were far more meaningful than her encounters with civilians:

> I think there was a special sort of a bonding that came together. Everybody knew that. Any time that there was a crisis or special news bulletin, we usually would get together and talk about it. And we all knew that we were in the same situation, and we could say what we wanted to say. Where I used to find that my neighbours and friends that weren't in the situation sometimes pussyfooted around the issue. They didn't want to say too much because, well, "Her husband's in the Gulf." Well, we all could be open about it.

Sometimes the togetherness amongst the wives could have the opposite effect and heighten anxiety. Sensing the mood of the other wives in her husband's unit, one wife decided that she would remain calmer if she spent the evening of 16 January alone:

> I stayed by myself, and about half an hour later the wives called me. They had all gone to one of the wives' houses, and they were crying over the phone, and they said they wanted me to go and sit with them for that evening. I said, "No, no, no — I'm fine. I'm gonna stay home and, you know, if I want to cry I'll cry by myself." Because those wives were like, "Ohhhh! my God." They were crying and screaming — I could hear them over the phone. So I said, "No — I'll stay here by myself."

Networking was also less successful when it appeared to replicate the military ranking system. Husbands' ranks often determined the leadership of support groups, especially those representing the three warships deployed from Halifax. Efforts were made to have all ranks represented in these groups' steering committees. But despite the initial importance apparently given to husbands' ranks, a number of women who led the groups believed that as the groups evolved, it was phenomenal how little rank mattered. It seemed that for the first time in the history of the Canadian military, wives were so united by their common predicament that they did not allow extraneous circumstances to divide them. Nevertheless, some wives of non-commissioned members felt that choosing the executive committees by husbands' ranks got the groups off on the wrong foot and that rank was, indeed, a factor that determined how individual women were treated. One navy wife says:

> There were some people there who thought they were better than other people because their husband might have been a Chief or something. See, what happened was the night of the first meeting there were executives picked, and I think that's what turned me off. This was an officer's wife and this was this and this and this. ... What Jesus difference does it make whose wife you are? You're in the same boat we are! They're all over there together! ... They said they wanted one from each, you know — Chief and POs or whatever. Garbage!

Similarly, the wife of an army member deployed from Germany, who was active in a telephone "fanout" network, was shunned by some of the officers' wives who had been assigned to her.

Despite such problems, most wives of deployed members found the military community more comforting during the crisis than they found the members of their own extended families. Most women who had a choice elected to remain in the military community rather than packing up and going home to parents or siblings. A non-commissioned army wife, whose husband was deployed from Germany, says:

> Everybody was concerned about the war, I think, here. It was a good thing. It's why I didn't want to go to Canada, because in Canada it would only have been my family. What would I have done? Just stay at home all day and watch television? I said, "No, I want to stay here. I know I can do something — everybody is concerned." So I was fairly comfortable here.

The fact that most wives made this choice made the military's job of containing their emotions easier.

One of the military's main objectives was to manage wives' reactions to the media. The military often attempted to prevent media-induced fear by putting its own informational spin on major developments before the wives heard about them on radio or TV. An army wife recalls:

I remember one morning they said, "Okay, a bomb just passed Qatar." "Oh, Qatar is where they are, so what's happened with them?" So they told us the bomb went 15 km near where they were. So we knew nobody was hurt at that time, before we had the information on radio or someplace else.

From her vantage-point, the director of a family resource centre adds:

It was very American, you know, that the Patriot missiles and all this hit a Scud. Well, these were all on the American territory, so you never really did hear what was happening to the Canadians. So those who did sit and watch it unfold were watching the American side. And they would get a little antsy because, "Is this happening to my husband?" ... So then we started letting them know that this isn't ... "Don't watch that! If you don't hear it it's not true. We didn't tell you it was such!" And that got to be one of our most famous statements at our briefings.

According to the husband of a deployed female member, American news was actually appropriate because Canadian forces shared both the Americans' role in the aggression and their physical space. He says:

The 416 was working with a squadron of American F15s using the same hangar. And so if they were going after the Americans, the Canadians were right beside them. ... I don't know how many people knew that they flew side by side with a squadron of F15s out of Qatar. I am sure most of the Canadian public didn't know that. They probably thought the Canadians were there in this little place all by themselves.

From the military standpoint, the strict accuracy of its information was less important than the fact that the wives trusted it and used the support groups to ventilate (and therefore allow the military to manage) their fears.

The military also tried to manage rumours, especially in PMQ neighbourhoods. The wife of a navy member recollects:

Harbour Heights was a bad place to live when the guys went to the Gulf. Because you couldn't go anywhere. Everybody knew your husband was away. And everybody would ask you things, and everybody was telling you all these different rumours. Oh yeah — it was hilarious down here. It was crazy. But there were times that I was scared.

Wives were encouraged to divulge frightening rumours they had heard so that the military could dispel them. A rumour that was out in the open could be parried and thrust aside; a rumour allowed to fester could weaken morale. One of the navy fiancées says:

At the beginning you'd watch TV ... or you'd call them and say, "Listen, I heard this rumour." They encouraged that. They said, "Listen, if you hear a rumour or something that you're not sure of, just give us a call." The ExO's wife was in charge at MarCom, and they had a good group. She'd call him every couple of days if she heard a rumour, and she would say, "Listen, this is what I heard," sort of thing. There were always tons of rumours and that floating by all the time. After a while you'd go, "Oh no, that's not for sure, that's not true."

Some attempt was also made to manage wives' expectations. The deployed members' return dates were uncertain, and many of the navy wives, in particular, hoped that their husbands would be home by Christmas. As it turned out, they were not. Through its various support mechanisms, the military endeavoured to make sure that the wives did not expect too much, realizing that exaggerated hopes followed by disappointment might bring despair, which on a collective basis could produce chaos. An active wife in one of the ship's support groups recalls:

Right at the beginning I told everybody, "Think six months, and then if it's earlier you won't be disappointed. Don't expect them home for Christmas."

Wives whose expectations could be aligned with military policy early were less likely to make excessive demands and even less likely to complain when their hopes were dashed.

The military's honest answer to the complaint, "I don't want you to deploy my husband," is that it is under no obligation to wives, that its only obligations are to the combat unit that needs to send its best members into battle in order to save the most lives. The Gulf War comprised one of many demonstrations to the military that the honest answer is counterproductive. An answer that somehow communicates the message "wives are important" is more likely to make wives feel that they are being well informed and cared for and that their own contribution to the war is appreciated. The military has increasingly come to reason that such wives will be more content, their husbands will be more content, and deployments will operate more smoothly. The fiancée of a navy officer summarizes:

> This past deployment, to me, has been, hey the family's been noticed. To a certain extent they do it to keep them happy. Mail! Like they wanted to get the mail through because the mail really boosts their morale and they wanted to keep everyone happy. … It really came into their consciousness. We have to look after these families sort of thing. Even the sports end, it really kicked into high gear. Like a lot for the children, there was a lot more awareness of the kids in school, how they were reacting. Which is a good sign. We're not like second-class citizens almost — we're a whole family unit.

The Mobilization of Wives

In order to motivate some wives to accept the Gulf deployment gracefully, the military mobilized the labour of others. The extra work created by the war in the forms of counselling, babysitting, homemaker services, telephoning, organizing social functions, supporting, and managing frightened women's emotions was largely done by wives. While this work distracted these wives from their own problems, it also produced new problems, including burnout.

Like most of the work that the military creates for wives, Gulf War support work was generally unpaid. Many military wives are available to do volunteer work because their husbands' postings move them around so frequently that they are unable to find paying jobs, especially wives posted overseas. An army wife on a Canadian base in Germany describes how her volunteer efforts evolved "naturally" into wartime support work:

> When I came here first I didn't find any work, so I said, "Okay, I am going to be a volunteer." So I came to volunteer to one centre for radio — I am doing a lot of radio shows. When the Qatar situation came, I became a volunteer for the Van Doos [the francophone Royal 22nd Regiment] to get women together

to make sure nobody was alone. When they had kids or something, they had a car to go someplace.

The most obvious work that individual wives did during the crisis
was to set up — and staff — support groups and services. A deployed
army officer's wife based in Germany carried out her support work
under the umbrella of her husband's company:[7]

> During the crisis period, I started up my own support group
> with my husband's company because it was his company that
> went to Qatar. I started up a support group and got very in-
> volved with the wives of the company. And then I also worked
> the Help Wanted [which] had been set up. Then when they
> came back, I still continued to volunteer for the wives whose
> husbands were away, and I worked for three months as the
> co-ordinator of the Help Wanted. ... And every week I put out
> a newsletter, and we met once a week. Every Tuesday night we
> met in the Women's Centre. It ranged from, say, 25 would be
> the worst to about 40 women. And there were 52 living in the
> company. And I'd write a newsletter after every Tuesday's
> meeting. That night I'd go home and write a newsletter of what
> we'd decided to do in the upcoming week or whatever. And we
> also had the fanout, we called it, where I would phone three
> ladies, and then they would phone and everybody would get the
> messages.

As this last wife mentioned, telephone fanouts were quite important. A fanout is a "hierarchical" system for quickly distributing
information to a large number of people. The person at the "top"
phones several people, each of whom phones several others, each of
whom phones several more, and so on, until the entire constituency
has been contacted. During the Gulf War, fanouts were ways of
informing wives about social functions, support functions, and important developments in the conflict that needed to be given the
military slant before the wives heard about them on the news. Because the women on the receiving end of the calls often needed
support as well as information, even calling a few of them could take
a lot of time. An army wife based in Germany recalls:

> I had a friend who helped me and I said, "Okay, you phone five
> or ten women." But it was a lot of work, because I found you

cannot count on other people any time you need them. Every week I had to phone a lot of people. And you cannot just say okay and that is finished. You are talking to them and saying, "Are you okay? Do you need something?" And just talking — they needed to talk about what had happened during the week. "Did you receive any letters?" And stuff like that. So you were talking about 10-15 minutes per person. And if you were friends too, you were speaking more. So I can remember passing a lot of evenings.

Sometimes, when it was bad news that was being disseminated, the calls were preludes to general invitations to callers' homes. A navy wife based in Halifax recalls a specific instance:

I think the most difficult thing that we all found was when we were told that they would not be coming home until maybe the middle of May. We got a call from MarCom saying that we had an hour to get to as many people before the media got it. I'd say we reached about 75 per cent at least of all the people to let them know before they heard it on the news. And I ended up that night I had open house here. It was wall-to-wall people. I just said, "Come." There were more people landed at my house that night than when war broke out. Because I think even when war broke out, they still were hoping that somehow those guys were going to get flown home.

Some of the telephoning was long distance to offer support to family members who did not enjoy the benefits of being surrounded by a military community.

All in all, although it was rewarding, the support work was often onerous for the women who did it. For some deployed members' wives, it proved so demanding that it overwhelmed their lives. One navy wife felt responsible for all the other wives on her husband's ship:

I felt that I was sort of responsible for all the other wives on the ship. ... I was on the phone all the time. A lot of [the women] still now call me Mom, because some of them are younger than my kids. And they'd never been through things like that before. So I sort of had a really extended family while the ship was away. Sometimes I used to come home and hope the answering machine wasn't playing, and hope that the phone wouldn't ring during the night. ... I found that I got through it better because of them, and the close friendships that were formed. But I also sometimes wished for my own time and my own space.

Another deployed member's wife was so involved in support work that she spent relatively little time with her own children. She blames herself for what happened to her oldest son in school:

He had always been an excellent student, and I really think that most of his problem stemmed from me being so actively involved with the support group. Like I was gone 24 hours a day, right around the clock, not realizing that my children needed me too. ... My oldest one, I always assumed that he was doing fine and that he had friends. He never talked to me about the Persian Gulf. He never had questions about it. ... He's not the type of person that opens up easily. I didn't see that, and I don't think I will ever forgive myself for that. Because what I did was I was so involved with other families and saw problems with their children and helped them fix those problems, but never noticed it with my own son. And that's when he started slipping. Everything started slipping in school, right down to everything, and I had a really bad day yesterday because I just found out that he didn't pass. ... We have better communication right now because we have taken action. We are going for counselling to get help to try to find out what happened. Because we lost it all.

Because of the time she spent being a support group co-ordinator, still another wife got no help for herself.

Men whose wives were deployed to the Gulf did not appear to suffer burnout, family problems, or loneliness as a result of doing too much support work because the military is a gendered organization, which assumes that support work will be done by wives. Speaking about himself, the husband of a deployed female member explains:

I think they thought, "Well, this guy's got a 2-year-old child at home — he's got enough problems." And, like I was one of the people that was supposed to get support. Myself and John [another husband of a deployed female member] were on the fringe of the support group. I think people said, "Well, they have enough problems — ... I am not going to phone them and give them some more."

From the military's standpoint it was crucial that most deployed members' spouses were wives.

Self-Reliance

Despite the support services the military mounted during the crisis, the self-reliance mythology about wives remained strong. Wives' continuing belief in it was essential to the conduct of the war.

The wartime support services provided an extra cushion that gave wives more confidence in themselves. The services also provided wives with a safe outlet for their loneliness and fear. The services attempted to maintain wives' feelings of goodwill toward the military and their willingness to conform to the military's demands. They appealed to wives' patriotism, their anxieties about their husbands, and their previous experiences of military community solidarity.

The support services were often buttressed by the civilian community and the media. Like the military, the civilian community and media nurtured the image of the brave wife. The wives were pleased with this image, especially as the war newly glamourized it, and they redoubled their efforts to emulate it. According to a navy officer, the community and media "flattered" wives into making an extra effort:

When this operation broke out and this war thing came along, what you saw happening was everything was elevated. The importance of the navy became very very high. I mean, the city went around in circles trying to do this. Therefore automatically the role of the spouse became very very high. The community started to focus on the spouse and became very concerned with what was happening with the spouses, trying to provide all kinds of things for them to do. [These women had had their husbands going away every year], and all of a sudden [people] were out there, and they were saying, "Wow, how can you do that? How can you cope with that?" And so I think for a lot of them, for the first time they felt really good about their role in that scenario. So if a problem arose, the last thing they were going to do is sort of blow this image.

The support groups themselves fostered wives' self-reliance and determination to cope during the war since they strengthened each wife's conviction that some other woman was faring worse. The wife of a deployed army member recalls:

> So you said to yourself, "Okay, here is a person who is worse off than you — you can do it." They were worse off than me, they had more problems than me — and some had kids. A woman just had a baby before he left. He saw his baby on video, and she said, "Look, it's your baby — she is growing, she is growing." He never saw his little girl for three months, it was so sad. For me it was a way to tell me, You can do it. There are people who are worse off than you, so you cannot complain. "You can do it."

Not surprisingly, many wives feel in retrospect that the war helped them to grow in their ability to be independent. A navy officer's fiancée summarizes:

> If someone said to me, "What have you learned, like him having been away?" I would say the biggest thing I've learned is that you can only count on yourself. To me, everything you have to do you can't solely rely on someone else. If anything, I've become more strong and realized that I have to do it for myself. It's nice having someone there with you and to talk to you and that, but when it comes right down to it, it's you — you're the one that has to do it.

Even more noticeably than during routine deployments, wives censored their communications with their husbands and tried harder to handle their problems and feelings on their own. An air element member's wife reports:

> I started a diary on the day that he left, and I wrote to him in this diary and saved it for him till he got home. When I was married before, we had a debriefing before the guys went to Cyprus in '76, and one of the things that the padre warned us about at that time was to be careful what you say in a letter — or if you got to talk to him on the phone, how you word something on the phone. 'Cause when they are 3,000 miles apart, it really gets exaggerated by the time it gets there. So I

tried very hard the days I was mad at him — or he had annoyed me or whatever — I tried very hard not to portray that to him.

Wives also constructed a polished front for the community. During the Gulf War, as perhaps never before, they were stoical about their husbands' deployments, and — except, perhaps, with one another — they did not speak publicly about their fears. An army wife says:

In front of the people you could not begin to say, "Oh, no — I am afraid." So, if somebody asked if you were okay, [you said] "Yes, I am okay." You could not say everything you felt in here — you had to keep it for yourself and deal with it. I think it's what I learned for three months — to deal with my own feelings.

An air officer's wife adds:

It's very common with military that you may share it with another wife, but to the outside community it's business as usual. "Oh, no — everything is just fine." I mean, just because they are over there and somebody is shooting at them! I mean we are all falling apart, and we are not going to let the rest of the world know it!

When asked why she did not tell the media how she really felt, another air officer's wife says:

There's no sense. Why bother? People don't understand. Why should I expose that part of me? Not because they'll hurt me or because ... It's just over their heads. It's in another world. ... Why should I cry about my husband going away and going to the Gulf in front of the cameras or anybody? I don't think people understand. There's no sense me trying. I haven't got the energy to teach them.

Certainly the "stiff upper lip" approach prevailed. Indeed, some women believed that stoical wives were handpicked by the base to talk to reporters while wives with negative attitudes about the deployment were discouraged. One such wife says:

They were having these interviews on the TV and the news — it was always certain individuals. And I said to Harriet [Family Resource Centre staffperson] one day. ... "Boy, you hand pick them all! Or somebody is!" And she kind of looked at me, and I said, "Well, Harriet — haven't seen you phoning me about an interview for the newspaper!" Notice those that were on the interviews, though — everything was rosy and red. Hey, they were right behind their husbands 100 percent — sock it to them and da, da, da, da!

Wives who did not project the self-reliant image were frowned on by the military, and efforts were made to muzzle them. According to a family resource centre staffer in Germany, wives who made a conspicuous fuss were not tolerated. On some occasions, their husbands were contacted in the Gulf and ordered to rein them in. She reports:

They would get hold of the husband and they would say, "You control your wife!" They would get a hold of the husband in Qatar and say, "Control your wife!" And certain conditions were given. I don't remember them any more, but these women felt very very insulted.

Wives were even criticized if they failed to arrest their children's fears. A family resource centre worker observes:

[The mother's attitude had] an awful lot to do with [the child's adjustment]. An awful lot to do. ... If the mother was agitated and she took in every single piece of information and just went up to Level 13 with it, of course her child was experiencing anxiety and stress and not doing well at school. But I knew some ladies who just turned off the TV and didn't listen to the TV, and if a piece of information came on, they sat down with their child and they talked to their child about that. And they tried to make the best situation out of something that just wasn't very good at that time. And those children. ... I'm not saying they didn't experience stress — I'm sure they did — but it was of a much reduced level than the others.

In general, wives were expected to do everything they could to bolster the self-reliance myth. This included not making a scene when the Associate Defence Minister Mary Collins visited the base to brief them. Wives who asked "dumb" or "morbid" questions at these briefings were considered an annoying embarrassment. One wife, who bluntly asked Mary Collins if her husband would be brought home in a body bag, was thought to have let the side down especially. Her outburst was mentioned in several interviews. Wives who asked Collins to pay for their phone calls or babysitters were also criticized. A deployed air element member's wife recalls:

> Her bottom line was that she felt she needed a break away from her three kids, and she really wanted Mary Collins to come up with some money to put into some sort of a pool or a pot or whatever that would pay for her to be able to pay a babysitter. ... And I found this girl inappropriate to some degree in the respect that, as she sat and complained about this and not having enough money and having to go and take out a personal loan to pay bills and what not, she probably went through five or six cigarettes.

Wives who emulated the self-reliance myth and did not tarnish the Forces' public image were as useful to the military as the wives who did the unpaid support work.

Reintegration after the War

Even more than other deployments, the Gulf War created extra work for wives when their husbands arrived back home. Prior to the homecoming, many wives embarked upon a significant gearing up process. The tight combat bonding that had existed during the war had been of a totally different order from the spousal relationship that was about to resume, and some of the wives anticipated their reunions with fear. The fiancée of a deployed navy officer recalls:

> One of these meetings where all the wives were out, we got together and we were laughing that it would be. ... Like all the wives would be in one corner and all the guys would be in another corner. ... They had been so close and they were so used to being together. That's why we were all laughing. ... Almost like a high school dance, you know. The old slow song comes on and everyone grabs their corner — the guys on one side and the girls on the other.

One wife who was taking a college course wrote her term paper on military members' readjustment after deployments so that she would have a better idea of what to expect. Other wives planned elaborate celebrations. A navy wife recalls the joint preparations she made with a friend:

> We were going to rent a limo originally for Jack's homecoming — and for Chuck — and then everybody else was into the limos. So I said, "No, we are going to do something totally different." ... We were going to see if we could try to rent a Brinks armoured truck. But by the time we came up with the brainstorm, it was getting too late. So we ended up. ... We bought all these yellow pom-poms, and we put the word "love" on the back of the car. And then we had the pom-poms on the windshield wipers and on the aerial. And then we made this great big yellow heart and put all the pom-poms on that, and "Welcome home Jack and Chuck." And we called it the love bug. And then we decorated Susan's bedroom — put all the pom-poms and the streamers, and took pictures, you know, the night before, sort of thing. And I said, "We'll see how long these streamers can last!" But we had a good time.

The homecoming itself was exciting, especially for the navy wives who went down to the jetty to greet their husbands coming in on the warships. A navy officer's fiancée recalls:

> It was just like pandemonium! They came in at 11:00, and I got up at 8:00. They came right under the bridge, and the cars here were honking their horns. You would have thought the Beatles were coming, or all these superstars were coming home. The whole city, you know — Welcome home! There were yellow ribbons everywhere. It was just pandemonium!

Another navy fiancée adds:

> I was near where the crew was coming off — the camera crew. And I just spotted him, and he saw me. And he turned round and looked at the Executive Officer, and he went, "See ya!" And he just took off! He left! He never went back! He came over to me, and he didn't know where his mom was. And his dad came then. And John said it was the only time he ever saw

his father crying. 'Cause his father's a military man, and he's very strict. ... He gave him a hug and he walked away. It was so sad. He was crying so much, and he didn't want John to see him crying. And then, of course, Mrs. Freeman, she had high blood pressure, and I think the crowds were really getting to her. So she stood back so she could see, get a better view. 'Cause there were a lot of people pushing and shoving. And she had a big umbrella up. ... And John went over, but she didn't see him coming. And he went under the umbrella and gave her a hug.

Since deployed members received several weeks leave after arriving home, many wives suspended their own lives to take holidays with them. Sometimes before their husbands returned, wives busied themselves planning exotic trips. One air officer's wife planned a family trip to Florida in order to avoid the tensions that might otherwise have erupted after her husband returned home:

I connived and figured out that we needed to be out of the house so we were all off balance. So we went to Florida for two weeks, four days after he got home. And we'd never done that. We never go on holidays like that. ... Anyways, we did the Florida thing. It was just great. They just laughed and had fun. They had no responsibilities or job descriptions within the house. And when we got back here, Ted was back on his throne again within their minds. So it resolved itself without any friction.

An army wife put off finding out whether or not a job interview had been successful so that she and her husband could go away together:

I said to them, "Okay, now I am leaving with my husband, so give me the answer when I come back." It was more important to go away with my husband than to have the job here. After three months like that, you need to be together.

After the homecoming and the holiday, many wives coped with the fact that for their husbands the Gulf War was not yet over. At least one returned member sat in front of his television set and played and replayed the network specials on the ships' homecoming. His wife recalls:

I had taped the news CBC did the last week. They had done a special every night on the CBC news about the homecoming. And there was music and all of this. For the first month he was home, he played that tape night after night after night. He would play the tape over and over. And then he'd play the one of the ship coming in. Like the day that they came in, there was a two-hour special, and he played that over and over and over. I'd come in at 11 o'clock at night, and he'd be sitting here with the tape player.

Another wife was taken to social gathering after social gathering at which the war was the only conversation topic:

At first, we spent a lot of time going out with people that were in the war — like over there. Like we'd go Friday night down to friends of his that were in the Gulf, see his wife and this other couple. And that's what they would all talk about. I got sick of hearing about it all the time. I'd heard about it four months, every day from work to home, you know. And then he came back and I thought it would be over, but that wasn't the case.

Some wives coped with their husbands' symptoms of post-traumatic stress disorder. One such wife recalls:

At first he was really nervous — flashbacks almost. He woke up in the middle of the night and he would scream, and that lasted for about two months. They got all kinds of needles and pills to take while they were there. They don't even know, you know, the side effects of those pills or needles, so I'm sure that's got a lot to do with it. And he was really tired when he came back. It took him a long time to make it back to his old routine.

Even more than in other deployments, wives needed to take special care after the members returned home to give them time to reintegrate into their households.

Sometimes the work performed by a wife during the war was done in vain because the war's strains and tensions proved to be too much for the couple's marriage. While military deployments are always hard on marriages, this war was especially so. The number of broken marriages that resulted from the Gulf War was unusually high. A navy fiancée reports:

> I talked to this one guy off the *Terra Nova* and he said, "Yeah
> — there are five divorces now happening on the ship." We're
> not talking separation, we're not talking breakdowns — five
> divorces in one area alone. That's a long time to be away — a
> very long time.

Some wives additionally report that their friendships with the wives of other deployed members suffered strain upon the members' return because for several months one woman or the other in the friendship was preoccupied with restoring equilibrium in her own household.

More effectively than previous deployments, the Gulf War provided an opportunity for the military to focus the time and energy of wives on the mission and reinforced wives' already ingrained practices of flexibility, loyalty to the military, self-reliance, and unpaid work. The Gulf War comprised a stunning exemplar of military organization in action. This was despite — partly even because of — the strain the war put on wives.

4

Postings

"You're supposed to want to get ahead in the military," a senior officer advised us tersely, just after he had finished explaining that members without ambition were frowned upon. He could not have spoken more accurately. Military members are not only supposed to adhere to the chain of command and bond with their unit-mates; they are also expected to covet promotions.

The military believes that the life-threatening character of its work necessitates extraordinary accuracy, enthusiasm, and esprit de corps. It expects each member to perform both technically well and in a way that demonstrates his or her commitment to the mission. Among other things, commitment to the mission means willingness to participate in military leadership.

Members who aspire to leadership jobs are considered to be merely normal. They take all the courses they are asked to — and more; they accept every assignment, they never complain or seek a redress of grievance, they never demand special treatment, and they are continually demonstrating innovativeness and initiative. According to one army officer, "natural" military leadership begins to show itself right after basic training:

> We go to the field. And if I have ten sappers — engineer privates — in my section, and I'm doing something, my section 2ICs [second-in-commands] are doing something, and there's enough split work for another three or four guys, usually if the guy has any natural skills he'll say, "I'll take those guys — I'll go do that." The kind of guy that volunteers not only to do something but to accept a little bit of responsibility. Like, I'll bring one of the guys with me. And you can very quickly determine if the guy's just going over to waste time, where he doesn't have a real supervisor to watch when he's doing things. And you can tell by his peers' attitude towards him. If the guy

is a natural leader, then he's one of the natural leaders even if it's organizing card games in the coffee room.

In contrast, members who shun leadership opportunities by refusing courses, complaining about assignments, asking to be removed from promotion lists, and showing excessive concern for the needs of their families are considered obstructionist. They often find themselves harassed by superiors or punished.

The most important military advancement prerequisite is geographical mobility. Members are transferred from one location to another every two to four years, sometimes even more frequently, and the higher the rank they achieve, the more transfers they can expect. While the normal military career involves 10 to 15 moves,[1] fast-track careers involve more. The stated military reason for frequent transfers is acquiring diverse experiences. The successful member evolves from a specialist to a generalist, carrying out increasingly diffuse and complex leadership tasks as he or she ascends the hierarchy. As a National Defence Headquarters general puts it:

> It is basic policy, you know, to do that. It is to pick up experience in different fields. And to be able to do this transition that I'm talking about from specialist to generalist. If you spend 20 years doing the same thing, that's no experience.

By moving around, the member learns his or her occupation or trade thoroughly, developing an understanding of how it is applied in many locations and circumstances. Officers also learn about military management and how to attain the maximum from subordinates as they graduate from platoons to batteries to battalions to bases to command headquarters to National Defence Headquarters in Ottawa. A former senior army officer's wife says:

> In the military you can't [just] be promoted up the operational line — there are tickets that have to be punched. They have to be a battery commander, they have to be, and they have to be it by a certain age.

Military moves also prevent members and their families from forging close bonds with civilians. Members' dependence on the military is accordingly ensured, and the military's control is strengthened.

Members who attempt to remain in one location rarely succeed in doing so. When they do succeed, they forego promotions, and they know it. The Surgeon General recalls giving the following warning to one of his physicians:

"I am not moving from Kingston," ... said one of our doctors. "I like it here. I have a practice on the weekend, my wife's got a job." [I told him] "You're doing a good job. Do you realize that the longer you stay there, the less you will be presumed to be competitive ... ? Are you satisfied to be, let's say a major, lieutenant-colonel, for a long long time?"

Members who wish to stay in one place are not always treated so gently. The proportion of such members is growing. They have become attached to a particular place because their children are happy in their schools and peer groups, their spouses have good jobs, one or other of their extended families lives close by, or one or other of their parents is ill. When they are transferred, they may not want to move. In such a case, the member's only recourse is to apply for a *compassionate posting*, a posting at or near the geographical location of his or her preference, that will last for a two-year period. If the compassionate posting is granted, it will arrest the member's career. For the two years of its duration, the member will only do his or her job; he or she will go on no courses and will be ineligible to receive a promotion.

Although implicit in the institution of compassionate postings is the acknowledgement that continual relocation causes hardship, applications are seldom successful. The fact that compassionate postings entail career delays is intended to discourage members from even applying for them. Indeed, during the present period of military downsizing, members have almost as much reason to fear early release as a result of asking for a compassionate posting as they have to fear early release as a result of developing a medical problem. If the various deterrents to application fail, military policy is that if the member could serve the Forces best in the location to which he or she was originally posted and no suitable replacement can be found, the original location is where he or she will go. Regardless of the member's circumstances, career managers are instructed not to sacrifice operational effectiveness, so even airtight applications are often turned back. Compassionate posting applications are also not even considered unless they fall within quite a narrow range of criteria. A medical condition, especially of a child, that would worsen or could not be treated in the assigned location is the basis of most successful applications. Illness of a parent succeeds less often, less often still if the illness is unlikely to be "resolved" within two years.

After a member has decided to apply for a compassionate posting, he or she usually makes an appointment with a military social worker. Although social workers are supposed to help members solve personal problems, regulations remind them that they are first of all military officers.[2] Compassionate postings are thus the first occasions on which many military professionals face the human implications of the fact that their primary loyalty is to combat readiness.

One situation that virtually never qualifies the member for a compassionate posting is a spouse who is in university, working at a good job, or making soon-to-be-vested contributions to a pension plan. The military has no interest in or sympathy for civilian spouses (usually women) with careers and treats them as threats. One reason for this attitude is the military's conservative adherence to the model of the traditional patriarchal family, in which women's subordination to the demands of their husbands' jobs is assumed. On this topic, a prominent general exclaims:

> Oh, spouses are in the military! If a person in the military marries somebody that doesn't understand that they are part of the military in the sense that they're going to have to move, and they're going to have to do a whole bunch of things that they normally wouldn't have to do if they married somebody who wasn't in a uniform, either the marriage breaks up or they're going to have to change their views. Because you're marrying an institution here!

The importance of dedication to the military and "the career" is so thoroughly ingrained in members, especially officers, that members are expected to put pressure on wives who threaten to "make trouble" about a move. When members fail to "handle" their wives, military authorities often try to do it for them. The wife of a noncommissioned member, who attended graduate school, recalls how her husband's career manager attempted to intimidate her at a party:

> He kind of sidles us into a corner, and what he wants to tell me is that he thinks I'm threatening my husband's status because I have changed status at this point. He is an enlisted man, and

enlisted men don't have women with these kinds of credentials. ... And telling me very clearly that I am not earning brownie points for my husband, that this is not the kind of thing that they like to see, especially when you are making an issue of it. You [are asking] to stay here because you are in university. Those are not reasons to stay here. Other reasons they might consider, but I was holding him back at this point. ... [He wanted] to remind me that I was headed in the wrong direction, and that this was going to penalize my husband.

The wife of an army officer remembers a similarly tortured interview with a military social worker, during which she was not permitted to state her career-related reasons for refusing to accompany her husband to his posting in Québec City and was forced to characterize herself as unsupportive:

When I went to see the social worker, she never asked me what I was doing or what I wanted. All she asked was why I wouldn't go to Québec and live with him there and how she couldn't understand that. I couldn't ask for [another] posting on the basis of my own needs. I couldn't talk about myself or what I wanted at all, because that wasn't relevant. They weren't interested in furthering my career, and they made it quite plain to me that I was a part of my husband's career. And did I see what I was doing here by refusing to go to Québec?

Wives are often further inconvenienced by the military's tendency to send members on "replacement" postings for eight or ten months or to put members on "standby" for new postings, on the understanding that when they are asked to relocate, it will be without the usual notice. These practices presuppose that wives' time is completely disposable and wreak havoc with their study and work plans.

Largely as a result of their frequent moves, military wives have a much lower rate of participation in the labour market than comparable women married to civilians. While the work of 53 per cent of Canadian military wives is confined to their homes, the same is true of only 23 per cent of Canadian women generally.[3]

Moves as Work

While being transferred is something that happens to the member, responsibility for the preparation, process, and after-effects of each move is mostly his wife's. Each move involves extremely hard work.

Posting messages usually arrive a few months in advance, at which time the couple finds out where it is going. Depending on the member's element, the posting will be to one of a number of possible locations in Canada. Until 1992, an army or air posting could also have been to a Canadian base in either Lahr or Baden-Soellingen, Germany. Some officers are sent on educational or exchange postings to the United States or England or on a NATO posting to a location in Europe.

While the move is often into a PMQ, sometimes no PMQ accommodation is available or the couple has decided that it would prefer to live off base. In that case, the work begins long before the move, since civilian accommodation must be found. Until about 1982, spouses had no input into this process. Members who were not going to live in PMQs travelled to the posting alone and were allowed to send for their families only after they had found appropriate housing. Wives began their new lives in homes they had never seen. At present, a member interested in buying a house is allowed a five-day trip for that purpose with his or her spouse.

Buying a house in five days is stressful. It is a terrific amount of money to commit in such a short time, much of which must also be devoted to getting to know the new city (including its schools) and arranging the house's financing. The fear of making a mistake or not finding anything suitable is invariably great. An army wife who bought a house in Canada while her husband remained in Germany recalls:

> I arrived in on Saturday night. ... Sunday I met the real estate agent, and he took me out and showed me stuff all day Sunday. I didn't see anything I liked. He showed me Monday. This house went on the market Sunday night, and I bought it Tuesday. On Monday I saw this house for the first time, and then I went and saw a couple of others. And then I narrowed them down and went back to this one and one other in the subdivision, and then I decided on this one. Put in my offer. You have five days to look, but that's it. You've got to get your banking and your financing and everything done in that five days, so

you literally only have two days to look because you've got to have enough time to do all the bank business.

An air element wife who has been through the process several times adds:

> I think [househunting] is in itself the biggest pressure of all. We've done it five times now. Gone some place, and, like my husband says, you shop around for everything you buy. $300 item, you look for two weeks to find a bargain on it. And yet in five days you spend the most money you're probably going to spend in your lifetime on a building. You hope you're buying something suitable, and you've got five days to do it.

Even when the move is to a PMQ, the preparation can be frantic if the amount of lead time has been unusually short. The underlying assumption is that the wife, whose only purpose is to support her husband, can mobilize herself at a moment's notice. A young army wife recalls:

> My goodness, we were given less than two weeks' notice when we left Valcartier to here. So you really have to be organized, and you really have to be able to think, and you have to antici-pate a lot. Have to plan ahead. Because you know at any time you could get your PMQ, your notice, the information could come through those lines, they could give you a call and say, "Okay, you can move, come on down, sign the papers, what-ever." You're like aahhh!

Although the physical packing is now done by movers, most other tasks are still done by wives. Most wives rapidly develop their own system. When the move is to an overseas posting, the wife must make an inventory of every item the family is taking (by year of purchase and cost) and divide all household items into four piles — storage back in Canada, advance boxes, arrive-later boxes, and on-the-plane luggage. For each electrical appliance, she must decide whether it is more practical to provide it with a converter or to leave it in Canada and purchase a European-voltage equivalent when she arrives abroad. Since postings are usually for several years, young women must often even consider whether or not they should pack the equip-ment they would need for a new baby. An air element wife recalls:

I packed all the boxes that went into storage. We had to do that. Like we had to pack red balls and green balls. Everything in the red balls — they are big boxes — that's the stuff that arrives first, okay? So that's got Paul's combat things in it, the kids' school clothes — things that we think we are going to need right away. Those are the red balls — they have to be packed long before the movers ever come. They go six weeks ahead of when you leave, about. Then you have to pack the green balls, which are several boxes of things that you can wait for, like pillows and maybe summer clothes — you know, things you don't need right away. Maybe some of his uniforms. He'll only take maybe two uniforms, and the rest will go in the green balls. So that has to be all done, and they have to be sent before the movers come. Then you have to inventory everything that's left. So you have to separate what you are going to store, what you are going to need right away, and what you are going to need a little bit later. It's a hell of a job. I thought I was going to go insane.

If the move involves vacating a PMQ, the wife must prepare the PMQ for a stringent military inspection called a "march-out." At march-out time, an inspector pronounces the PMQ clean or unsatisfactory; if the latter, the PMQ must be cleaned again. Until a few years ago, march-out inspectors wore white gloves to ensure that they detected every possible speck of dust. The idea that wives' main purpose is to do unpaid domestic work for the military was thereby underscored.

The wife's work in preparing for the move is often aggravated by the non-participation of her husband, who is away on an exercise, course, or unaccompanied posting. Since his absence is of benefit to his career and he has already been defined as the primary breadwinner, she usually feels powerless to protest.

Travelling to the new location is rarely straightforward. Sometimes it is on the other side of Canada and involves several days driving with cranky children. Other times it is overseas. Travel to overseas postings is usually on a military flight, which leaves from CFB Trenton. The previous night is likely spent at a rundown military establishment called the Yukon Lodge. Although the flight normally does not leave until the next evening, patrons are evicted from Yukon Lodge at the customary check-out time. The ensuing many hours, spent sitting either in the Yukon Lodge lobby or at the AMU

[Air Movements Unit; in civilian parlance, "airport"], are arduous, especially for wives travelling alone with small children. The flight itself is sometimes in an uncomfortable military aircraft called a Hercules. As a former navy wife describes it:

> You sit, strapped in the bulk of this bulk carrier aircraft, which is five rating and is lopsided. ... You are facing the two sides and you are sitting in sling seats as if you were a paratrooper. And back behind a curtain somewhere there is a loo — behind a curtain, in the tail of this thing. But the only way they have of keeping you warm is to take this big pipe out of the ceiling and shoot hot air at you, like a dryer exhaust. So they shoot hot air at you and everybody starts peeling off. And then they pull the pipe up, and then it freezes and drops 20 degrees like that. And then when everyone is sitting there freezing and being jiggled to death, they shoot the hot air at you again.

In the case of some overseas postings, a long bus ride remains at the other end as the final stage of an exhausting journey.

For a variety of reasons, the end of the journey is not always the end. Accommodation may not be ready when the posting begins, yet it may have already terminated at the previous place. The result is that the wife (and possibly children) will float in limbo while the member begins his new job. If the posting message provided little notice and there is a waiting list for PMQs, the family may have no accommodation until civilian accommodation can be found. Or the couple may wish to buy a house but had insufficient time to sell its house at the last posting. Or, as sometimes happens, the couple may have been catapulted into the new posting without a househunting trip. An army wife remembers the loneliness and alienation she suffered after relocating in this fashion to the other side of Canada:

> We got to Fredericton, and Andrew had an aunt who lived in Newcastle. It's about three and a half hours from Fredericton. And she had said that we could come and stay with her. Miles and I could stay there until we got an apartment, because Andrew had tried every avenue to see if we couldn't get a Q. There was a ten-month waiting list for PMQs. They said, "No, there's no way" — nothing rated it. ... We arrived there on the 13th of January and we didn't get a place to stay till the first of March. ... It seemed like forever.

Sometimes the move has been handled incompetently, and the wife must immediately confront the reality of damaged or stolen possessions. At other times housing has been secured and possessions have not been smashed, but chaos awaits the wife because the new PMQ is too small, bug-infested, or otherwise substandard. Sometimes even another move awaits her because a last-minute posting change occurred after the first move, a sudden promotion has provided the opportunity for more prestigious quarters, or a PMQ has suddenly become available. The former wife of an ambitious army officer recalls:

> We went straight into PMQs that were on the outskirts. We used to call them the chicken coops. Very very very tiny houses. We were there for exactly three weeks. I'd just finished putting all the curtains up, washing the crystal, we had had our first reception, when he was offered another job. And with that job came a huge house beside the Armouries Club in downtown Montréal. "Well," I said, "I don't want to move there. I've just got this place all fixed up and the neighbours are nice." And he said, "Well, we're moving." And that was a major move, even though it was just from the outskirts of the city into the city. It was a major move. And changing the kids. I had had the kids enrolled in school. I had done all this, and then for his ego we moved into the city.

Once the move is completed, the wife's first task is unpacking and settling in. If the family has moved into a PMQ, she must inspect every nook and cranny in the house and report problems to the base authorities so that she will not be charged for the fault if it shows up during march-out. Some overseas PMQs are completely furnished, which makes this job even more onerous. An army officer's wife recalls about a posting in England:

> They count the silverware, they feel every dish in the house. They expect you to take every glass and run your finger around the top and the bottom to make sure it is not chipped. Every glass. ... I said, "I'm not doing that — I can't be bothered." And of course they said, "Well, you have to do that, because if it is chipped and you don't tell us, then you'll have to pay for it." I said, "I'll pay! Get it over with! I'll pay!" You know, I

wasn't interested in spending the time. ... And you have to count all the blankets and all the sheets and all the towels, and you have to make sure there are no holes in them. Take the slipcovers off the furniture to make sure there are no stains on it. I found that difficult.

If her husband is sent on a course or exercise immediately after the move, which is often the case, the wife unpacks and settles in alone. An army member was deployed to the 1990 Oka "Operation Salon" immediately after he and his family had been repatriated from Germany. His wife remembers her frustration:

We arrived the 9th of August 1990, and it was a Friday night. And Monday the military police contacted him and said, "You are coming with us." And he said, "No, I'm on vacation for three weeks; I have to buy my house; my family's in a hotel — I'm not going." And they said, "You're obliged — you're coming with us." You always have five days of debarkation when you arrive, and that was all cancelled. So who had all the problems to fix? That was me.

When the move is to an overseas posting, the wife's problems are compounded by extra difficulties and unfamiliarities. During the first weeks, while her husband is settling in to his new job, she struggles at home without many of the amenities she has been used to, such as telephones, cars, TVs, appliances, and furniture. She is often handicapped by being unable to speak the local language. She is socially isolated in a village and/or must cope with the fact that conditions in PMQs or apartments are worse than she had expected. The wife of a former military social worker recalls:

I remember that young family that arrived shortly after we did, the second time we were over, and she was out in that little village. They had no phone. They had no car yet. She was stuck in this sort of semi-furnished apartment, and only the baggage she came with. He went on exercise, and then finally her baggage came like about a week later, and it had wire straps on it. All her stuff was strapped with wire, she had nothing to snip it with, and she couldn't speak to anybody. She was the only Canadian in this little village. He was away, and she couldn't

get into the baggage. And she didn't know how to buy the
German food. ... It was just a disaster. It was abandonment.

Although many wives' narratives refer to "we," overseas postings
are experienced quite differently by their husbands, for whom the
continuity of military and mess existence has been uninterrupted. In
fact, according to one retired female officer, members spend even
more time in their messes during overseas postings to escape from
the unhappiness of their wives:

> I think generally the men spent more time in the Mess, because
> I suspect that very often when they went home they would get
> really dumped on. ... Because it was the wives who were
> having the problems, not the husbands really. The husbands'
> lives went on very much the same as they did here in Canada,
> because they were doing the same jobs and the Mess was there,
> and everything was there — the base was pretty much the same.
> But it was the wives who were trying to cope with all these
> differences, you know, and living in a country whose standard
> of living was not as high as Canada's. Like they'd move into
> these apartments. There wouldn't even be a light bulb, there'd
> be no fixtures — nothing.

Overseas, military wives are more dependent on their husbands
than they are in Canada. They are also more dependent on the
military. Language, cultural, and legal barriers make civilian medical, social, and legal services largely inaccessible to wives in most
overseas countries, and they must survive on whatever the military
offers them. Not infrequently, it is not much. Medical service personnel who are most likely to be used by wives — such as psychia-
trists to treat depression — are often either non-existent or else they
speak only one language. A French-speaking air element wife recalls
the experience of being severely depressed in Germany:

> I asked them to send me to Canada [so I could] see my own
> doctor over there. They said no. They said, "We have good
> specialists for you." And it took four months before they de-
> cided to do something with me. Four months, maybe five. I
> started to feel bad in February, and I started to take those pills
> in August. So it meant that there was a lot of time where I felt
> bad. Enough to think about suicide.

Even anglophone wives find that there is virtually no counselling for serious problems. A wife whose daughter had been sexually abused just before the family left Canada reports:

> There's nobody over here. If you have a rape, if you have incest, if you have anything like that, there's nobody to help them. ... In other places in Canada, you always have access to specialists. But here, I don't know why they think that it is not important. There's one psychologist for the entire base. And you can't get in to see that person. That person only has a certain knowledge about things. So you have got 5,000 people here. We have case after case after case of abuse and all this stuff. I don't know how it is handled. They didn't help us very much.

Postings in remote areas within Canada can be expected by members of many air element trades even though many of the old "radar chain" bases have been closed recently. Remote postings share many, if not all, of the disadvantages of overseas postings. Although medical, counselling, and social services exist, as do diagnostic facilities for children with learning disabilities, they are at least several hours away by car. If they need to be accessed frequently, they are of no use to the wife.

Despite the community fun mentioned by some wives who have lived in remote postings, the fact that they have nothing to do, relative to their husbands, and few social outlets can subject them to serious depressions and tax their marriages to the limit. The effect of several remote postings can be devastating. For one air element wife, the third remote posting in a row was the last straw:

> Both my babies were young there, and he was hunting and fishing. He went to mess dinners, to which I was not invited. We saw the same people all the time ... and I didn't have a job. And then he extended without telling me. ... You see, to him it was a very wonderful posting ... but I can't ski. ... And you can't get away — you have to drive 150 miles to get to [the nearest city]. To go out for our anniversary, we'd go to a gas station type of thing. You can only live that life for so long. And then he extended the third year, and that was it. I went home to my mother. I took the kids with me, and I said, "I am not coming back."

Another wife, who had become clinically depressed during her first remote posting, recalls how she felt when she heard that she was going to another one:

> It was a Thursday the day Jake was told that we were going to Moisie. He came home early to tell me, and he came in and said, "Well, we got posted." I said, "I knew it. I knew it. So where are they sending us?" He said, "Moisie." I said, "Where?" He said, "Moisie." I said, "Where is it?" And he brought out the map of Québec, and then he went to the insert, and he said, "We are on the insert." I walked away from him. And I looked at it, and I said, "You are kidding." He said, "No." "How long?" He said, "Three years." "No way — we can't go." And he said, "Yeah, we have to." I went to my room and I cried.

Some postings, even in Canada, entail language hardships. French-speaking wives posted within English Canada, or (formerly) to Baden-Soellingen in Germany, experience the alienation of inhabiting a largely anglophone world, and anglophone wives feel likewise when their husbands are posted to bases in Québec. Attempting to overcome the alienation requires tremendous effort. A French-speaking air element wife recalls the laborious process of learning English at the Baden base:

> Là-bas il y a beaucoup de femmes de la région, et ici dans la région on n'a pas souvent l'occasion de parler anglais. Il y a beaucoup de femmes qui arrivent et qui ne parlent pas du tout anglais, et là-bas c'est beaucoup anglais. Et pour travailler, il faut que tu parles anglais. ... Les personnes avec qui je travaillais parlaient toutes anglais et pas du tout français. Mon travail exigeait de parler français, mais à leur contact j'ai appris à parler anglais. Au début, je ne parlais pas beaucoup. J'écoutais, j'écoutais. Comme les films là-bas, les vidéos, sont tous en anglais, donc on se louait des vidéos en anglais puis j'ai appris comme ça.[4]

Apart from the problems associated with the moves and the special difficulties stemming from particular locations, the money, labour, and stress required to make continual transitions from one place to another are enormous. Each move typically involves selling appliances — at a loss — buying new curtains and decorations and finding new doctors, dentists, hairdressers, mechanics, cleaners, retailers, and veterinarians. As an air element wife summarizes, "You have to change everything that is part of your life."

Always Starting Over

Postings entail enormous upheavals in wives' relationships. While members also move, their new situation furnishes them with an instant life: job, similar workplace, Mess, and congenial companionship. As a former air element member says:

> To me it was the same job. Different equipment, you know, but the same basic scenario. You went to work and ... it was the same job.

An air officer adds:

> On the member's side, there is a natural built-in network. You have the professional associations, because the members that you tend to form friendships with are those that are within your own environment or classification. And you have a natural network to keep track of them.

Wives are not so fortunate. When they move, they give up their affiliations, especially the friends they made at the last posting and the commitment they invested in those friendships. It is a loss that always hurts. An air element wife says:

> You just get to meet new friends and make some good friends, and then it's time to pack up and leave again. It's very hard. You meet a really good friend and you share a lot together, and then all of a sudden you find out you are getting posted and you are not going to have her. Sure you might see her some other time throughout your life, but it's just not the same. You know you're not going to be there. She's not going to be there. You can't just pick up the phone or just run across the street and see her.

Contrary to what many civilians think, most military wives do not experience their existence as a continual accumulation of friends. For them, each move represents the permanent loss of a closeness that will be unable to surmount the obstacles erected by geography. The wife of a former member says:

> Anybody that says, "Oh, it's wonderful being in the service! You've made so many friends all over the world!" They *are* all over the world. They are not anybody that you can talk to. You get these letters at Christmas, telling what they've accomplished that year. That's not my idea of friends. You've lost them. And sometimes they are people that you had a really really close bond with, and they are gone. It's not like a childhood friend or something. Something else has made that, and that's gone.

She adds that as military wives get older they have problems even making friends because the shared predicaments of being newlywed, pregnant, or struggling to raise young children no longer exist to bond them together immediately. Wives' pools of potential friends are also often limited to the military community because many civilians are reluctant to become involved with persons who will soon move again. An air element wife says about her present civilian neighbourhood:

> They know your husband is military, so they know you're going to be leaving, and they all have their family and friends. Like they're people from the area, so they go to visit mom and dad on Saturday, or their sister and brother or whatever, and they have their friends that are established. So they're willing to chit-chat with you, but they don't see any need to make friends. … I've been here three years, and we don't have that many close friends. There's a few ladies who have children that are the same age as my children, so we go for walks, or we'll go shopping in the afternoon. But close friends? François speaks to them, you know, but we don't have one couple we know that we can relate to or go out.

The heartache of leaving friends who were hard to find in the first place is too much for many wives, and they eventually decide to avoid contact with women who look like they might become friends. Some wives conclude that they cannot be bothered investing time and energy in friendships that will soon terminate. The wife of a former air element member says:

As you spend longer and longer making friends and having them go away, and making more friends and having them go away, or you moving or whatever, you don't want to do it any more. It's not worth the effort. You can be acquaintances. You can get along with people. But you don't want to invest the time into being friends with them.

Other wives have been hurt by terminating friendships in the past, and their present decision results from their wish to avoid experiencing more pain. An army officer's wife says:

It was the first year I was in Kingston, and I was really lonely, and I ended up meeting a girl across the road who was six months pregnant, and this was before I got pregnant with Sarah, and we got very very close. We just suddenly bonded. I mean, I needed somebody. I was lonely. I needed a friend to talk to and everything, and I just latched right on to her. And she ended up getting posted away the next year, and it was devastating. And I always swore I'd never do that again because it hurt too much.

Wives who have decided that the rewards of short friendships outweigh the costs nevertheless often find themselves becoming distant from a friend in the months before posting time in the hope that by the time the move actually occurs the loss will have stopped hurting. An air element wife says:

I've noticed — I've done it the last time we moved and this time too — that I've really tried to distance myself from my friends the last couple of months. Not to see them as much. Not to socialize as much. ... I'm thinking, "Well, if I don't see her as much now, maybe I won't care for her as much when we leave."

Perhaps not surprisingly, many wives report that even if things used to be otherwise, their only close friend is now their husband. This situation adds to the hardship created for wives by absences and increases their overall vulnerability.

Some wives look to their families of origin (parents and siblings) to provide the emotional continuity they are unable to receive from friends. For them, the growing up years represent the only period of

their lives that they stayed in one place and enjoyed the same relationships over time. Or their first families are, they believe, the only
people who are unlikely to hurt them by walking out of their lives.

Parents often stand in for an absent military member to help their
daughter through a difficult time. They also sometimes help her
through the trying parts of a move by providing accommodation
during a period when the couple has no housing or by visiting her or
otherwise keeping in close touch during the months she is newly
arrived at a new posting and her husband has been sent away. An
army wife recalls the time her husband was sent to Cyprus for six
months a few weeks after they had been posted to an unfamiliar city:

> When they found out Simon was going, they were upset that I
> was all the way out there. So Dad said, "Call collect. Any time
> you're the least bit upset or you want to talk, you call me." I
> called him this one night. I was in tears and I said, "I want to
> come home."

Looking back over her years as a military wife, a former army wife
recalls:

> My mother was very very supportive. She came to Europe four
> times when we were there. She came to Gypsumville. Wherever
> we were, she made an effort and did come and travel. All the
> time I was in Europe, my mother sent me the local Brockville
> newspaper. The whole paper, every day.

But for most wives, the assumption of a mobile lifestyle means a
net family loss. Moving far away from their extended families means
that what was once a crucial source of affiliation and support has
suddenly vanished. One wife says:

> You could dial home, but you don't want to get your family all
> upset too. "You're having a rough time, I wish I was there, I
> could take the kids off your hands for a day or two, we miss
> you, we love you." This sort of thing, and of course as soon as
> you get that sort of thing on the phone you're all tears anyway.

Another wife adds:

A Noël, c'est dur. C'est pour ça qu'on faisait des voyages. On étaient dépaysés, et ça nous rendait moins nostalgique. En Tunisie il n'y a pas de neige et ça ne ressemble pas à Noël. Mais si tu restes chez vous à faire jouer des cantiques de Noël, là tu t'ennuies.[5]

An especially frustrating part of being uprooted from one's first family is feeling cut off and helpless when a crisis happens. An officer's wife lost her mother to cancer just two weeks after she had travelled to Germany to take up a posting with her new husband:

My mother was diagnosed with cancer about a year before we were married. She had a recurrence we discovered two weeks before we were married, and when I went to Baden, we extended our stay in Canada. And it was my understanding that she would be all right, but two weeks later she died. So we had quite a time. I had quite a time. We were very close, my mother and I. ... That was tough — newlyweds, strange country, and that loss. ... I think I was very angry at not being there. My family was all with her when she died except for me.

Wives feel equally upset at being cut off from their families when the crises happen to themselves. An air element wife wishes that her mother had lived close by when she was learning to care for her first baby:

When Monica was first born, I did really miss that. So many times I wanted to phone my mother and say, "What do I do? She's crying." And you just can't, because they're that far away and it's another long distance call.

The mother of a child who died mourns the fact that she had no true "home" community to bury him in:

What do you do when your son dies suddenly? Where are you going to bury your son? Where he was born? Where you are living now? Where are you going to be in five years? There is no focal point. There's no actual home.

Military life does not simply put a geographical distance between wives and their original families. Its closed and distinctive nature erects social barriers as well. What happened specifically during the Gulf War often also happens during peacetime; some wives come to feel alienated from their own families, relative to other members of the military community, and to believe that only the latter are capable of understanding them. An air element wife says:

> Tu ne peux pas en parler à ta famille, ça c'est un autre problème que tu as. Parce que eux ne peuvent pas comprendre, ils ne l'ont jamais vécu. Tu parles de ça à tes soeurs, et puis ça leur passe dix pieds par dessus la tête parce que eux ont toujours leur mari, elles ont toujours quelqu'un pour les aider quand elles ont de la peine. Les responsabilités plein les épaules, elles ne connaissent pas ça par ce qu'elles les partagent tout le temps.[6]

Military life thus has several ways of loosening connections between wives and their original families.

For all these reasons, the degree of personal isolation caused by moves can become overwhelming. An air element wife summarizes:

> You are segregated by rank in the military community, both on and off the base, so that you will only communicate with young women exactly like yourself, and not either the senior enlisted or senior officers' wives who might have provided some insight and support. You are separated from your own families. You are separated from civilian women because you are perceived to be part of a separate community. You are separated often from your spouse, who's God knows where in the world, and you are not sure when he is coming home, and he will only be home two weeks, and he'll be gone again. So the isolation is absolutely crippling in my mind. And it's easy to say we'll get out and make friends and stuff like that, but I think there has to be a recognition of the different levels of social skills of people. Some people do that very very well. They are gregarious. They can make friends with a stump fence. But other women find that very very difficult, and never really break out.

Postings and Military Kids

The fact that members spend so much time away from home means that their wives must perform the double duty of single parents. They must also do most of the work that is needed to help children adjust to moves.

The most poignant loss military children experience each time they move is the loss of cherished friends. Military children suffer real pain each time they wrench themselves away from their friends in order to begin what they are convinced will be a friendless existence in a new place. It invariably falls to their mother to help them deal with it. An army wife says:

C'est difficile. J'ai mon plus jeune qui est en troisime année à l'école. A chaque année scolaire il se fait un ami, même s'il n'est pas dans sa classe, mais qui est de son niveau à l'école. A chaque année l'ami part, il recommence à zéro à chaque début d'année scolaire. Je le regarde aller et ça me fend le coeur. Je me dis, "Il recommence à zéro à chaque fois." Dans mon coin il n'y a pas beaucoup d'enfants de son âge. Parce que je suis dans le civil, il n'y a pas des enfants tous collées comme dans les PMQs.[7]

A navy wife recalls:

One of the hardest things I went through ... was the first day of school, when she went into Grade 7 at Shelburne. I drove her up to the school and she said, "Don't stay — leave!" And she was standing there by the school all by herself. It was awful.

Like their mothers, children truly give of themselves and make large investments in their relationships outside the family. They are perhaps even more hurt when moves have the effect of ending these friendships because they lack some of the adults' understanding of why the moves are necessary. Apart from the pain of losing individual friends, one of the most difficult (and common) military childhood experiences is trying to fit into a civilian school in which the children have all known each other for years and are not interested in making new friends. Military children in these situations often feel like outcasts. An military child who is now grown remembers the first time her family lived in a civilian neighbourhood:

When we moved to Ottawa, onto civvy street, I just felt like I'd hit a brick wall. ... You'd walk out and smile at people in the street, kids that were on the street, and they'd just walk by: "What rock did you crawl out of?" You'd go to Junior High, and most people had pretty strong little cliques before they ever

hit Junior High. They'd grown up together for six years before.
I felt very out of place for about half a year, and tremendously
stressed by it — just tremendously stressed. In fact, I remember
at one point thinking I wished I was dead.

A teenager, living in Germany at the time of our interview, recalls
her hurtful send-off from a civilian school in Canada:

So people asked me, "Where are you getting posted?" Germany. "Oh well — that's nice." And they went on their merry
business. They were staying there and getting ready for the next
year, because they were going to be there and I was going to
be gone. It made me feel kind of left out. In a way I had always
felt left out, because here were all these kids. They had been
going to school together since elementary school, and now they
were just going into Junior High, and I was going to be leaving.
I was sort of like an oddball, because I had come in Grade 6
and now I was leaving after Grade 7, and here were all these
kids going to Grade 8. And I was going to Grade 8 in some
foreign country.

Some military children are shunned by their civilian friends even
before they move so that their friends can suffer their own pain
gradually. The mother of an army child recalls a difficult birthday
party:

My son, he was in Grade 8, and a little boy that he met when
we first moved there, his mother said to me, "Well, we didn't
invite John to Jimmy's birthday party this year because he is
moving." And I said, "Well he's not moving until July, and this
is an April birthday party." And she said, "Well, I just thought
it was better for Jimmy to start breaking away from him." And
I said, "Well, it was very hard for John to be left out of the
party."

The children often develop intricate strategies for making friends
quickly and otherwise making the most of the fact that every friendship they have will be short. One now-adult military child remembers:

I became very good at it. I'm very good at making friends. I think that was a strength of my background as a dependent. It was an art. I looked at every person as being a kind of a book, and that I had a limited time to get through this book. And that I'd better get going on it the first day. And I had a whole rhyme of an introduction. I knew exactly what the important parts were to tell people about me and to make it really interesting, so that people would want to get to know me. And then I did a lot of the coaxing of the information from them, and I think I taught a lot of people how to make friends quickly.

Other military children, like their mothers, reach a point where they retreat into themselves and decide that making friends is not worth the pain of having to lose them later. Since this strategy makes them feel even more isolated, their mothers usually try to coax them out of it. Still other children become so angry at the disruptions of their lives that they act out against their parents, becoming involved in drugs and other "taboo" activities in order to retreat or draw attention to themselves. The mother of one teenager recalls:

Rick put Mary Anne in the truck and locked it and said, "You're coming to Trenton with us." She just didn't want to come. My son is all right. He can make new friends and stuff, but Mary Anne thought she would die. She had left all her friends behind. That's when she started misbehaving ... smoking and staying out all night.

A navy officer's wife recalls her children's return to Canada from an overseas posting:

They came back thinking their friends would be there. Their friends here would sort of be standing at the doorstep waiting for them. ... David was not too bad. David is really a scholar, so he'd go down and read books, and sort of after three months his friends started drifting back. But Trish wasn't ready to wait for that, so she got into a real loud crowd, and she ran away from home, and she got involved with drugs, and it was a whole bad scene for about three years with her.

Friends are not the only people that children mourn for when they move. They also miss their extended families of grandparents, aunts,

uncles, and cousins or regret the lost opportunity to develop relationships with these relatives that staying in one place might have given
them. One wife, who was also a military child, remembers a time
when her grandparents were visiting when "all my friends came to
see what a grandparent looked like."

Because they are always moving, military children experience
many problems in school. How members' children fare in their
school careers does not appear to be a high military priority. Moves
make impossible for military children the smooth, ordered passage
through the school system taken for granted by most civilian children, in which one's teachers are always building on the knowledge
one obtained last year.

Military children find it most difficult to move during their high
school years, both for scholastic reasons and because the peer group
is so crucial during the teenage years. While military policy allows
families to remain in a posting for an extra year so that a child can
finish high school, in practice the policy is seldom adhered to. Even
when the consideration is granted, it may entail a significant career
cost. The former wife of an ambitious army officer remembers a
move that, while benefiting her husband, was extremely difficult for
her teenage son:

> Jason doesn't make friends easily, but he had two good friends
> and he loved the cottage. So he didn't want to go. And I had
> my job. I didn't want to go. So. That took about two nights until
> Jack said, "Well, if the family wasn't going to follow, he was
> going alone." Oh my god! There again! So I left my job; we all
> moved to Calgary. Jason hated it. He almost flunked his year,
> we had to get tutors in for him. He hated going to school — he
> was crying.

Military children must, unfortunately, often move in the middle of a
school year or in the middle of a high school career. Even in the
course of a "normal" military move (i.e., during the summer), they
may miss a lot of school owing to the upheavals of postings and
settling into new accommodations. An air officer's wife, who used
to teach in Department of National Defence (DND) schools, remembers:

> A lot of military parents used to get posted in at the end of May.
> So they moved for the whole month of June. The kids didn't

get school for that month. It was happening in the 70s. Later on, they would post people only in July if they had school age children. But the parent would say, "I'm starting my new job in July — I've got to be there, so we're gonna take our leave for the month of June." And they'd just leave. They'd just drag their kids right out of school. September was a lost month as well. Like you're supposed to hand in the number of students that you have for a final count to the board September 21st. September 21st they finalize all the numbers. Everybody settled in. Not DND. You'd be getting your kids till Hallowe'en because they'd just moved in. Or they'd been living on the economy in a hotel somewhere, waiting for their PMQ to be readied. And when they finally got in the PMQ, then their kid could come to our school. They just wouldn't go to school. That's why there'd be these great big blocks of stuff missing.

The teacher's account omits the fact that wives often work extremely hard during their weeks in temporary accommodation precisely to make sure that their children will not miss school. An air officer's wife whose family had to evacuate an ant-infested PMQ in the middle of the school year afterwards drove her children back and forth from their civilian housing to the base school until the school year was finished. Another wife, living in a hotel, spent her mornings and afternoons sitting in an unheated, unfurnished PMQ during the winter waiting for her daughter during the child's first nine days at her new military school:

I didn't want my older one to miss too much school, because then she would be far behind, because it took us a week to come here. I sent her to school, and I would come in the PMQ and wait all day for her to come home. [With] no furniture, no nothing. And I only had a little jacket and jeans. ... So I'd wait in the morning, pick her up at lunch, make sandwiches — I would buy my stuff at Canex or whatever — and then drop her off at school again and wait all afternoon with my younger one. Minus 39. Nothing to do. No toys. That was the weirdest thing I've ever done. Sitting on the stairs and waiting.

Across the Canadian provinces, and even more so across different countries, variations in the importance and timing of kindergarten, French language teaching, extracurricular activities, and diagnostic tests are large. Often, as a result, military children completely miss out on important experiences. Or they struggle for an excessively long time — or forever — with undiagnosed learning disabilities. Or they develop keen extracurricular hobbies in one place only to have to discontinue them at the next posting. Constant moves also produce gaps in the children's knowledge that their new teachers do not understand, and they may consequently develop problems with self-esteem. A non-commissioned member's wife, whose daughter failed Grade 2 because she had never been taught to read, believes that the effect on her self-esteem has been permanent:

> About halfway through Grade 2, we talked to her teacher, and the teacher said, "She's going to fail." And we went, "What???" And she said, "Yeah — she can't read or write." And we went, "Okay — why didn't we know this before?" But the tragic thing was, not so much that she had to repeat a year, but that all through this time where she was struggling to try and do what the rest of the kids were doing, she was turning off. Because she gets this syndrome where the other kids can do it and I can't and I'm stupid. ... So she really had a hard time and she wouldn't read. She absolutely fought and refused to read. It turned her completely off school. ... And she still hates to read. She only reads when she has to.

It is the wife's job to struggle with all these problems. Some wives feel compelled to become assistants in their children's classrooms to help them with their difficulties in coping.

The enormous work involved in moves and the adjustment difficulties experienced by mothers and children are usually invisible to the children's teachers. Teachers are trained to teach children who relocate seldom or never; their pedagogical preparedness rarely extends to children who move every two years. Teachers only see the finished product: a group of children who are not in step with the others and appear to be chronic discipline problems. The teachers, who are extremely busy, are often tempted to ignore these "problems" instead of giving them the extra attention they need, rationalizing that they will be moving on to other schools soon anyway. A woman who has taught in DND schools says:

> The majority of the military kids they get in their classrooms belong to other ranks.[8] And so they say, "That family, I mean,

really! The mother drinks. The father's always drinking. The mother's stupid." The kids are poorly dressed, probably because their boxes are still in Europe. You know. But they don't take that into consideration. They say, "We'll get rid of them next year." And when posting season comes in April or May, the whole staff room just takes these big class lists. Cross off, cross off. "Thank god we're rid of that fellow! Look at this — I can cross off seven kids! That stupid family had seven kids!"

The fact that military absences are hard on wives is likewise invisible to teachers, who often label wives who try to discuss their problems as complainers. The former teacher continues:

> The complaining wife is someone whose husband is gone and who comes in and says, "Well, Johnny couldn't get his homework done because his father's away and I'm so busy with the other children that I can't possibly help him at the kitchen table, blah, blah, blah." And they just won't listen. The teachers won't listen. She has a serious problem. And the teachers are not willing to be flexible in any way. They say, "What a whiner! What a complainer! She stands up for her kid — the kid is a loser! When is she going to figure that out?"

Some wives attempt to counteract the impact of moves on their children's relationships with teachers by struggling at each new posting to acquaint each of their children's teachers with their children's aptitudes and problems. Quite understandably, however, many wives react to the lack of empathy they sense from teachers in the opposite way. They provide only grudging co-operation to each school system they fleetingly encounter and, in some instances, even withhold their co-operation altogether. Already overburdened with the other impacts of military moves, these wives treat school difficulties as the "last straw," the one obstacle they have no energy to surmount. The combination of late starts because of postings, longer holidays spent becoming reacquainted with geographically distant extended families, and even (at times) longer-than-normal periods being kept at home for minor illnesses provides military children with many missed school days with their parents' blessing and conveys the message that the school is the parents' last priority. The school, as a result, reacts even more negatively to the children, and so the spiral continues further downward.

For all these reasons, it is impossible for most military children to enjoy trouble-free school careers. For children who have special needs, the situation is even worse. Moves are especially unsettling for them. Life is already so frustrating for such a child that the loss of a trusted doctor, teacher, or counsellor can push him or her to the brink. At the very least, this kind of loss may undo all the good that has been derived from his or her education or treatment so far. The emotionally disturbed stepson of one officer became so disruptive after a posting had snatched him from a good residential treatment program that his mother had to commit him to a psychiatric hospital. She reports bitterly:

> John was in a residential treatment program in Edmonton, and they posted us here anyway. And Dave went to the Colonel and said, "Look — John is not ready to get discharged. If you post me, we will have to pull him out of the program before he is ready." And now, look, he is in hospital. Never mind the proper treatment program. Now he is in a psychiatric ward because of the move. They pushed him too far.

Each time a military wife with a special needs child moves, she must learn what facilities will be available to help her care for her child in the new community. Even after finding the facilities, she must often fight to get her child into them, and her difficulty is compounded if — as is often the case — the local specialists will not accept the assessments that were done in another province. Her child will consequently wait a year for placement, and she (the mother) will have to school the child at home in the meantime. When language problems are added, the situation can become unbearable. An anglophone non-commissioned member's wife, whose son is learning disabled, recalls her husband's posting in Québec, where her son was adjusting unsuccessfully to an integrated class and there were no English-speaking professionals available to ease the transition. In order to force a solution to the problem, she had to threaten to take her son out of school:

> When he went up to the Grade 5 class, it just didn't work. He didn't have a teacher that had the patience with that sort of thing. So at that point we had a real argument with the school, and we found out then that there was no English psychologist, there was no English speech therapist — anything in Québec.

There was nowhere we could go. Because at this time Michael
was at the point, he couldn't go to school — he was vomiting
every day. Like he was ready to just, I am sure, have a nervous
breakdown at that point. And it wasn't working. And it was at
the point we were back to the fits and the tantrums. ... I was
making him go, and then it just got to the point that it was too
exhausting for both of us to go through this every day. I think
it was just that it was never a win situation at school — it was
a lose, lose, lose situation — he could never succeed or achieve
anything. And so I went in and I just said to them, "Either you
take him out of Grade 5 and put him into a level that he's
capable of working at, or I am taking him out of school." And
I mean, prior to this I had gone in and tried to negotiate pleas-
antly with these people, and it hadn't worked. They hadn't even
gotten back to me. So I just phoned and I said, "Michael won't
come back to the school — he'll be staying home." And it was
the next day I got a call from the principal that the adjustments
had all been made and he was to report to the Grade 3 class on
Monday.

Not only do wives do the work of helping their children settle in
to each new posting; they also tend to be blamed in the military
community (and to blame themselves) when their children settle in
poorly. Indeed, the mythology of "Mother Attitude" circulates almost
as widely on bases as the mythology of wives' self-reliance. This
fact should not be surprising in an organization that takes for granted
that wives will assume total responsibility for housework and child
care. For wives it means an additional pressure. One army officer's
wife describes acclimatizing her children to moves as one of her
more important jobs:

[My role is] showing them that it's a positive thing. Get to meet
new people. Visit different areas of Canada. Just keeping them
up. That's my role. And helping them. Making sure all their
needs are met. I'm sure if I moped around the house and cried
every five minutes, and was in a foul mood all the time, then
they would pick up on that and say, "Oh, mom's not coping."
And probably they wouldn't be coping either.

Another army officer's wife believes that in fulfilling her responsibility of acclimatizing her children, she must, if necessary, perform

a "con job," even when doing so means camouflaging her own feelings:

> You have to prepare the kids. And even if you are going some-
> where that you know is going to be absolute hell, you have to
> find something positive about it. ... We are the adults. They are
> the children. There are ways we can get around them in the
> sense of talking it out. I mean, I didn't want to go to Toronto
> for that year. I knew it was going to be an upsetting year. But
> when I told them about Centre Island, and when I was young
> and had been a student there, and I could show them where I
> had gone to school — you know, that kind of thing — they
> thought that was great. I hated every minute of it, but it's up to
> you.

In sum, moves often create enormous difficulties for military children, and it is their mothers who always cope with them.

Myths about Postings

Strangely enough, military mythologies abound, boasting of the
enormous rewards that wives derive from postings. Like all myths,
they contain some truth. But, like the myth of wives' self-reliance,
these other myths come to enjoy an independent existence, which
allows the military to use them to wield an impressive measure of
influence and power.

The essence of these mythologies is adventure. Variety is the spice
of life, and wives who take advantage of the learning opportunities
that postings provide are adapting most successfully to the military
lifestyle. Clearly, wives who take a positive attitude toward continual
relocation and who believe that its benefits outweigh its costs make
the military's work much easier. It is thus in the military's interests
to nurture the attitude that military wives are "special" women who
find anything less than constant change boring. Hence, the opening
words of a traditional military poem are: "Who said that 'Variety is
the spice of life'? / No doubt 'twas first said by a Military wife." At
the festivities held on every base each spring to mark the departure
of the members who have been posted, similar tributes to wives are
always reiterated. At these ceremonies, wives who speak positively
about their new postings are lauded and praised. Wives who complain are conversely denigrated. Using the example of overseas post-

ings, a retired officer speaks approvingly of wives who overcome the hardships and learn to appreciate the cultural novelty:

> I know there were problems with daily living over there for a lot of these spouses, but at the same time there were spouses that enjoyed it immensely because of the difference. It was my understanding at the time that the ones who expected France to be like Canada were unhappy. The ones who just took it in their stride — "I am in a different country. I am going to make the most of it while I am here and see as much as I can" — were relatively contented.

Experience in the military community teaches wives to internalize the adventure myth and to put the best face possible upon the disruptions in their lives. Hence, an air element wife reports that since she does not want to be like those "complaining" wives, she has tried to regard every single posting positively:

> I have always decided, ever since we were married, that I was never going to approach a place with a bad attitude, and that the place is what you make it. ... I met a lot of women who were very unhappy where they were living, and they complained constantly. You heard total complaining all the time. And I decided in Falconbridge that I was not going to be one of those women who constantly complained about where they were posted and where they lived. I have always decided that I am going to like where I go.

Wives almost always mention adventure when asked to characterize the best aspect of their lives. The way in which they speak about the adventure depends on their ages and backgrounds. A young army wife from one of the hinterland areas of Canada believes that the military option was her husband's best:

> We both knew what the alternatives were. Like, down around where we lived there was no employment. And, like I say, he could have went to Connors Brothers, but he would have been working shift work. And we both like travel — we both wanted to see the world. The military's the best way to see the world, as far as I can see. And neither of us is shy. We're both outgoing.

A young air element wife adds:

> Home for me is where my suitcases are stored, so I have always
> looked on it as an adventure. Like I'm going off to a different
> part of the country to meet people, find out about them, and do
> all the touristy things. Just go and get as much out of it as I can.

Some long-time wives, who have never developed a career — and
probably never will — have learned to regard their travel as an
adequate trade-off. A senior army officer's wife says:

> I have accepted the fact that I'm never going to be able to have
> a career, being married to a military person, so therefore what-
> ever I do is a job. And if I wanted a career, we would have to
> get a divorce — or Keith would have to get out of the military.
> But I have accepted the trade-offs of some of the things I have
> enjoyed in his military career ... moving around and seeing new
> places and being in new situations and being able to adapt.

And military children, who otherwise find adjusting to postings difficult, nevertheless absorb the message that adventure is a palatable
compensation for lack of personal control. A teenager who was based
in Germany during the Gulf War boasts:

> We are world travellers here. We've got much of the advantage
> over the people in Canada. Like most of the kids in Canada just
> dream. What they do is when they are done high school, they
> take a year off and travel to Europe. Well, I won't be doing
> that. I'll jump right into university, because I've already trav-
> elled for five years in Europe. ... I've been to the French
> Riviera. Next year we want to go to the Canary Islands, or my
> mom wants to go to some faraway place like China or some-
> thing. I've been to three communist countries, one of which is
> now not a communist country any more. I was here when the
> Berlin Wall fell. I was here for the Gulf War where all our
> soldiers were going, where on the airfield the hockey arena was
> turned into a morgue if it was needed. I heard everything,
> because all our soldiers were going. My dad even thought that
> he might have to go. ... I like what my dad does.

The adventure mythology helps the military to acclimatize wives and children to moves, and helps some wives and children to regard their military experiences positively.

Postings loosen relationships among friends, families and spouses. For members, this loss is replaced by opportunities, long-term associates, and bonding. Wives, in contrast, undergo isolation, arrested careers, and the proliferation of their unpaid work. The military meanwhile extracts enhanced loyalty and dependence from wives, and tightens its already extensive control.

5

Missed Opportunities

Military wives rarely have the opportunity to pursue a "career" in the middle-class sense of acquiring extensive training or experience, applying it in a challenging job, learning to do the job well, and enjoying a measure of public success. Of course, many civilian women also never develop careers — because of factors related to their social class, lack of education, and/or childrearing responsibilities. But to all the factors that disadvantage civilian women, military wives must add the demands of their husbands' jobs. Very few of them ever manage to develop themselves through meaningful paid work.

The wife's first sacrifice often coincides with her husband's first posting. Although at the time her relationship almost always seemed more important, looking back years afterward she recognizes what the sacrifice meant. The former wife of a navy officer remembers:

> I thought, "Well, I can't afford to go back to university in the fall so I'll go out to Victoria," 'cause he had said, "Come out to Victoria." ... I had graduated, just a straight BA. I knew I couldn't do anything just with that, so I wanted to go back and do postgraduate work, 'cause I felt, really, that I was just getting started. I rather enjoyed studying. ... [If it hadn't been for him] I probably would have worked for a year and then gone back.

Another navy officer's wife remembers:

> I got a job at the university and, thinking back on it, this job could have worked into something really good for me. I was secretary to the new Dean of Graduate Studies — the first Dean of Graduate Studies they had there — and I could have grown with the job. I was basically a stenographer just out of business college, but I could have grown with that job if I had had a

chance to stay. But a year later we were posted to Virginia for three years.

When an opportunity is relinquished later in the marriage, after the important parts of childrearing have been completed, the wife's anguish is intense more immediately. An army wife felt that her life had just begun again, when her husband was abruptly posted to Germany:

> C'était vraiment une nouvelle vie pratiquement qui avait commencé. Au moment où Jean-Paul a commencé l'école, un autre horizon m'est [ouvert], quelque chose de différent. Je me suis rendue compte que j'étais capable de faire de quoi, moi aussi. C'est venu tranquillement, pas vite, mais même si j'étais rendue à presque trente ans, bien regardes donc ça je ne suis pas juste bonne pour les tablettes et rester à la maison à servir n'importe qui et tout le monde. Je suis encore capable de penser, de réagir, d'écrire. J'ai dit, "Ma petite fille, tu as trente ans; aujourd'hui une nouvelle vie s'ouvre à toi; on part." Ma vie s'est arrêtée à trente-quatre ans quand on est reparti pour ici.[1]

An air element wife, who had finally begun her first career in Edmonton when her husband was transferred, remembers:

> When we had to leave Alberta, that was absolutely devastating. When Henry came home and told me we were transferred to Ottawa, I didn't know whether to throw up or cry. I felt sick about it. I thought that things were just finally coming together, and that I'd found something that I was going to be happy doing.

Indeed, as the wives of ambitious members find out, their own first career chances often coincide with their husbands' ascent up the steep (and geographically mobile) hierarchy of senior officerhood. Almost invariably, the member's career wins. Even after the first few moves, his salary is high enough that, on monetary grounds alone, nothing his wife has developed can compete with it. Several moves later, the odds are stacked in his favour even more. A former navy officer's wife summarizes the dynamics that disempowered her in her marriage:

You have to be flexible. You have to be willing to be flexible, to move. And really not to question. Because as soon as you start to question, then that might bring up some doubts or maybe some disagreements with certain things over which you really don't have that much control. I mean I could say, "I don't want to move to Halifax." ... [But since] he was the breadwinner, what choice did I have?

Giving up a good job or job prospect is only the beginning. When the wife arrives at the next posting, she faces even greater obstacles. At remote and overseas postings, for obvious reasons, there are often no — or few — jobs for her to apply for. And the jobs that exist are unlikely to match her training. According to an air element wife, the situation at one of the Canadian bases in Germany was so bleak that most wives were unable to find paid work at all:

There are only certain jobs that you can get over here. You can be a gate guard. Lots of the women are gate guards. They stand in front of the gate and they check people's IDs — that's what women do here. You can be a bus monitor, which means you supervise the kids on the school buses. Or you can work at the Canex part time, stacking boxes, or work at the LX. There's some jobs for nurses. Most of the teachers are hired from Canada. So you can substitute over here, but you can't teach full time. Mostly, you know, if you are a secretary and you are bilingual, then often you can get a job with the military. But that's it for anyone who doesn't have specialized skills or has too specialized skills. We have lawyers who are working as gate guards 'cause there's no jobs for them.

At a number of postings, language differences bar many wives from the job market. To be eligible to work at the former Canadian base in Lahr, Germany, wives had to speak both English and French. And francophone wives who are posted to English Canada are required to speak English, just as anglophone wives who are posted to Québec must speak French. A francophone air element wife recalls her husband's first posting outside of Québec, where she found work but suffered because she did not know the language:

In Trenton I had to work [as a] dispatcher, which I hated. Which was really hard on me, because during that time I spoke English maybe one or two words: yes and no and how are you and fine thank you. But I didn't start to understand English. ... And I worked with mostly English-speaking people, and I had a hard time. I remember coming back home the first week, and I cried and cried. I never understood. It was really hard on me, and it wasn't even in my trade.

A common problem wives encounter is discrimination against military families. Employers are reluctant to hire people who will leave town soon, and they often say so to the wife's face. A navy wife, who applied for the same job in Victoria that she had just resigned from in Halifax, recalls:

When I got there, I was very politely told that I was not a permanent resident of Victoria and I could not guarantee them that I would be there for six months or two years or five years, and that they would not give me work because I was not a permanent resident. I was a military dependent. I could be posted with my husband at any time, and the job should go to people that were born and bred on the island and needed the money more than we did. And at the time we did need the money terribly.

At overseas locations wives are almost completely dependent on the base to provide jobs, and getting base jobs frequently depends more on who one's husband is than upon one's own experience and qualifications. A non-commissioned army member's wife, who was trilingual and had impressive qualifications as a travel agent, was assured that when she went to Germany she would easily get a job on the base. On this basis, she turned down a good job that she had been offered in Canada. She believes that she never got the promised travel agency job because her husband was not an officer. She reports:

I never had the job. I always went to give my name, and they always told me they had all the people they needed, but some times I went back and there were new people there. And the thing I knew — I can't certify that — but most of them were wives of officers, who had pull to get in. And they didn't have any courses in tourism or geography, most of them. And not all of them were speaking both languages. ... So I didn't have any chance. They never called me. Nothing.

A non-commissioned air element wife recalls a job interview in Germany at which virtually every question pertained to her husband:

> They started asking me what was my husband's rank, where he worked, what his place was in the military, how many years he'd been in the military, if we planned to have children, and how many years we'd been married. And after a while I said, "Look — do you want to know where I studied, what I can do?" "Oh," she said, "there's no point." I said, "You're not hiring my husband!" I knew after that I wouldn't get the job, I was getting so mad. "Don't ask about my husband, he's not looking for the job, he's not going to do the work — I am!" That was the first year. After that they were more careful, because they had lots of complaints.

The consequences of such abuses are serious, especially since all Canadians who are living either overseas or in remote areas of Canada are ineligible to collect unemployment insurance benefits.

Even if discrimination, job scarcity, language, or the military ranking system does not prevent the wife from getting a job, the wife who does find work starts each new posting at the bottom of her occupational ladder, irrespective of the experience she has previously acquired. Or she is unable to get the training she obtained in one region of Canada recognized in another. Or she begins a course, only to be posted somewhere else with her husband and forfeit the time she invested. Or she finally loses all her motivation. One wife who has spent her entire adult life trying to qualify as a teacher reflects:

> I only had a two-year permanent teaching certificate, from when I went to university the first time. And had I stayed in one place, I would have continued to teach and just upgraded as I was going along. But when you move every three years. ... Well, fairly soon I was totally obsolete. I could substitute, but I couldn't teach full time any more. I had to go back to school, and of course it turned out that none of my credentials were good. I had to start from the beginning, all over again.

An officer's wife who is a nurse says:

I always start back down. I'm the first one hired, but I'm always back down at the bottom of the heap. Maybe they give me pay incentives and that, but not a lot of authority. And no pension.

Another officer's wife, who hopes to train to be a lawyer, says:

You cannot have a law practice in Ontario, and establish a clientele, and suddenly two years later you get posted to Winnipeg. You have to write your bar exams again, you have to set up a new practice or go in with somebody. And nobody's going to take in a two-year law person. ... If you go in with a bigger firm, you'll never get a partnership — ever. If you go out on your own, you'll never get any clients.

An army officer's wife whose nursing training was interrupted by a posting recalls:

I just started my first year there. I'd only taken one course. And then in university my second year I decided that I was going to apply for the Bachelor of Nursing. ... So the second year I took all these science courses. And in October he flew home [from a course] to tell me, "Guess what — we're going to Germany!" So I'd taken all those science courses for nothing.

A non-commissioned air wife describes her missed opportunity to become a hairdresser:

I remember in Trenton when I went to apply for a hairdressing course. The guy looked at me and said, "You'll be at the end of the list." I asked why. He said, "Because you're a military wife, my dear, and we cannot expect to train you and after that you leave. You won't even work here. So don't wait for us to give you a chance." So I said, "Put my name on the list anyway — I'll wait." And do you know when I got news about it? I was in Germany! I got a letter in the mail saying I was accepted.

For want of career alternatives, most wives settle for mere jobs, which are temporary, poorly paid, and tedious and fail to provide pension plans or other important benefits.

Wives who are overseas often cannot find even these kinds of low-paying jobs. Sometimes, they cannot even find volunteer work.

The most adventurous of them resolve to enjoy the novelty of being in Europe, and if they can afford it, they travel. Others become interested in crafts. A Family Resource Centre staffperson at one of the former Canadian bases in Germany observes:

> That's one thing that's very big over here is crafts. They are time-fillers, so you get a lot of people that are otherwise not craft-oriented becoming that way over here.

Still other wives have babies. According to Family Resource Centre personnel, 500 babies were born at the two Canadian bases in Germany in 1990, out of a total military population of 20,000, in comparison to the normal Canadian birthrate of 295 out of 20,000 during approximately the same period.[2] This difference is very significant. According to a navy officer's wife, it was circumstances like these that largely motivated her to start a family during one of her husband's overseas postings:

> If I hadn't been in a strange country and on my own, it's something I would not have done. He wanted a big family when we got married — and I don't want any. I had no desire to become a mother. But because I was there and lonesome all of a sudden, it became something to do.

Although having babies is something that most wives do eventually, military wives often become pregnant in overseas and remote locations because they don't have much else to do. Wives invariably describe overseas postings as the times that they felt most compelled to set aside their own goals.

Long-term Consequences

The long-term implications of not having meaningful paid work can be profound. First, many wives fail to follow through on what promised to be an excellent start to their lives — their high quality professional training and experience. The consequent economic and personal wastes are enormous. Other wives get married before they receive any training, or even fail to find out what they would have done with their lives if they had been in a position to do anything. This loss is perhaps even greater. Looking back on her life, a francophone air element wife reflects:

I've tried a lot of things, but I've never finished one. Never said: "I'm going to be that." Like my work. I'm nothing really, because today I'm a secretary, tomorrow I'm going to be a C-dispatch, another day I'm going to be ... but I never finish anything.

An anglophone air officer's wife says:

I wanted a career, and you know I'm 35 now and I just don't have it. I don't consider what I'm doing as any kind of a career. It's a nowhere job. ... I want a career — a business career — for myself, and I feel very bitter because I haven't had any jobs all these years through the military. And I feel like my life has just been kind of wasted.

Some of the long-term consequences become deeply rooted. Like other women, military wives who do not work outside their homes are vulnerable to low self-esteem, and they often remain in this state until they have found meaningful work again. Some wives never achieve it. An air element wife describes a depression she suffered at a remote posting:

I think because I wasn't working and associating with making my brain work or whatever you want to say, I got depressed a lot out there. I gained weight. I did all kinds of dumb things. I got so I didn't want to go out of the house any more. I lost all my self-confidence, because I can say when we moved back here I was really not ready to go back out into the world. I couldn't even sit down and carry on a conversation with a normal person half the time.

An officer's wife describes how she slid into alcohol abuse at an overseas posting in order to repress her anger at her husband that because of his career her own life was going nowhere:

Drinking at the parties. I think it started socially, but then the marriage problems got worse. It stopped being a social drink, and I'd have a couple before he came home in the afternoon. ... I don't know — it was just a very tense atmosphere. I don't think either one of us knew what was wrong with it. I felt like I was walking on egg shells a lot of the time. And I don't know

— I think too — it's hard to explain. Maybe I should have tried to prepare for this better. I felt I was in sort of a limbo, because I had started to think of going to work or doing something for myself before we went to Brussels that time. I felt like I was marking time.

A professional woman, who is also an army officer's wife, describes how she feels every time she is unable to find work that is commensurate with her skills:

As a military wife I don't cope well. ... Just as a military wife with my children, I feel trapped. And that's the way I am. It is two totally different things for me. My self-esteem goes on the ground, and that is the way it is.

A civilian woman who works on a military base theorizes that repeated postings eventually make some military wives feel so powerless that the deepest spirit inside them simply "gives up":

I really sympathize with the fact that they have to move every two, three, or four years. And change. And start all over again. And after a while, I think, there is just no more energy to fight back and try to get what they want out of life. They are so tired. So, they are sort of: "Well, I tried — I am tired of trying." The world passes them by.

These psychological consequences are tragic — and predictable. The work postings extract from wives is staggering, and almost none of it contributes toward developing their own lives. Much of the work wives do actually serves to destroy what they had constructed at the last place in the way of relationships and jobs. It should not be surprising when this destruction exacts a mental health cost.

The consequences of the wife's loss of self-esteem become most apparent when her marriage breaks up and her shaky self-confidence is exploited by her ex-husband and his lawyer. During the divorce negotiations, her ex-husband often skillfully contrasts her sporadic employment history with his career success. He asserts that while he was gallantly defending his country, she was *choosing* to "do nothing." In her weakened state, she believes him and actually reduces her demands for support.

Unpaid Work

If postings create a self-esteem vacuum in wives, the military is quick to try to fill it with volunteer (or in some cases poorly paid) work on the base.

Wives' volunteer or semi-volunteer "base work" serves three purposes for the military. It gives unemployed wives a way to fill their time. It provides most of the free or cheap labour that the military uses to support the wives of absent/deployed members through such measures as family support, regimental wives' organizations, and wives' clubs. Finally, and most important, "base work" secures unemployed wives' loyalty to the military and encourages them to look to the military community for solutions to the problems military life creates.[3]

The military does not try to hide the fact that it is delighted to have wives' volunteer labour. For example, a non-commissioned navy officer expresses glee that one fancy dinner a year is sufficient to thank the wives who volunteer on his base. He believes that the military has underutilized wives as an unpaid resource:

> Sometimes I think we've really missed the boat in taking advantage of women as a resource. ... There's a handful that run my local little newspaper, which is critical to disseminate information. There's two of them up there, and they put hours in — absolute hours, you know. So once a year we have a dinner and: "Have some more madeira, my dear, and Do you want some more duff for dessert?" ... No, I think we've missed the boat. I just think we've missed the boat.

The national Director of Military Family Support admits that his program would be unable to run if it were not mostly staffed by volunteers. He exclaims:

> It's got to be! Like I said before, there's almost 2,000 volunteers in this program. We've got some centres that have got a list of 300 volunteers. And they use 'em, oh, in real unique ways. So yeah, it's got to be volunteer-based.

He justifies his reliance on volunteers by connecting the program's "community ownership" philosophy with self-help:

I mean, if you look at community organization and community development, as I said before, the best way to do that in the community is to turn it back to the community. "What is it that you need? We'll help you! But you run it, you decide, you program it, and it's yours. And you really own it." And so self-help is, I suppose, another way of saying that.

But, as an air element wife points out, the director is using "the community" to dress the military's traditional exploitation of wives in deceptive new clothes. She says:

It's going to legitimize the kind of band-aid work that has always gone on in the military community, which is women accepting women's burdens. You turn to your neighbours and friends in your own community first, and the military family support centre in some ways is going to legitimize this band-aid system. Women have always carried the military community on their backs.

While volunteers are especially important during major deployments like the Gulf War and Oka, bases use them continually. A family resource centre staffperson at a large base reports:

We did a survey last year, and we had almost 1,000 volunteers between recreational clubs and our services and other things that were going on. But we usually average around, for our own facilities, around 400 that do different things.

The volunteer co-ordinator at another base lists some of the things she obtains volunteers for:

Well, for community projects like the Easter parties, the Army Day — we have had to have people come out for that. Emergency homemaking we have had people go out for; people to come in and run courses that we are offering; people who are willing to do child care on short notice for one reason or another; people to drive. One of the big ones with the fellows in Cyprus was people to cut these women's lawns. We had a fellow go over and fix a lady's dryer. There has been so many things — anything you can think of — people phone in and ask if someone will volunteer.

Although some volunteers are male members (e.g., for lawn cutting), the vast majority are wives because wives who are unable to find paid work have the most time on their hands. An army officer's wife describes her hectic volunteering existence, making it clear that volunteering provides her with a needed respite from her small children:

> Totminders right from the word Go. I was a volunteer there on Thursday afternoons when we first came. And now I am also on the Board of Directors of Totminders. And I am on the executive of the Wives' Club for the second year running. Everybody else disappeared fast at the end of their year's stint, and I said, "I'll do it again — why not?" And now I've put myself onto the board of the Family Support Centre just last month. Because wives' club has come to an end now, and if nothing is happening, if everywhere you turn it is closing down, it is horrendous. So I thought if there is something else I can belong to and get myself out in the evening, I'll belong to it.

A non-commissioned member's wife who runs her base's community council[4] for low pay instead of having a civilian job has kept herself busy by allowing her job description to expand indefinitely. In the process, she has provided her base with an unlimited source of cheap labour:

> The job started out as seven hours Monday and Friday, three hours Tuesday, Wednesday, Thursday. It has turned into 35 hours a week. The job description has changed dramatically, which a lot of is my fault. My boss says, "Take care of this," and rather than saying, "Look, that's not on my job description," I'll do it. ... The job has gotten to the point where I'm going to put a bunch of hooks on the wall for all the different hats that I wear. My office has taken on Block Parents. The person that was running Block Parents was posted out and nobody was there to run the program. ... That's part of my job now. The information centre was being run by someone else in PMQs. They got posted out — nobody to run it. Well, all right, put the hat on — let's do her. Because of these additional jobs, I put in a request for and got the additional hours. I prepare budgets for the community council. Now on paper I have noth-

ing saying that I'm qualified to do this. I should have courses
in accounting and business admin. I haven't got the courses,
but I've done it for years. "Would you take care of this?" "Sure
— no problem!"

Wives' volunteering not only provides labour for the military's
own community, but also it often widens the military's sphere of
influence by bolstering its image in the outside world. The Protestant
Chaplain-General reports having found "useful" community work
for the wives of some generals in Ottawa:

> The former CDS's [Chief of Defence Staff's] wife, for exam-
> ple, was thinking that the women should do something more
> than just meet from time to time and chat and lunch together
> or play bridge. She thought they should do something. She
> phoned me and said, "Can you find us something that would
> be useful?" I phoned some of my women United Church min-
> isters in the area, and there's Interval House for abused spouses
> here in Ottawa. And we've hooked up the general officers'
> wives and Interval House. So they work with one another.

The military does not find it difficult to recruit wives as volunteers
or cheap labour, especially in locations where wives can find little
"real" work. The adventure mythology provides part of the pressure
for wives to volunteer, with its implication that a wife can enjoy
absolutely any posting if she will only put a little effort into it. The
self-reliance mythology, with its insistence that wives are responsible
for their own happiness, helps too. According to both reasonings, a
wife who can't get a good job should be almost as pleased to have
a poor or unpaid one. An army wife who does a lot of base volunteer
work says:

> Any place is what you make of it. If you're not willing to get
> out there and do something to occupy your time, I'm sorry [but]
> I have no pity for you. You have to make do with what you've
> got.

Many wives feel compelled to volunteer as a way of reciprocating
the support they have received, as if this support had been a privilege
and needing it had been the wives' "fault," rather than a consequence

of the military lifestyle. An air element wife and long-time volunteer articulates this view:

> I feel that everybody should in some way give back to their community, wherever they are, something of use, especially if they have something to give back. And if they haven't, they must learn to give something back.

But the military does not need to provide an extra incentive to encourage many wives to volunteer. Postings have already created enormous voids in many wives' lives, which they have an urgent need to fill. For one young navy wife, volunteering on base has helped her feel needed and enabled her to believe that there is more to her life than marriage and motherhood:

> It has given me so much pleasure. I like people. I like getting out of the house, and I am not a person to sit in the house and just idle away. I can't do that. My volunteer hours have given more to me, I think, than I've given to any organization that I've volunteered with. I feel better. I enjoy doing something for the community and seeing it come together. It gives you a feeling of self-worth, of not being just a housewife.

The wife of a former air element member argues that her low-paying job in the orderly room enabled her to claim an independent social status on the base for herself that she would have been unable to claim if she had been an "ordinary" wife:

> I wasn't just a wife. I was somebody that had worked with them, and it made a difference. ... I had worked with these guys in the orderly room at headquarters. I had done their typing for them, so I was a person, whereas they didn't treat me like that at other bases. They viewed people that were working differently than they did people that were staying at home. Just totally. There is no other way to put it.

Whatever volunteering provides for wives, it realizes very high dividends for the military. At little or no cost, some wives' "base work" helps the military to contain the problems that military life has created for other wives and their children.

Officers' Wives as Corporate Wives

For officers' wives and, to a lesser extent, senior non-commissioned members' wives, unpaid base labour also includes participating in the unceasing rituals of military social life, whose demands intensify as their husbands climb higher. The social expectations of officers' wives serve at least four purposes for the military. First, they constitute a mechanism through which senior members' wives provide "mothering" support to the wives of more junior members (e.g., through the regimental system) so that members will be freer to concentrate on their jobs. Second, they enable the upper echelons of military life to mirror the upper echelons of corporate, political, and diplomatic life, into which wives are customarily "drawn in" to help out with the expressive aspects of their husbands' jobs. Third, they provide the military with an additional criterion to use to separate the "promotable" from the "merely average" senior officers. Fourth, the social expectations of officers' wives provide an outlet for the energies of women who are too geographically mobile to develop their own careers. They therefore supply the military with an additional method of controlling wives and securing their loyalty to the organization in a manner that is calculated to ensure the officers' own enhanced dedication and devotion.

Just as they openly admit the military's desire for all wives' "base work," senior officials are candid about the additional unpaid expectations of officers' wives. The military expects the officer and his wife to function as a team so that the services of two skilled workers can be mobilized for the price of one. The spousal expectations escalate as the officer's rank rises. Apart from all her other responsibilities, his wife is expected to play the roles of escort, gracious hostess, regimental mother hen, trouble-shooter/problem-solver within the wives' community, family support volunteer, charitable good works organizer, and socialite. She is additionally expected not to entertain her own career aspirations or to complain about the military lifestyle. If she fails to fulfil these expectations, her husband suffers. The 1942 edition of the American *Army Woman's Handbook* read:

> Numerous instances are on record where an officer's efficiency has been discounted heavily, where he has failed to achieve positions of trust and distinction, and even where transfers have been made, entirely because of the fact that the wife was indiscreet in her speech or showed too plainly a lack of knowledge

of military customs, ordinary social customs, or customs of good breeding.[5]

A contemporary Canadian National Defence Headquarters general puts the point more baldly:

Take, for instance, an ambassador. I mean, if an ambassador has a turkey wife, we're not going to put him in Washington, are we? We're going to find him a backwater somewhere.

He continues:

My predecessor, when he invited a colonel to go and be an attaché, he'd invite both the husband and the wife into the office. And he'd talk to both of them. And if he thought that the team wasn't gonna be effective, or he'd perceive, you know … I mean, the last thing you want to do is have a family problem in the middle of Zimbabwe or somewhere!

The general adds that wives of senior officers are often specially trained for the adjutant roles they will assume during keynote postings:

That's why we invite them every year to listen to our briefings, so they can be part of the team. God, we give them special language training because they're part of the team! We give them training in how to take photographs and not get caught by the KGB and all this sort of stuff. I mean, we do it! So they *are* part of the team!

Even wives of non-commissioned members are taken into consideration when their husbands are posted, if they are deemed to have extraordinary abilities. A senior army officer recalls how the military recently made a posting that would ensure the participation of a particular corporal's wife in the execution of an overseas peacekeeping mission:

There was a corporal in the PPCLI [Princess Patricia's Canadian Light Infantry] force, who was posted to Calgary, not because he was the greatest corporal in the world, but because his wife was capable of organizing the ladies' auxiliary in preparation for a major deployment on peacekeeping duties. And that's very much the way it is operated when it is effective.

The military's expectations of officers change as the officers go up the ranks, and these changes are reflected in the demands on their wives. Whereas the junior officer (lieutenant, captain) supervises non-commissioned members, the senior officer (major, lieutenant-colonel, colonel) supervises officers. By this time, he has learned to regard himself as a "system man" and has thoroughly internalized the demands of the operational standpoint.[6] At the lieutenant-colonel level, the officer becomes even more of a system man as the focus of his management shifts from persons to resources.

Command and Staff College (which trains lieutenant-colonels and colonels) and National Defence College (which trains generals) put the finishing touches on the ascending officer's transition from specialist to generalist. Staff College prepares officers for the Forces command level. Officers emerge from this experience ready to be base commanders, NDHQ directors, managers at the command headquarters for their own element (land, sea, or air), or occupants of NATO positions overseas. At Staff College, officers learn to work in a larger environment than their own element. They enter the world of "joint operations," which means offensives (such as the Gulf War) that are mounted by a combination of elements and/or a combination of NATO countries. At Staff College, officers thus begin to learn about NATO and about military organizations in other countries.

National Defence College[7] is an even broader experience for the relatively few full colonels who manage to be sent there. These colonels, the military cream of the crop, share their educational experiences with the cream of the crop of keynote civilian organizations, such as the civil service, powerful industries, and academia. They study the "big picture" of how the military interfaces with political, economic, and cultural life in Canada and elsewhere. They also learn to generalize their management skills so that they could (if necessary) transfer them from the military to other situations. Colonels make important contacts at National Defence College, and they often use the experience to begin to position themselves to assume high-paying civilian jobs when they retire.

As they ascend the hierarchy, officers not only learn new skills but also become increasingly dedicated. No longer merely loyal to the military, they begin to personify and represent it. In order to climb to the military's top jobs, officers must — even more than non-commissioned members — willingly subject their personal lives, homes, wives, and families to 24-hour-a-day scrutiny. They must also become even more committed to combat readiness. Whenever it is necessary, officers must sacrifice all other priorities to "the mission," without believing that they are sacrificing anything. A senior officer who was commissioned to officer status from the ranks explains:

> Certainly an officer never says no. ... If the CO comes in at 4 o'clock and you're ready to go off on your leave to go off to Gracey Lake to go camping, and the CO says, "I need this done by tomorrow morning," then you'll work. You'll do it. You'll cancel your leave. There's no doubt that you will do that. ... The expectation is that you won't volunteer. You won't have to. You won't say, "I'll stay." There's no question of whether you'll stay or not. You'll stay. You'll be there. And that's the difference. An NCM would volunteer. And you'd go, "That's great — he volunteered!" An officer who didn't stay would be deficient. There's no doubt about it. And now that I'm a senior officer, it's even higher. What it is is that you shouldn't even think it. You shouldn't even think that you wouldn't be there.

As a male officer ascends the hierarchy, the military expects his wife to make up the difference at home. The military also steps up its demands on her. And the ambitious officer develops a growing vested interest in pressuring her, if necessary, to comply. At the lieutenant level, the social demands are limited primarily to mixed dining-ins and other similar functions on the base. Entertaining at home is usually confined to friends and colleagues one likes. The real demands start at the captain and major levels, when the wife is expected to entertain the members of her husband's unit and their wives regularly. At the major level, she is also expected to organize social events and perform mentoring roles for captains' and lieutenants' wives. If her husband is occupying an exchange posting in the U.S. or overseas, she is expected to entertain Canadian military personnel who visit on business.

At the lieutenant-colonel and colonel levels, depending on her husband's job, the wife assumes more high-profile leadership toward junior wives, entertains significantly larger groups of people (e.g., everyone on the base), spends more time hosting visiting military personnel, and, if she is overseas, represents Canada at important events. Visitors who have travelled a long distance will often spend

one or more nights at her home. If they are VIPs, the wife's responsibilities will include planning a daytime social calendar for their
wives as well as an elaborate mixed dinner party for every evening
of the visit. By now the wife will likely be moving at least once every
two years, and it is most unlikely that she will have a paying job.

At the general level, in many locations, the wife entertains every
important dignitary who visits the area, including chiefs of defence
staff from Canada and elsewhere, NATO officials, ambassadors, and
heads of state. Again, she hosts these visitors in her home and plans
and carries out exhaustive day and evening itineraries. Even during
a "slack" week, she may host or attend more than eight functions.
Like many head-of-state wives, she may also be encouraged to perform visible charity work. She almost certainly will not do paid work.
A former general's wife recalls her husband's NATO posting in
Brussels:

> You were out six days out of seven. And the seventh day you
> were doing the entertaining. See, in NATO you have all the
> NATO countries represented there, through ambassadors and
> mil-reps [military representatives]. Okay? Ambassadors, mil-
> reps. So there's two per country. There's 24 countries — there's
> 48. You're on the circuit every day. And these are all dinners,
> cocktails. The same people all the time. And then twice a year
> the NATO meetings go on. And so representatives from all the
> other countries come over. Like the Prime Minister, Minister
> of National Defence. Then they all come from each country. So
> you've got great big dos then.

At its highest levels, the military needs wives in the picture partly
for appearances. Since heads of state, ambassadors, NATO officials,
and Chief Executive Officers all bring their wives to functions,
military officers must do so too. But, as in other senior management
contexts, military wives are also needed at social functions to exercise social skills that men are traditionally believed not to possess.
Wives' "person-work" at military functions helps their husbands
with their own jobs in many ways. Wives' presence and congenial
hospitality relaxes the atmosphere around the men and facilitates
alliances and "deals" that might be less likely to succeed, even in the
male-bonding context of the Mess. Wives extract important information from people they talk to at functions and pass it on to their
husbands. Wives form their own opinions about people they meet

and pass these on to their husbands, so their husbands gain an additional valuable perspective on the members they command and their families. Wives impart information to other wives that their husbands would actually like the other husbands to know, thus providing a conduit for delicate communication between members. This last point is especially important for husbands who have something to tell officers of higher rank. Good officers are very cognizant of the social engineering feats effected by their wives. A general indicates that his wife's community volunteering provides him with valuable information for his own work:

> My wife's very much involved in volunteer work with food cupboards, food banks, and things of this nature. She's very involved in a general officers' wives' club in Ottawa. Through this — her contact with the church, with the community and the military — people get to know her and they talk to her. And then she talks to me. It's a dimension that I find is very positive because of my position, being married with my wife out in these areas.

A senior air officer says about his wife:

> Helga's very sensitive to people. Listens very carefully to what they say. And tells me things. She can assess how a person is feeling on the basis of a two-minute conversation. And can give me some pretty good insight into what that person is feeling or thinking. It's partially a case of me simply not being as good at it as she is, [partially one of] her seeing somebody for the first time, whereas I'm close to them. I'm talking about her meeting people that I work with at my house at a gathering. I don't know how significant it is, but it certainly causes me to look at that aspect that she's suggested a little more closely.

A general's former wife recollects:

> At cocktails and receptions, dinner parties, any time that you're out with other people, we women have a very strong gut feeling about other people. Much stronger than men do. And after any reception, I can remember going home and we'd sit for an hour, two hours, going over the whole evening. And he'd say, "What do you think of so and so?" And I'd tell him. And he'd listen

to my gut feelings. And it was like a tipoff. My reaction to so and so would tell him something different than what he thought of them. ... And the fact that I got to know the spouses quite well through wives' club and different circles, I heard an awful lot. I would tell him an awful lot. So he was aware of an awful lot. So a wife can be very important.

Apart from the direct reasons for wives' usefulness, the military uses their participation in its social life as a yardstick for judging their husbands' suitability for promotions. When everything else is equal (and occasionally even when it isn't), the wife's performance can be the deciding factor when the promotion board must choose between Officers A and B. A senior air officer explains:

If the two that accept the work as a unit screw it up, he's not going to be promoted. But he's never even going to get looked at if she doesn't play the game. And those are the rules.

A non-commissioned navy officer specifies further:

I mean, he makes one slip, it's over. Literally! It's such a tight race. Literally, yeah, if you are looking at the old navy that I joined. Receptions, functions, parties, new dress, new dress, new dress. That's not the lower ranks, but I mean, yes, I can see that.

The negative consequences to members whose wives opt out (or members who have no wives) are correspondingly severe. A complaint was recently made to the Canadian Human Rights Commission by an officer who believed he had been denied a promotion to base commander (and the rank of colonel) as a result of becoming separated. Military witnesses at the Human Rights tribunal corroborated his story.[8] And an army officer was understandably dismayed when his wife announced to him that she no longer wanted to play the social game. She recalls:

Towards the last year [of that posting], I sort of took a stand and decided to do my own thing and just not attend anything I didn't want to. ... [My husband] was upset at first, that's for sure. Because I mean, let's face it, wives are sort of an adden-

dum to their military careers. And to have a wife consciously
make that choice was quite political.

Playing the game by the wrong rules can sometimes damage an
officer's career equally. Another army officer was told that his career
might be in jeopardy after his wife had challenged the military's rigid
dress code by asking permission to wear a pant suit to a Christmas
function. His wife reports:

> I have — or had — this really gorgeous heavy satin pants and
> matching jacket, like a sparkly top or whatever. And I went to
> Harry's boss and I said, "Look — I know it's formal, okay, but
> because it is more of a party, could I wear this pant suit?" I
> said, "I'll bring it around so you can see, okay?" And I said,
> "We are looking at buying a house and I don't really have much
> cash around." ... He said, "Tess, if you come to the Mess in a
> pant suit I will ask you to leave." So I said, "Okay. All right.
> Fine." ... [And the Colonel] threatened Harry with writing that
> he had an unsuitable wife for any overseas posting.

Officers are thus provided with powerful incentives for having wives
who conform.

The social demands on some officers' wives are so high that
military life virtually prevents them from taking on paid jobs. From
the military's standpoint, it is extremely convenient that military
mobility makes it difficult for wives to find such jobs. High-ranking
officers' wives frequently find themselves so busy with their husbands' careers that they hardly even think about the paid work opportunities they are missing. The former wife of a general who once
commanded Canada's forces in Europe recalls succinctly: "The wife
of the Commander could never have an outside job. That was full-
time."

But other officers' wives attempt to develop careers, and as a
result, they need to be overtly pressured to toe the expected line. Until
the 1960s, officers' wives were actually forbidden to seek paid employment, so that their time would be completely free for volunteering. A retired air officer's wife recollects about that period:

> I remember my first officers' wives' meeting in Cold Lake,
> where the Colonel's wife looked at me and said, "You are going
> to run the Thrift Shop." It wasn't a question of, "Would you

like to?" or "Draw up a plan for volunteers." "You, Martha, will run the Thrift Shop." Which I did. We did other stuff — volunteer stuff — that we chose to do. But we were expected, and required, and indeed ordered, to do certain jobs.

During the last 20 years, military tactics to achieve this end have been more subtle; they have consisted mainly of veiled threats about the negative consequences of non-conformity for husbands' careers. Sometimes the threats have not been so veiled. As recently as 1990, an army officer's wife was reprimanded for having a paid job on her husband's base:

> I was at a mess dinner last February. I had started the home-maker project, and another major's wife was telling me that majors' wives should [not] be working. I mean, we were in 1990. I had just started the homemaker project. ... I was the first one of our majors' wives who had taken a job in years, and they ostracized me. They never talked to me for the rest of the thing. So my husband in November was called into the CO's office so that they could talk to him about me. That was in 1990, yes.

On other occasions, officers' wives who have managed to find low-paying jobs have been pressured by their husbands' commanders not to accept them on the grounds that such jobs would not qualify as suitable officers' wives' pastimes.

Peer pressure within the wives' community is another factor that can discourage officers' wives from paid work. Wives who do not conform to the non-paid work norm are frequently ostracized. An army officer's wife who is a career woman reports:

> I always felt bad that I never adjusted. Not conformed, but I never seemed to get along well within the military community with the wives. Like I always felt that I wasn't a part of it, that I was somehow different. And they didn't like it when I went to things. And they were sort of, I don't know, disdainful of what I was doing.

While the indispensability of wives' unpaid socializing may pro-vide the best military rationale for ostracizing career women, from the wives' perspective the reason is often resentment. According to the former wife of an army officer, the "career" wife violates the unspoken "misery loves company" solidarity that is supposed to cement wives' interpersonal relations:

> Why should she go out and be able to earn money when we can't? Our husbands won't let us. And if there is a tea or something, she can't come because she's working and earning money. Well, we're all over there in the same boat, so why should one and not the other?

Since moving around has already deprived officers' wives of families and long-term friends, many of them may lack the internal resources to withstand the onslaught of other wives' hostility.

Despite military and peer pressure, some officers' wives nevertheless do find paid employment. Some of them, in fact, work professionally on a base as teachers or nurses, as do some non-commissioned members' wives. But the military does not appear to be comfortable with the idea of wives having professional status. It goes to considerable lengths to remind such wives that within the military community they will always be regarded as dependents. For example, there is a tradition in the military that a wife's place is in the mess of her husband. For this reason, civilian professionals who work on a base are permitted to be members of the Officers' Mess, while military wives who work on the same base are not. Officers' wives forego the privilege of a bar bill and must use their husbands' identifications when signing meal chits. If the husbands of these professional wives are non-commissioned members, the wives may be prohibited from even going to the Officers' Mess.

An important reason for the military's social expectations of wives — especially officers' wives —is that wives' participation in the military social milieu buttresses the conservative patriarchal notion that wives derive their status and identity from their husbands. Wives who conform enhance their husbands' and the military's control over them. Wives who have their own professional careers conversely threaten that control. Control is thus an important motivation behind the military's expectation that officers' wives will not have careers.

Typical officers' wives might well envy their paid work counterparts, who have built-in excuses for missing get-togethers, because the officers' social whirl is relentless. The fact that officers and their wives are usually invited to parties because they are on "lists," rather than because the givers of the parties are their friends, makes many

officers' parties superficial affairs that are dreaded by the wives who
attend them. An army officer's wife says:

> Stuff that I still have trouble with is the places that we *have* to
> go, you know ... I don't always feel like going. And most of
> the times you know that the only reason you're going is you
> are on a list, and they just as soon probably didn't want you —
> not you, but the group — to go. They are giving an obligatory
> thing, and you are going out to an obligatory thing. And I mean
> that's not exactly the makings for a great social [time].

Apart from the superficiality and tedium of military functions, the
continual requirement to entertain acquaintances and strangers can
be exhausting. At foreign postings, entertaining can be especially
stressful because customary cooking ingredients are unavailable, the
work involves research about other countries' customs, or the military expects the wife to be a model ambassador for Canada. A navy
officer's wife recalls her husband's posting at a British staff college:

> There were 13 foreign students on every course — us being one
> of the 13 — and there was another Canadian couple with us.
> Sally Nicholson and I tended to do a lot of the entertaining with
> the other foreign students. We were kind of all grouped in one
> little section of town, so we did a lot of very difficult entertain-
> ing, because a lot of these nationalities can't eat pork or beef,
> or they can't drink alcohol, or whatever. So you really have to
> sit down and read up on your dos and don'ts for whatever
> nationality. I mean, we had Arabs, Pakistanis, Uruguayans. I
> mean, they were from all over the world, and they all have
> different religious type of things. Anyway, the safest thing you
> could serve at one of these places was a chicken! We learned
> how to do chicken many different ways.

The same woman recalls Canada Day at the same posting. It was the
Canadian wives' responsibility to put on a big party:

> Six wives threw the Canada Day party for three years for 350
> people. We did all the cooking, all the foods, all of that kind of
> stuff. We would do a Canadian Ladies Luncheon, and the six
> of us would get together and we would decide on a menu. And
> we would try to make it as Canadian as possible with Canadian

flags on the table and provincial pictures up all over the walls. And we'd have Canadian books. Hit all the houses in London, like Nova Scotia House and those places, and do all kinds of things. Write to any kind of a Canadian company and get whatever we could from them for raffle prizes. And the money would go to charity.

At any posting, a lot of the preparatory work for parties is done behind the scenes and is not something the officer's wife generally discusses. One such item is her wardrobe. As in many other high-profile settings, it is an unspoken military rule that officers' wives should attempt to avoid wearing the same outfit twice. While a new posting can come as a godsend from this standpoint, within the context of each posting, where one typically attends social event after social event with the same people, the amount of time and money that wives spend on shopping or sewing can be staggering. The wife of a former army officer recalls her courtship:

> I was only a girlfriend — or a friend — and, god almighty, I had to get another outfit! It wasn't like *them*! *They* could wear the same uniform! Every time you went to a party, if you weren't wearing something slightly different from the last time — well! They knew! Here we go again!!

Officers' wives also do behind-the-scenes work on their homes to transform them into appropriately elegant backdrops for military parties. This task typically involves putting considerable effort and money into choosing furniture, draperies, rugs, wallpaper, china, and crystal — and doing so at every posting. An air officer's wife recollects the early years of her first marriage:

> I remember it being very important to spend the money I got teaching on crystal and good dishes and good furniture. Well, acceptable furniture for that time. Because people were coming in. And because he was an officer, it was really important that the house look right. At least the downstairs area that people could see. It had to look right.

Senior officers' wives, who entertain important people in their homes, additionally often spend several hidden hours before each party attempting to ensure that its social interaction will proceed smoothly. A former general's wife recalls spending hours before each dinner party constructing a seating plan that would bring out the most amiable qualities of her guests. She explains:

> It takes hours to prepare a seating plan! Because you've got a table for 18. And say one doesn't show up or the wife can't make it or somebody's sick. Then you're down to 17, so at the last minute I'm on the phone, phoning one of the majors' wives to see if she can come and fill in. Otherwise, the whole seating plan is thrown off. And then you have to decide: "Are you going to sit this way at the table with your guest of honour here?" It's really complicated to do a seating plan. And so I had it made — a seating plan in velvet.

Another behind-the-scenes job officers' wives do is devise a system that will help them to entertain on a large scale with the least possible work. For one former senior army officer's wife, the key to successful unit parties was starting her preparation far enough in advance and then spacing her tasks out over the time:

> I started preparing for these 35 people two weeks before the event. I borrowed card tables from all my friends. Then I prepared the menu. I had a menu that was easy to serve, and I made it early. Like we started with quiche, an entree of quiche. So I made about six or seven quiches and froze them. And then I made sweet and sour pork. And tons of rice. And a huge salad. And then for desserts, I made banana bread, fruit cake, and all the other things that are easy that I could freeze ahead of time. So every night I would do something, weeks ahead of time, until it was all done. And then I would set up all the card tables, I remember, on the Thursday, and the candles and the flowers. And got all the chairs from friends and arranged it. Arranged it all beautifully. And then when it was the day of the dinner, it was just a matter of thawing everything and heating it up.

All military wives' work is invisible from the standpoint of the economy, and officers' wives' entertaining is no exception. This fact becomes especially apparent when wives' contributions are assessed by divorce judges. The preparation that officers' wives do behind the scenes is merely an extreme instance.

Although entertaining is very demanding, officers' wives are expected to reap their rewards when their husbands get promoted. Each promotion proves anew that the couple has been an effective team, and wives are expected to feel gratified. They are also meant to derive pleasure from the growing respect that is shown them by more junior wives. An army officer's wife says:

It isn't easy, but also it can be very enjoyable and very rewarding, especially when you see your husband getting promoted and, you know, getting up there. And, you know, it's nice to see him get up there, because also you are part of it. I mean, if he gets promoted, I feel, without me wearing his rank or anything, [that] I have been promoted too. And I am rewarded by his promotion. It's hard to explain. Being a senior officer's wife is nice because you are looked up to by the lower ranks, and that's really quite nice without being snobby. And you get respect from the younger ranks — the NCO ranks and also the other ranks too — you are respected.

Promotions are also associated with visible privileges that wives enjoy, such as higher salaries and more opulent PMQ accommodations.

But, apart from all the work it involves, military socializing costs wives dearly. Wives who lack a natural talent for cocktail party life suffer when they are forced into it, and the stress sometimes makes them ill. An officer's wife attributes her alcohol abuse phase partly to her dread of these parties:

When we went to Europe the second time, he was an officer. So we had to have all kinds of parties and we had to go to all kinds of parties. And I really hated some of them, because I am very shy and have no confidence. And I had to have about three drinks before I could go to one of these things. It was a big strain, and drinking became a big problem.

The hectic pace of military socializing can also wreak havoc upon the other important parts of one's life. An army officer's wife reports that the combination of socializing and paid work during her first marriage meant that she neglected her children:

Sometimes I used to feel like you spent your whole week coming home to get ready for a dinner party on Saturday night. Cleaning the house all day Saturday, and then on Sunday you had to clean it all over again because you had made a mess from having a dinner party. And there was never any time for the kids.

Most obviously, the time wives put into socializing costs them many opportunities that they might otherwise have had to develop their own careers.

Officers' wives' participation in the military social life provides the military with — among other things — an expressive backdrop to its instrumental functions, a conduit for essential intelligence, and heightened social control. What socializing provides for the wives themselves is far less evident.

Social Life and the Rank Structure

Military social life is one means of selecting officers for higher ranks. It is also a theatre in which the formal protocols of rank are acted out (amongst wives as much as amongst members), rank distinctions are rigidly reinforced, and the negative consequences of rank are endured.

Military wives are often reputed to "wear their husbands' ranks," in a manner that can be savage. The stake that these wives have in their husbands' careers is a poignant manifestation of the fact that they have been cut off by moves from the relationships and jobs that might have supplied them with their own sources of self-esteem. But it is a stake that the military intends. A non-commissioned army member's wife describes her first (rather traumatic) introduction to a mixed ranks' wives' club:

They had a wives' club for the members of the service battalion. And I'll never forget. I went to their first meeting. And I walked up and said, "Hi, how are you?" and "Where did you come from?" That type of thing. I walked up and I talked to about six different people. Maybe I picked the wrong people, but every one of them within three questions asked me my husband's rank. Within three. One lady, it was the first question out of her mouth. Not even, "Hi — where are you coming from?" or "How do you like it here?" It was, "What rank is your husband?" And I thought, "This is a wives' club meeting.

Like what does that have to do with anything?" And after I got to know these women, every one of them were upper ranks that asked, and most of them were officers' wives.

An air officer's wife describes her attempt to join a wives' club when she was accompanying her husband on a course:

> I was so lonely I decided, "Well, I will go to the Wives' Club." So I got him to drop me off at the Mess, and they gave me a name tag saying, "This is Captain Smith." I gave it back and phoned him and said, "Come and get me."

While wives' gatherings have the potential to be havens of support, this potential is often thwarted because the competitive nature of the rank system has turned the occasion into a minefield. Some wives fear, and have reason to fear, that what they say at wives' gatherings will be repeated elsewhere in ways that will harm their husbands' careers. The outspoken wife of a former non-commissioned air member recalls:

> If you bitched, you only bitched to those you really trusted. I never attended those stitch and bitch parties, because it was very common for people to take what you said and stab you in the back with it. And that's how they tried to propel themselves upward.

Wives who wear their husbands' ranks help to maintain rank discipline among the men.[9] Senior officers' wives also do such unpaid work for the military as schooling their junior counterparts in military etiquette and protocols. One such protocol is the expectation that officers' wives will not work seriously at developing their own careers. Another is the tradition that members and wives who attend a mixed dining-in must sit through the entire evening without getting up to go to the bathroom. The fact that it is virtually impossible for pregnant women to comply with this requirement guarantees that many wives transgress and receive harsh reprimands afterwards. A former army officer's wife recalls:

> I was pregnant with William, so it must have been '58. In '58 there was a mess dinner. And I remember the Colonel's wife calling me over to her house. She wanted to be sure that I would

be able to sit through that whole mess dinner without being excused to have to go to the bathroom. And I was so defiant. I said, "I will sit through and I will not go to the bathroom." And I had a special dress made. It was quite expensive to go to this mess dinner. And I sat through the whole dinner, big as I was. And one of the other wives, who wasn't even pregnant, had to excuse herself, and the Colonel's wife got after her for that, for [her] lack of self-control.

Senior wives also orchestrate the ostracism from the group of those wives who have, or are deemed to have, engaged in immoral behaviour. Such ostracism is meant to remind the wives who remain that the punishments for misconduct in the community are severe. An army officer's wife recalls an incident from the years that she lived in Germany:

Each month, the Major's wife of the squadron, with her officers' wives — who may have been two or three captains, two or three lieutenants — would get together and organize a dinner in one of the gasthauses [restaurants] for all the other wives of the RCD. And the Colonel's wife always came to this organizational meeting. Okay? So [when] we sat down to organize, the Colonel's wife said, "We can't invite Bridget — don't send her an invitation." Because it was suspected that maybe she was having an affair with one of the young single officers.

The spatial arrangement of military housing affords the military an additional opportunity to structure its social relations by rank. PMQ neighbourhoods normally segregate members by rank, and the quality of housing improves as the ranks get higher. Both considerations minimize the possibility that mixed-rank friendships will form. The easy comfort of officers' housing, relative to the more humble quarters of non-commissioned members, acts as a formidable barrier to social intercourse. The fact that the rank structure is thus replicated in members' non-work lives deepens its influence and enhances the military's already pervasive control. Officers who do live in mixed-rank contexts often feel compelled to counteract this situation by telling their wives "not to talk about work," presumably so that the mystique junior members attribute to their superiors will remain intact. A senior air officer recalls a conversation he had with his wife during the years he was a captain living amongst sergeants and warrant officers:

> We had a discussion about [her] not getting too closely in-
> volved with them. That, as far as I was concerned, it was all
> right for her to talk at any level, but that she should stay away
> from work-related topics. ... Now that's why we segregate
> officers and senior NCOs — to avoid that problem.

An officer's wife recalls being forbidden to allow non-commissioned parents to view the interior of her house before, after, and during the piano lessons she was giving to their children:

> I had to set it up in such a way that these people would come
> by for a specific half hour lesson, and the parents didn't wait
> in the house. Because [otherwise] I would be seen as an offi-
> cer's wife entertaining a corporal's wife, or a corporal, what-
> ever. And the corporal probably would become far too familiar
> with my home, my husband, any phone calls, any business that
> was going on. So they came to the front door, they dropped off
> their child, I taught them piano, they picked them up, I received
> a cheque once a month.

Sometimes the rank structure of military relationships spills even beyond the base into the surrounding community. A common exam-
ple is a mixed-rank grouping of wives who work for the same civilian employer and find that their workplace pecking order does not jibe with their pecking order on the base. The wife of a former non-commissioned member, who worked in a bank, recalls her unfortunate experience of supervising officers' wives:

> A lot of the wives in the bank felt that they had the ranks of
> their husbands, and they tried to actually pull rank in the bank.
> And what I really resented was I had seniority in my position,
> and I had more knowledge and experience in my position. And
> when some new person came in whose husband was an officer,
> it really annoyed me that they thought that I wasn't as good as
> they were because my husband was not an officer. ... I can
> remember very clearly a woman who had just started in the
> bank. She had not been in the banking system for over nine
> years, and was starting all over again as a teller. And she was

trained by me. [Her husband was a] major. And her behaviour and her remarks implied that I was less than she was. I don't know how to say that. She put me down.

An analogous thing happened to an army officer's wife married to a captain, who was in the process of receiving the proceeds from the settlement of her divorce from her previous husband. She planned to spend this money on a piece of real estate that she thought would make an excellent site for an innovative small business venture. However, her real estate agent, a colonel's wife, assumed that no captain's wife could possibly afford to buy such a property. She therefore did not show the property to the captain's wife, and the property sold for a reasonable price without the captain's wife having had the chance to make an offer on it.

Perhaps the most poignant impact of rank on wives' social life happens in the area of friendships. Members are instructed not to make friends outside their own ranks and pass these instructions on to their wives. A wife often loses a close friend simply because only one of their husbands gets promoted. A wife also sometimes makes a new friend, only to discover afterwards that her husband is the "wrong" rank and the friendship must end. For example, a non-commissioned navy member's wife, who was accidentally assigned to the officer section of a PMQ neighbourhood, was in the process of making friends with some of her neighbours when they discovered her husband's rank and stopped speaking to her. A non-commissioned army member's wife made friends with a major's wife when their husbands were both away, and the major's wife had no discreet way of finding out the other husband's rank. When the two husbands came back, the confusion was ended, along with the embryo relationship. The non-commissioned wife recalls bitterly:

Not only did I not see her, she didn't say hello to me when she saw me. I'd walk to church behind her on a nice winter's day, and she wouldn't acknowledge my presence.

Wives who transgress the same-rank friendship code are rapidly brought back into line, either by their husbands or by other, usually more senior, wives. A young army lieutenant's wife who became friends with a major's wife was admonished by the wife of her husband's colonel. Many years later, she recalls:

I became very friendly with a major's wife. And she was very very good to me. She had three children of her own, and here I was with Jamie — a baby. I didn't know anything. I didn't have my mother there. And she'd come over, and she'd help, and we'd talk about everything. The Colonel's wife called me in, and she said that I was becoming too friendly with a major's wife, and that was not allowed. That would not be tolerated.

After having received such a reprimand, many wives capitulate completely. Others embark upon a hypocritical project, which consists of seeing their "inappropriate" friend secretly but refraining from being seen with her in public. While this strategy is a diplomatic compromise, it is difficult to execute without causing pain and resentment. A non-commissioned wife remarks:

You know that major's wife that I chum with? When she has a function at Christmas, she can't invite us. She's told whom to invite. And the Base Commander on this base — it's his policy [that if] they have a function at the Officers' Club for the officers' wives, she cannot invite me. He will not allow me to go to a function that is for the officers' wives.

Wives' likelihood of enjoying lasting relationships, already lessened by postings, is diminished still further by the rank structure. The linking of friendships to ranks and promotions inhibits the possibility of their occurring along spontaneous and natural lines and bars wives from important opportunities for personal growth. By drawing wives into the ranked world of their husbands, the military clearly intends to provide them with a pseudo-power that will replace the real achievements their military life has deprived them of and give them a strong motivation for helping the military do its work. But women suffer, economically and personally, when they are confined to a social milieu in which the primary measure of their value is their husbands' success. A senior army officer's wife summarizes:

People are not real. They really are not real. A lot of hypocrisy, a lot of hello and knife in the back. You know, a person would be nice to a lady because her husband happened to be a colonel. And the first thing they ask you when you go to functions is What does your husband do? ... I am my husband's wife. I'm not Evelyn. And this is what frustrated me at the beginning. I saw that I was not important. That I was nothing.

From the moment the wife gives up her first job, the military begins to exploit her derivative status. The derivative nature of the wife's position increases with each move and with every promotion her husband gets. The result is that the military's control over her is strengthened, while her own political and economic autonomy erodes.

6

Cover Ups

Military culture is a breeding ground for some disturbing problems, which have especially damaging effects on wives. The problems most commonly associated with military families are alcoholism, wife battering, and the physical and sexual abuse of children.

Perhaps even more noteworthy than the fact that these problems occur is that the military handles them in a manner that makes their impacts worse. A contradiction exists between the military's stated attitude to social problems — its traditional "need to know" — and its actual way of dealing with them, which is a propensity to cover them up. At times, the military truly wants to know that one of its members is an alcoholic or a batterer. Knowledge is usually desired when one of these problems, for example, alcoholism, has impaired the member's functioning on the job. But when the member is valued by his unit, the military does not want to know how he behaves during his hours off the job and has ways of ensuring that it will never find out. This military need *not* to know stems from specific operational requirements. Its frequent result is that the wife of the alcoholic or batterer, who has already been isolated by the rank structure and postings, receives no help or support and becomes even more isolated and vulnerable.

Alcoholism

The military's alcoholism rate is high — about 50 per cent higher than the rate for civilians.[1] Military alcoholism is partly attributable to unit cohesion and to the use of drinking to reinforce combat bonds. Remembering a remote posting, a male air member says:

> We worked our asses off up there — in between being drunk. I was drunk the majority of the time, I'd say. When we weren't working, we were drunk. When it came down the hill from work, the bus stopped at the Club. They would lock the door to the Club, but they would leave a window open so that the

stoop game that was going on continuously could continue. You just came in and out through the window.

The social pressure to drink in the military is overwhelming. A young army wife notes:

> It's available, it's cheap, and it's expected. ... Drinking is part of the event, and anyone who doesn't do it is stupid. It just becomes part of the story of the event. It's expected. It's part of the lifestyle.

An important element of military pressure to drink is that career success is difficult without it. One reason is the emphasis placed on cohesion. Another is the requirement that members pass all the information they have up the hierarchy to their superiors. Getting together for drinks is one of the main ways that this is done, especially amongst members who already have drinking problems. An air officer recalls:

> The CO of my first unit was an alcoholic. And he thought nothing of staying up all night in the Mess and drinking. And he expected his officers to do that with him.

One consequence of military alcoholism for wives is that it can also reach out to entrap them. Years of attendance at mess functions can result in wives themselves developing dangerous drinking habits. An army officer's wife confesses:

> I was drinking a lot. I think as soon I knew I was going to the Mess, it was an excuse to drink. And it started to get out of hand. I do not think I was an alcoholic because, I mean, I stopped. But I think I had like a red flag saying, "Okay you can drink as much as you like — you are in the Mess." So I had a problem.

Although most wives do not become alcoholics, relatively few escape the fate of spending many evenings waiting up for their husbands without knowing the state they will be in when they arrive home. This is especially true on Friday nights, when the military's renowned TGIF celebrations occur. A former air officer's wife recalls:

He'd go out to the Mess Friday night. And, you know, they'd start conducting business at the bar at 10 o'clock in the morning, and then 5 o'clock the next morning he'd roll in. Then he'd wake up and say to me, "Where's the car?" "In the driveway." "Who drove me home?" "Well, you must have." "Oh." You know, this type of thing. And I'd wake up thinking, "He's lying in some bloody ditch in the middle of winter."

Later on in the chapter we will examine how alcoholism, like absences and postings, is a feature of military life that creates special work and difficulties for wives.

Battering

Training for violence is the cornerstone of military life. Violence is also especially revered in specific military subcultures. These are probably the major reasons that wife battering and other kinds of violence are significant military problems. In the United States, one spouse or child is reputed to die each week at the hands of a military member relative. A recent survey also indicates that one out of every three American army families has experienced domestic violence — twice the rate for comparable civilian families.[2] Army members in particular are skilled practitioners of violence, and they can usually hide whatever damage they do. A retired army officer reports:

We learn how to hurt people badly. With our hands. You know, I can hit you on the shoulder and it's going to hurt. Might not show, but it's going to hurt. And there's other things I can do with two fingers, from your shoulders up, that are going to hurt you a hell of a lot more and still won't show.

The military's objectives are mastery and control. Perhaps even more than other husbands who batter, military batterers are men whose primary orientation to intimate relationships is control. The former wife of such an air element member remembers:

[He tried to control] every aspect of my life. What I wore. He'd come shopping with me and pick out my clothes. How I wore my make-up, the clothes I wore. He used to make me pose on the bed for him, in clothes that he had bought me, and take pictures of me. ... And then he'd check me to make sure, before I went out, that I didn't have anything that might have a little stain or anything. And if it didn't come out, it wasn't anything good to wear.

The former wife of a pilot says:

My husband was the type [that] kept everything from me. I was more or less a prisoner right in the home for years. He would only tell me what he felt I should hear. And if there was something he didn't want me to hear, I wouldn't hear what was going on. I'd hear about the flying, but I really wouldn't hear very much about the other things. ... I couldn't make a really really close friend because he interfered. I mean, it was to the point where he would mail my letters. He would even get the groceries with me.

She adds:

I think it was that I started to lose weight and I wasn't pregnant any more, and I looked quite attractive. He called his men in because he was the instructor. And he said, "If anybody asks her for a dance, they have to ask me first." So therefore I became a wallflower. I couldn't understand why nobody would ask me to dance. And the fights and the battering started after every do.

We will elaborate on battering later.

Sexual Abuse

Sexual abuse of children is another problem. Like military members who batter, members who abuse their children may do so out of a need for control; they may exercise either too much or not enough control on the job. Their behaviour may also reflect the way they were treated as children.

A number of the wives we interviewed told us that their children or stepchildren had been sexually abused either by their fathers or by other military members. Some of the husbands of our interviewees had been abused themselves. One wife we interviewed believes that childhood sexual abuse is what caused her husband to join the army in the first place. She says:

I think he figured this was the only thing he could do, 'cause he wasn't that good at school. And I guess, just being so messed up, he didn't know what else to do.

An air officer's wife recalls the moment she realized that her second husband had been sexually abusing his daughter:

When he was making love to me in August, he blurted, "Come for Daddy, dear." ... Patrick and I never called each other Mommy or Daddy — always by our first names — so I thought, "Oh, Oh."

An air element wife describes how she felt after her teenage daughter revealed that she had been sexually abused by one of her father's colleagues:

I was devastated. I couldn't sleep for weeks. I can't even hardly talk about it right now without feeling bad, because I didn't protect her. I felt like I had failed her because I didn't protect her. I feel that this is my little girl, and I owe her her safety.

Sexual abuse of children is one of the most disturbing — and hard to document — aspects of military life. It is a problem that requires further study.

The Military's Need to Know

How does the military respond to these problems? Our knowledge of military imperatives would have us believe that the correct answer would be "aggressively." After all, commanding officers need to know their members intimately in order to be able to determine which of them could not perform adequately if they were sent into a dangerous situation. The military also surely recognizes that social problems weaken the family unit and jeopardize combat readiness.

When military leaders are questioned about how they respond to social problems, they indeed espouse an aggressive line. A general explains:

The reason that happens is because you don't want to deploy overseas, or on an operation, with an administrative problem behind it that you're not aware of. I mean, why should we spend $5,000 taking a person to Cyprus, to turn around because we

weren't aware of his problem? I mean, we ask a person: …
"Have you got any personal problems?" "No, sir." "Fine. Sign
here." He gets over there, and we find out that two weeks before
he said "No, sir" he punched out his wife. She's actually suing
him! So we've got to take him back out and bring somebody
else in. I mean, we haven't got time to fool around with this
garbage!

The military claims that it is not only the commander's responsibility
to know his men; it is also each man's responsibility to "come clean"
about the salient negative features of his life, especially if these
include alcoholism, abuse, or violence. The general adds that any
member who tries to hide his difficulties is jeopardizing the country's
security and should be punished:

I would send him back. And I would discipline the guy. I mean,
if you've got a problem you've got to be upfront about it. I
mean, what they're doing is they're being dishonest. Right? So,
as far as I'm concerned, you take the necessary corrective
action for the dishonest person. If he signs knowingly on a piece
of paper saying he has no personal problems, and he does, I'd
charge the son of a gun! Okay? I would! I mean, they're lying!

When the commander has determined that a particular member
has a problem, he is empowered to intervene in the member's life to
"fix" it to an extent that in the civilian world would be unthinkable.
According to the Surgeon General, the military's ability to intrude
in its members' lives is so efficient that intelligent civilian employers
envy it. He says:

We think that as a team we can resolve this. That's the model
that society is aspiring to in treating — the team approach.
We've got it. Everyone is envious of the model that we have
of providing health care in the broadest sense, because everyone
works together. We're not working for dollars or fee for service. Everything's basically transparent and free and everything
else. So the access, the whole thing, is actually, you know, quite
a positive arrangement.

The military's willingness to intrude on privacy often even extends
to spouses. For example, after a member's wife had attempted suicide

in a PMQ, the military tried to intimidate her civilian doctor into revealing the details on the grounds that the event had happened on military property. The doctor recalls:

> She was brought to the base hospital, and the military people followed the ambulance in and said, "What's going on?" And they became actually quite aggressive to the nursing staff who were there, who were saying no, they couldn't give out this information. And some of [the nurses] were asked, "Is your husband in the military?" And, in fact, they even at one point said to me, "Well, you have to drive on this base. ... If we want, we can make it miserable for you."

The doctor adds that if she had disclosed the requested information, her patient would have been entitled to sue her.

In line with its stated need to know, the military has recently proclaimed, and in some instances practised, a renewed determination to identify and treat its alcoholics. It has established regional ARC (Alcohol Rehabilitation Centre) programs, trained officers in early identification of alcohol problems, and developed a formal policy for dealing with alcohol abuse. Identified alcoholics who fail to recover are now frequently released.

The military also considers a supervisor who does nothing about a wife-battering problem in his unit to be doing a deficient job. The military's monitoring of its supervisors to this end has recently become more pronounced. The military's Chief Social Worker says:

> This whole issue of wife abuse, we are scrambling to make sure we are responsive, because we have been perceived to be, you know, very conservative on how we respond to this.

Speaking about wife battering, a non-commissioned navy officer boasts:

> If it comes to my attention, I will do something about it. Don't read into it I "have to." I will! I will expect my peers to do something about it! And if they don't do something about it, they will answer for not doing it! Failure to perform a military duty! Move to the right in threes, and we'll have your arse in the COs office! ... If he doesn't do it, doesn't report it, then I'll have him — because he's not taking care of his people!

The military's official response to its wife batterers is now moral outrage, a resolve to solve the problem, and an eagerness to see the perpetrators punished in civil courts. An army adjutant reports:

> Everybody that I'm personally involved with gets one chance, and usually it's a very small chance. The second time I will take away his rights, including moving him out of his own house. His wife and family can stay, and I'll move him out and confine him to base and put him in quarters. And at the end of the work day, he doesn't even get to breathe fresh air unless he sticks his lips out the window. 'Cause that's where I'll keep him. And I can do that for an unlimited period of time!

Members who batter their wives are sometimes punished by their peers, just as prison inmates attack child molesters. The adjutant relates how such a retaliation happened in his own unit:

> It was at the Junior Ranks Club. They knew he was being counselled for it. It was a happy hour, Friday afternoon, and he was over there having a couple of beers with the boys, and one of the guys brought it up. And he said something back to them like, "Don't worry about it, it's none of your business." And within a couple of minutes it came to blows.

But the military's official position on battering and other problems is frequently stronger in words than it is in practice.

The Military's Need Not to Know

In order to understand why this is so, we need to examine yet one more aspect of military control — an aspect that directly contradicts the military's need to know.

As we have seen, the military has certain reasons for exercising control (e.g., obedience, solidarity, commanding officers knowing their men). But the military is also interested in control *for its own sake* because control is at the heart of combat. Control is, in fact, *synonymous* with effective combat. As Mary Edwards Wertsch observes in her book, *Military Brats*:

> A good military outfit is one that is prepared to control any situation, no matter what the variables. And of course a good military outfit should look and act at all times as if it is in tune

with that mission. It's as though, in their polished appearances and rehearsed behaviour, the warriors were saying, "Observe how we control ourselves, and you'll know we can control the enemy."[3]

As Wertsch points out, military control for-its-own-sake is essentially the *appearance* of control. That is, appearances are in many ways more crucial to combat than the realities they conceal. The appearance imperative operates at every military level. The unit must appear in control to destroy the confidence of the enemy, just as the Commander must appear in control to maintain the confidence of his men, and the wife must appear to control the domestic front (i.e., espouse the self-reliance mythology) so that her husband can remain focused on his job.

The "flawless appearance" requirement of combat dictates that everything on the base follow the prescribed authoritarian plan. The Commander must be revered by everyone, commanding officers must be revered by their units, members must be revered by their families, the Commanding Officer's wife must be revered by the wives of her husband's men, and every PMQ must appear spotless. From this perspective, the major's wife who refuses to play the mother hen role threatens national security almost as much as the corporal who is insubordinate. Similarly, the fact that the Commanding Officer *appears* to have confidence is what inspires the confidence of his men, just as how formidable the fighting force *appears* to the enemy is what fundamentally wins the war. Using the example of the Oka "Operation Salon," a navy member explains how a formidable appearance is targeted at the enemy's confidence:

Oka, okay? You show up with 5,000 troops — a brigade. Okay? What are you doing? You are destroying their determination, their will to fight. ... That's what you're doing. That's sort of the reverse of self-esteem. That's what we are talking about. You show up — overwhelming force. "You haven't got a chance." You just destroy their will.

The quest to control appearances is fundamentally different from the control that is sought through knowledge. But it is no less important militarily. Indeed, it frequently seems to overshadow the military's oft-cited need to learn the truth. In other words, the requirement that members present for public scrutiny only a flawless

version of themselves and their families often supersedes the requirement that members "come clean" about their personal difficulties.

Right from the beginning of boot camp, covering up errors is
inculcated as a military norm. At boot camp, members learn to cover
for their platoon-mates' deficiencies in order to get the platoon's job
done and win the all-important awards and prizes. At boot camp and
long afterwards, covering for mates' deficiencies creates solidarity,
contributes to readiness, and promotes the kind of polished collective
exterior that is considered essential to successful wars.

Members also learn to cover for the deficiencies of their superiors,
whatever those deficiencies are. Those who fail to do so are deemed
to have compromised unit morale. For example, an air captain was
commanded to do whatever it took to get members to attend an
unpopular dance so that his colonel would not lose face for having
planned it. A navy member who received a brain injury from a
superior during a brawl was told to keep quiet about the matter or
face discharge. Another navy member suffered in silence after his
daughter had been sexually abused by a superior's son.

Members learn to apply the same cover-up principle to their family lives. Implicitly or explicitly, they are expected to keep their
family problems "under control" and to do whatever is required to
keep them segregated from their work. Members — and their wives
— therefore learn to maintain a flawless image. They learn that
military knowledge of a family problem is likely to mean career
catastrophe. They therefore become extremely reluctant to disclose
their problems. For this reason, a padre says:

> I've had people told to come and see me, and they haven't
> opened up. And I've said to them, "Why aren't you opening
> up? Are you afraid of something?" And if they're honest, the
> odd one will say, "Yes — I'm afraid that this is gonna go right
> back to my boss."

A Family Support Centre staffperson adds:

> They think it will hurt their careers. They think that if you
> should come to the FSC for counselling or financial counsel-
> ling, or anything to do with the FSC, that somehow it will get
> back into the divisional system, and they will end up going to
> the career manglers[4] in Ottawa, and it will hurt their career.

An air element wife who had marital problems at a remote posting remembers having to drive 150 miles to receive counselling so that no one on the base would find out. An army wife whose son's learning disability became apparent when the family was in Germany chose to take him quietly back to Canada rather than inform the military that the family had difficulties. Secrecy about problems also separates wives from one another and deprives wives of what might have been a crucial source of extra-familial support. A navy wife confides:

> I mean, I run into people. I see them and, "Hi, how are you? How are you doing? How are things going?" "Oh, things are fine." They stare at you like a scared ghost, and they don't want to give you too much information in case you might use it later and say something that they might — that so and so down the street is having a hard time with this, this, and this. They just don't divulge a lot of information. Because they think that the military will look down on them, or the system will look down on them. Because they have to be strong.

Fears of disclosure do not belong exclusively to members and their wives. Supervisors also tend to encourage their subordinates to cover up problems for fear that widespread knowledge of these problems would reflect badly on their units. There is thus a contradiction between supervisors' requirement to "know their men" and their inculcated obsession with keeping up appearances. Supervisors often resolve this contradiction by attributing the problems they hear about exclusively to the stupidities of wives, rationalizing that the military therefore need not think about or try to remedy them. The connections between family problems and military culture have yet to penetrate these supervisors' thinking. A former military social worker summarizes:

> The military ... are still stuck in the old conservative ideology of rugged individualism. This is your life. It's your problem, your wife, your children. You handle it. There's no recognition in the military that they have created this community, this society. That they've created the problem that this family or these people are trying to handle. There's always the thrust to internalize the problem, that the problem is an individual, per-

sonal thing. Well, this individual personal thing is being recreated by the thousands.

Hence, an air element member in a remote location received a deaf ear when he tried to discuss his marriage problems with his supervisor. He speculates:

> If I had been doing something that I couldn't perform my job, I think the guy would have really taken an interest. But as long as I could perform my job, that was it. He couldn't care less, as long as every day at 8 o'clock in the morning I was there, at 4 o'clock I came home. ... As long as I was performing for "the corporation." The hell with what else was going on!

An army wife who tried to talk to a padre about the fact that her husband had been sexually abused by his father was admonished by the padre:

> "Well, wives get like that! You're sitting at home all by yourself and things get blown out of proportion. You sit there and your mind just creates mountains out of molehills. Your husband will come home, and everything will be fine!"

Supervisors often blame problems on wives to the extent of trying to turn their own husbands against them. They also slough off military responsibility for wives' problems by ignoring the problems until they have become serious, and at that point, they banish the "difficult" wives from the community or release their husbands as "ABs" (administrative burdens). This strategy never solves the problem because its purpose is to maintain the veneer.

For example, when a navy member was thrown in military jail, his wife had a difficult time coping. When she asked the military social worker for some counselling, she was told that the social worker was too busy. At her wit's end, and having no friends or family members to talk to, the wife decided that the only way she could get attention was to call the padre and tell him that she was on the verge of harming her children. Although this strategy worked, she did not receive the help she needed. Instead, the military doctor had her confined, against her will, in a mental hospital. Similarly, after trying — to no avail — to get the military to do something about her husband's battering and murder threats, a non-commissioned member's wife feared so much for her baby son's safety that she left him at a police station with a note saying that the police should take care of him until her apartment could be searched for a gun. The military had her locked up, too.

Overseas Cover Ups

The military's "see no evil" approach to problems has especially debilitating consequences overseas. Since members (and wives) who are posted overseas are unlikely to have access to civilian resources, they must usually make do with what the base provides. Wives who are overseas are not even considered inhabitants of a province and must spend a year upon their return to Canada re-establishing residency. In the meantime, they rest in a dangerous limbo, lacking access to child welfare, family courts, safe houses, child support enforcement, foster homes, or (should they ever need it) social assistance.

Given this paucity of support mechanisms, one might expect the military to try to prevent families with problems from being posted overseas. But this does not seem to happen. Indeed, every report we have received indicates that overseas screenings are perfunctory. A military social worker says:

> Oh, yeah — the screening process. It's easy. I can do an interview to someone, he can lie to me. I mean, I don't read minds. And a lot of people, they do pass a screening and they shouldn't.

An army wife who was subjected to such a screening before being posted to Germany agrees. She recalls:

> We went on an interview to see a social worker before we were allowed to come. But they didn't really dwell on anything or delve into our past. It was just a few questions.

Failing an adequate screening mechanism, one might still expect the military to provide its own comprehensive set of services as a way of offsetting the lack of civilian resources and trying to cope with the number of problems that overseas families have. But this does not happen either. Indeed, the interventions the military applies overseas are minimal. A military social worker explains:

You don't have the facilities. You don't have a safe house. You don't have a foster home. You don't have anything for the families. You don't have a shelter for the women. I mean, there's wife beating. I know it's going on. Everybody knows it's going on. Where do they go? ... I mean, you get very frustrated. Like, I mean, how do you deal with that? How can you help the wife if the abuser is still in the house? So, I mean, to me it just seems like you are knocking your head against the wall.

A former military social worker adds:

I don't think anybody gave a damn. I don't think anybody knew I was there. That was, you know, the feeling I got over there. There was this unreal kind of a feeling. It was unreal. Like: "Geez, we're over here to party it up for a while."

At overseas bases, a contributing factor to the "unreal feeling" is the absence of community news. At the former Canadian bases in Germany, the only source of news was a paper called *Der Kanadier,* which reported sports tournaments, recreational events, visiting dignitaries, shopping and travel tips, and selected military happenings. It did not report local wife assaults, rapes, or other crimes. Nor did it provide discussion of social issues. The military radio station, similarly, combined rock music, community announcements, sports scores, and extremely brief snippets of international events.

When overseas problems finally become known, the most expedient — and frequently used — military solution is repatriation to Canada, a solution that is consistent with the military's ostrich-like tendencies. For the members affected, this solution entails career costs. For their wives and children, it means another move. It also causes irritation for personnel at the affected Canadian bases, who resent being treated like "dumping grounds." A senior army officer exclaims:

I have sent so many good soldiers to Germany, to have them come back as drunks two years later. And I'm sitting there saying, "Well, wait a minute — I sent this guy and he was the cream of the crop! What did you do to him?" And what they did to him was actually they didn't do anything to him. They didn't check up on him, they didn't do anything. They just said,

"Okay, fine." Because in Germany, you see, they can slough their bad actors back to Canada, and they can just send them back to where they came from. They say, "You sent us this guy — he's an idiot." And they don't have to deal with that. They just send him home.

Whenever possible, the wife is defined as the problem. A francophone army wife relates the story of a member who beat his wife, sexually abused his daughter, had them both sent back to Canada, and as a reward received a promotion:

> Lui, y a fait un abus sexuel sur sa fille, y battait sa femme. Y l'ont retourné. Elle avait demandé: "Moi, j'veux m'en retourner." Y sont pas occupé d'elle. Y l'ont retourné. Y'a pas eu d'suivi pour lui; y'a resté ici. Y a eu une promotion. C'est pas grave; y'a plus d'problème.[5]

But most problems do not even surface overseas where the cover up principle is adhered to with particular rigour. A civilian social worker who has done military contract work in Germany says:

> There's a tremendous pressure on younger women not to ruin a career. And that means, "Don't ask for early repat. Don't call the unit. Don't make a fuss. Don't stick out." And I think that pressure comes from the men going home and saying, "Don't do anything because you'll ruin my career."

An air element wife who has been clinically depressed overseas adds:

> You can't even ask your husband for help, because if you do he can have problems with his job. So he cannot even help you because he will have problems. So you have to fight with it alone.

Military Professionals

Overseas and elsewhere, an important aspect of the military's "see no evil" orientation is that the human service professionals who help and counsel members and their families are, themselves, usually members. This means that military people who are products of military culture help members identify and cope with the problems military culture has caused.

The military eloquently defends its longstanding stipulation that its padres, doctors, and social workers be full-fledged military members on the grounds that only those professionals who are members can understand members' problems. The military adds that only those professionals who are members can win other members' trust. A padre reports that his thirteen weeks of basic training, embarked upon after several years as a civilian minister, helped him — more than any other experience — to minister to members. He says:

> I'm not much of a pastor if a private or a corporal is describing the sense of aloneness that he or she feels when they've just been dressed down by their corporal or sergeant. ... And I think I can identify in at least a small way with someone who's at the bottom of the ladder and can only look up. An immense hierarchy of people, all of whom have authority over him, that's what the officer cadet feels. And for thirteen weeks I felt that.

One of the Chaplains-General adds that civilian ministers who work on contract for the military are insufficiently able to comprehend military life:

> Usually they're good people, you know. They do their very best. But we know through our military people, and those clergymen themselves have told us: "We don't have the full grasp of what those families — those people — are going through and living, because we're not part of their system."

Nevertheless, the military membership of human service professionals means that these professionals work for, and are loyal to, the military, and they are required to advance the military's interests rather than the interests of their clients, when the two sets of interests conflict. Hence, if it is in the military's interest to cover up the fact that military life fosters wife battering and sexual abuse, military professionals are positioned to participate in this cover up. Military culture perpetuates male bonding, the importance of "controlling one's wife," and a conservative patriarchal vision of the family. Yet the padre or social worker who is a product of this culture steps in to "help" the wife whose husband has battered her.

An army wife therefore reports that the social worker from whom she sought help during the Oka offensive could only be a military member:

> Like when he came [to our house, he said], "I can see you have
> a problem, but you have to understand he is a military [man]
> before everything. And if there is a war he has to leave."

A former military social worker admits that she spent far more time
doing policing and screening work for the military than she did
providing meaningful counselling. She says:

> I think my biggest problem with military social work is that
> you don't get to do much social work. You work for the com-
> pany store.

The flawless appearance dictum often motivates the military to
hide its social problems. Loyalty to — and dependence on — the
military provides an incentive for its human service professionals to
do the same.

Cover Ups of Alcoholism

Military members try to keep their alcoholism secret, to avoid having
to confront the consequences of disclosure. Since alcohol consumption is considered a necessary part of military culture, military supervisors who find out about it tend to turn a blind eye. The normal
military method of dealing with alcoholism is to ignore — indeed
encourage — the problem until it has become visible and embarrassing.[6] By this time, the problem has also become advanced, and it is
often too late for the member to receive effective help. A former
army officer rails against the military's hypocrisy in this regard. He
says:

> If you want to talk about alcohol abuse in the Canadian Forces
> and how it was covered up, I could go on for days. It was awful.

The most important cover up operates in the member's unit, owing
to military solidarity and the commitment the supervisor usually feels
toward his men. An army officer's wife reports:

> They will cover up, and they do a wonderful job of covering
> up. They will do the work. They will do the man's work if he
> is not performing up to par. If he makes errors, the department
> will cover the errors. ... It's this macho one for all, all for one,
> male bonding.

Wives are drawn in to this cover up (and its ensuing isolation), too. The army officer's wife continues:

> [The wives] will hide it because they don't want the other wives to know about it. And so it becomes a real conspiracy, and you get very alone in this situation. In fact, when I decided to go to Al-Anon I wouldn't go to the one on the base, because I had my own pride.

A wife who does try to inform the military of her husband's alcoholism is often not listened to until the military has acquired its own reasons for wanting to get rid of him. Only when the military loses its commitment to the member does it stop covering up his alcoholism. It is at this point that the member is discharged. A former army officer recalls:

> It was accepted until it got to the point where you couldn't function. When you couldn't function on the job. When you became dangerous or you didn't function. That would put you over the edge. If you started missing work, you started missing parades. Then you got two chances at the dry-out centre. And if you couldn't dry out and stay dried out, then you were released.

In effect, the discharged alcoholic is punished for having been an exemplary member of military culture. He and his family, all of whom have served the military, find themselves suddenly abandoned. The military's present project of downsizing may exacerbate this trend.

Cover Ups of Battering

The cover-up principle particularly applies to wife battering. The member has a lot to fear if the military discovers he is a batterer, especially now that the military has taken an interest in battering. Many wives have endured years of isolated hell as a result of battering, and some of them have lost their lives.

Fear of the consequences of disclosure motivates some military batterers to keep their families living off base, to make sure their wives will remain isolated. The former wife of an abusive navy member recalls:

We were going to go to Victoria, and he was going to send for
me as soon as he got established — me and the baby — and he
was going to have a house for us there. I said, "PMQs?" He
said, "Oh, no — I'd never put my family in the PMQs! You
don't know the kind of stuff that goes on in PMQs — they're
dreadful places!" I know now it was his way of keeping me
isolated and removed from the other military personnel.

Even before getting married, this member had instructed his wife to
keep quiet about family problems:

He said, "You realize that this is a different world you're
stepping into. You don't ask questions." And also: "If we ever
run into a problem, you cannot go to the military. You cannot
go to the CO. You cannot go to the public. To do so will mean
that not only will I be kicked out of the Forces but I'll never
be able to work again." So I was brainwashed beautifully. I
didn't dare open my mouth.

Other members intimidate their wives with threats of worse beatings.
When asked why she did not report her husband, a former navy
officer's wife says:

Because it was something that if I did, I knew that I would get
an even harder beating. ... It would [have gotten] back to
Richard somehow. In the military things always seem — especially when it comes to like abuse, drugs, alcohol — it always
gets back to the individual. ... His boss would have found out.
And Richard was very career-minded.

Still other members fabricate evidence that it is they — not their
wives — who have been assaulted. A former air officer's wife says:

I had this white night gown and I was blue from there to there
— breast and all. And I looked at him and said to him, "Sam,
look at these — these aren't right. What are we going to do
about this?" And he took his service shoe and hit himself over
the head. And I thought, "Great — he is showing remorse —
there's hope!" ... I found out through his commanding officer
two or three months later that he went to his career manager

that day, showed him the laceration on his scalp, and said that I had attacked him.

Wives often fear disclosure about battering for their own reasons. One of these reasons is shame. A former army officer's wife says:

Most of us, even in these interviews, won't tell. And it's not because we're not assertive. It's because we are assertive. We don't want to admit that somebody would dare do something like that to us.

The former wife of a non-commissioned member says:

I was embarrassed. I was afraid to get close to anyone when we moved back here to Kingston, because I didn't want anyone coming to my house. I didn't want anyone to know what was going on. ... I was just embarrassed about it. I thought it was all my fault.

A former pilot's wife says:

I didn't want too much of the story to get out. I mean, I'm part of this too. I didn't want that story to get out. And I was frightened because I was ashamed. I wanted that perfect picture of the good squadron leader and the pretty wife.

A recent American study estimated that for every military wife who reports being battered, there are at least ten others who do not.[7]

The military wife who is battered lives a secret, isolated existence, and her isolation is deepened by the discontinuity in her personal life that has been caused by postings. Her isolation also contributes to the isolation of other battered wives. The belief of each woman that she is alone is heightened by the silence of the others, and so each one's silence is reconfirmed, and the vicious cycle continues on. A former navy wife remembers:

All the people that I knew, like my girlfriends and their husbands, they seemed to be happy. There wasn't any violence and no accusations. I mean, they didn't seem to be bitter or twisted about anything. And I know I was getting that way.

Some wives who are not battered would like to help, but are restrained by the intangible "keep out" message that battered military wives transmit. The result is still more isolation for the victims. The wife of a former air element member recalls:

> There were quite a number of women that I recognized right off the bat. I came from a very very protected home life, but I slowly started to recognize abused women at these parties. But you really couldn't discuss certain things, because you would touch the wrong buttons and you would — emotions would come out and you couldn't discuss things like that because it was just. ... Well, I wouldn't do it because I wouldn't want to hurt their feelings.

Despite all that has happened to them, many battered wives remain paralyzed with fear about how disclosure might affect their husbands. They choose to endure rather than be the catalyst for the destruction of a career. They also fear being on the receiving end of the violence of a man who suddenly has nothing left to lose.

Despite the military's supposed new vigilance, machismo military culture continues to ensure that wife battering remains secret. Some members are so enmeshed in this culture that they do not consider wife battering important. In their view, every man knocks his wife around a little, and battering is a normal part of marriage. Military culture also encourages unit members to close ranks rather than believe the stories of "mere wives." Social workers and padres are themselves members of this culture. The former wife of a non-commissioned batterer was thus advised by a padre before her marriage not to worry that her fiancé had almost killed her. She recalls:

> We were at Jim's cousin's place out in Smith's Falls, and Jim strangled me and I was unconscious. We went to see Padre Allen about it, and he said it was just pre-wedding jitters. Don't worry about it — right?

Added to this is the solidarity and fraternal feeling that envelops the members of a unit. Supervisors are aware of what has been invested in the creation of a good member, and they are reluctant to pursue allegations that might destroy the member's — and the unit's — good name. They thus frequently turn a blind eye. For this reason, those few wives who are courageous enough to approach military authorities often find their efforts blocked. Even the Chief Social Worker admits to having been intimidated by supervisors. He says:

> The frustration in this for me as a social worker is that I have been in at least a half a dozen situations where in fact I have helped the woman get out of an abusive situation, get downtown to a shelter, go home, or whatever. And guess what the boss has said to me? "What the hell are you doing, social worker, breaking up my man's family? He's distraught, he's upset. You, I'm told, told his wife to leave him." Okay? I mean, ... how do you stop the violence without infringing on the man's situation?

The former battered wife of a pilot corroborates this view. She remembers:

> No matter who I talked about it to in the military, they always took his word against mine. The last beating I had, which was one of the worst, that's when I knew I had to do something. When he pulled a knife and I called my girlfriend, she came and picked me up and we went to her place. And they called in his commanding officer. John Smith took a look at me and said, "Oh my god! They have to see the bruises, otherwise they won't believe you!" He went to see Jack. I have no idea what Jack told him ... but I'll never forget what John Smith said to me when he came back to my girlfriend's house. He said, "Joyce, you should quit your job and go home and be a good wife to Jack." I was licked.

A francophone army wife adds:

> Y vont être portés à croire sur l'homme. C't'un bon soldat, c't'un bon militaire, c't'un bon travaillant. Y peut pas battre sa femme. Fait qu'y va aller voir son sergent: "D'après toi, tu penses-tu c't'un gars violent?" "Ben non, c't'un bon gars." Y vont aller faire enquête pour savoir si c'est vrai.[8]

Batterers frequently take advantage of this situation and use it to taunt their wives. A former air officer's wife recalls:

After each assault I told him, "I'm going to the doctor." And he would laugh and he would say, "Nobody will believe you — you are just a mere nurse. I'm a lieutenant colonel."

One military method of turning a blind eye to a suspected batterer is to ask the man's wife outright, in the hopes that she will be one of the majority who denies it. In this way, the supervisor avoids having to deal with the problem and at the same time appeases his conscience. A former pilot's wife recalls:

He'd swat me in the Mess. And it was starting to be observed. However, his commanding officer phoned me and said, "Patricia, is there any problem? Is there anything you want to say?" And I said, "No." Because I was terrified that he would lose his job.

To make sure that the wife provides the "correct" answer to his question, the supervisor sometimes tells her that an affirmative response would mean her husband's discharge. A former navy member's wife remembers a call she received while her husband was in military prison:

He asked me whether my husband was a good husband and father. But before he asked me that he said, "Now I have to warn you that your answers are going to depend on whether or not I recommend that your husband be dishonourably released." … So of course I said, "He's a good husband and a good father." He said, "Well, that's really all I wanted to hear, Mrs. Twaits. Your husband will be home in about a month." And it was life as usual when he came home.

Another related military strategy is to get rid of the problem by passing it to another base or otherwise claiming geographical immunity. An air officer who worked at the base in Edmonton lived (with his battered wife) in another city. His former wife has this to say about her attempt to talk to his commander:

The colonel in Edmonton said, "Well, it really never took place here in Edmonton, so it is out of my jurisdiction. Good luck to you." And I said, "In that case I won't bother you again."

The military is extremely reluctant to discipline its batterers. Yet a civilian professional who receives a wife's request for help normally refers it back to the military, thus killing the wife's one last hope. It seems that as in the case of alcoholism, the military's overriding preoccupation is the unit's image.

Sometimes the battering has gotten truly out of hand by the time the military — or anyone else — has heard about it. By this time, the wife has gone for so long without support and become so disoriented, that she has acquired many of the symptoms of post-traumatic stress syndrome. She no longer appears cool and rational enough to be a credible witness, whereas her husband, with the military behind him, appears polished. So the member's original prophesy that "No one will believe you" becomes true, and the military easily convinces itself that yet another allegation has proved false.[9] One former wife we interviewed experienced "flooding" memories of her abuse while she was being cross-examined in court and then sat and watched helplessly as the Crown dropped its charges against her husband.

As a group, military wives are enormously vulnerable to being battered and having nowhere to turn. The isolation this experience creates for them is indescribable. For even the lucky ones who eventually find their way out, the emotional pain of what happened to them always remains. A former navy member's wife says:

> I got lots of bruises. But I could live with that more so than I could live with the pain inside. 'Cause he used to make me feel sick. 'Cause I couldn't understand how if somebody loved you they could do this to you. That was more hurtful than the physical part of it. Because that heals. The inside pain doesn't heal.

In many ways combat discipline requires a "see no evil" approach to family problems until the problems have taken on unavoidable public and/or embarrassing significance. At every military level, the need for knowledge is contradicted by the need for flawless appearances. Increased official vigilance about family problems only seems to redouble the efforts made to keep them quiet. The requirement for the member to appear "squeaky clean" is mirrored by the same requirement applied to his unit, and the combination leads to mutually reinforcing fabrications.

Military culture thus creates severe social problems and despite formal policies and official claims to the contrary, organizational military mechanisms work to cover these problems up. The result is that these problems are skilfully prevented from becoming public knowledge.

7

Endings

Enduring the military lifestyle is a formidable challenge; as a result, many military marriages end. In 1979, in the United Kingdom the military had a higher divorce rate than any other occupation.[1] Although comparable statistics do not appear to be available for Canada, it is reasonable to assume that the Canadian situation is the same.

The years preceding the end of the member's career are particularly stressful. Free for the first time from child rearing, the wife gears herself up for self-development just as the member is beginning to wind down. Or she dreams of freedom, just as he struggles for that last promotion, taking for granted her continued investment in achieving the pinnacle with him. A former navy member's wife recalls:

> He was at sea. I was working at K-Mart. I had managed to work myself into advertising, which meant that it was a little more prestigious. It wasn't any more money, but I could see that I was starting to get out of the rat race, and I was starting to become, I don't know how to put it. I was feeling good about myself, and I knew that I could do better than just being a cashier, standing there punching numbers all day.

A former navy officer's wife adds:

> He started talking about some things, maybe moving to Victoria. Or: "What are we going to do next, after the French course?" And I'm thinking, "Well, we just moved into our house. I'm just getting to a point in the school where they know me and I might be able to get a full-time job. The kids are growing up. Maybe we'll have more flexibility in terms of money — we'll be able to do things together." And I got the feeling that I wasn't being heard, or he didn't want to hear anything. And when he was in St. Jacques it came that he would

be posted to Victoria as the Commandant of X-Cell. That was a really good job — a very good job — and that was the first time that I didn't want to go.

We have seen how the "see no evil" aspect of military culture often pins the blame for problems on wives. Children who fail to adjust to postings and wife battering are two such problems. Officers who are passed over for important promotions are a third. The military encourages such officers to blame their wives, especially if they are wives who have opted out of military socializing. It often happens that an officer's bitterness at being turned down for a promotion precipitates the end of his marriage. A former army officer's wife recalls:

He didn't get it [an expected promotion]. And I think that's where everything started to fall apart for him. He was away a lot, and I thought he was away in connection with his job. And it turns out that there was a lot of absenteeism on the job. And he was really in Vancouver with this woman friend of his sister's.

A former army general's wife adds:

Henry believed that he was becoming the next Chief [of Defence Staff]. Well, he didn't. And that was the beginning of the end.

Other members — especially navy members — simply drift away from their wives. The combination of military bonding and years of extended separations have taken too heavy a toll. A former navy wife explains:

The marriage couldn't come together because he was spending too much time away. There was no way we could learn to live and communicate. It was impossible. A marriage that's on rocky ground anyway needs attention. ... This was an escape for him, always going to sea. [An escape] from a marriage that wasn't a good marriage. If things weren't going well, they would send him away.

The fact that members are encouraged to socialize in their messes after work instead of going home to their families means that many of them never learn to bond with their wives. Another former navy wife speculates:

> Maybe that's the problem — that enough isn't done together with the wife and husband socially. Maybe it's too much of the husband going to the Mess with the guys, and going there after work on Friday nights, and not doing things together, that leads to all these things that happen — these marriage breakups and things.

For a number of understandable reasons, many military marriages lose the intimacy that is needed to keep a relationship strong and thriving. A former navy officer's wife confides:

> [The counsellor] said, talking about our relationship, "You don't have a relationship." He said, "You really don't have a relationship." And I started to think about it, and I thought, "Yeah — we probably don't." He said, "You really need to start all over again and get to know one another." I think that's what we really needed to do. And we didn't take the time.

Wives who have spent years enduring members' alcoholism have special reasons to consider ending their marriages, as do wives who have been battered. Some battered wives are afraid of what their husbands might do if they tried to leave. Lacking the money to leave with their children, they fear that if they left without them, they would permanently lose custody. For these reasons, at first, many stay. A former navy wife recalls:

> He said, "If you leave, you will not get your children." All he had to do in the '60s was pay a sailor a case of beer [and] he would have sworn in court that he had slept with me. Therefore I [would have been] a non-fit mother, and I would have lost my son. So every avenue that I wanted to turn to was closed. So I bided my time, because I was not going to lose my son.

A former air officer's wife did leave without her children but only to save her life:

It's really hard to tell somebody how you feel at the time, that
you have to have the courage to leave, and leave your kids
behind. For a month I'd get up every morning and cry before I
went to work. I knew I had to do it, but it is so hard to make
that move. Because you know you have to. And I knew that I
could not take them with me. There just wasn't any way he
would let me. I really think he might have killed me.

Many wives indeed leave as a result of facing the fact that their
husbands might kill them. Another former air officer's wife, who had
often tried to bring her husband's battering to the military's attention,
recalls the last weekend she spent with him:

The last beating, when he did it, I went to run out of the house.
He grabbed me by the ankles, he slid me backwards by the step,
I hit the back of the step, and all I hit was my shoulders and
my neck and my elbows here. I heard "Snap!" and I doubled
like this. He went to kick me in the kidneys, and I thought, "Get
out." I knew if I didn't get out, that was it. I don't remember
where it hurt, but I got up and I tried to get out of the house.
That's when he tore my coat, and he kept me in the house three
days, from Friday till Sunday. I was not able to even open a
window. People would come to the house, the phone would
ring, there was no way I could reach anything. After that happened I thought, "This is it, this is it, you're changing the
combination of the alarm." It was after he left, I called them
and they changed it. And I said, "From now on if you come
into this house, the alarm is going to be set off. This is a lockout.
You are physically locked out. And nobody will force me to
allow you to come back in."

A former pilot's wife found that her recovery from a nervous breakdown gave her the strength to leave:

You don't know where you're heading. You don't know what's
going to happen. And I think that the end result is a breakdown
because you can't go on any longer. ... I just sort of went
through a wall, and I came out the other side and all the pieces
started fitting. It's amazing. ... And then once I got well I
became a totally different person. I just changed. I didn't recognize at the time that when I started getting well I became this

very rebellious person who would say F-U-C-K. And I would fight back. ... Maybe that's really who I was. This person who could speak up. Who was assertive. Who really wanted all of this for herself. So I just got on with it.

Invisible Labour

Wives who leave — or are left — often realize for the first time how much the military had dominated their lives. After years of having their entire lives organized by the military, newly separated wives discover that the civilian world meanwhile left them behind. Suddenly, in their forties or fifties, they face a future with few or no marketable skills, few or no civilian friends, and often tenuous connections with their original families. They have lost many of their old military friends and learned that what they had thought was a joint existence had all along just been his life.

As we have seen, military wives' work is mostly unpaid. Although the military acknowledges its inability to function without wives' work, like other corporations and government departments it does not believe that this work should be compensated. The military's convictions are fortified by its patriarchal attitude toward marriage. In a 1992 letter to the wife of an overseas attaché, former Associate Minister of National Defence Mary Collins explained:

> Although the spouse of a Canadian Forces attaché, like the spouse of other such Canadian representatives, is expected to be part of a "team," and the contribution of that spouse is, as you have indicated, very important, the spouse is not considered a direct employee of the Crown in this capacity and cannot be paid a salary, or equivalent compensation for a civilian job left behind.[2]

On the same topic, a National Defence Headquarters general adds:

> The problem is, Canadian society isn't geared to recognize that, whether it's military or in External Affairs or anything else. I mean, they're not prepared to recognize the contribution that the second part of the family — spouse in this case, more often than not a lady — contributes to the post. ... But, I mean, you expect there to be a team there — right? Now, she doesn't get paid as part of the team, but everybody expects it!

Although a woman who is still married to a member is not remunerated, her contribution is occasionally rewarded with poems and flowery tributes. But from the moment she becomes separated, it is as if she had never worked for the military at all. The military suddenly treats the wife as if her work had merely been a personal service to some inconsequential man.

If the wife had a job on the base that was earmarked as a "dependent's job," she is abruptly fired.[3] If the couple had been living on the base, the member normally moves into barracks, and his wife — even if she has been battered — is given 30 days' notice to leave.[4] A family resource centre staffperson explains:

> I think it's negotiable, but it's pretty much sort of 30 days. A military member is not allowed to have two places. So if they're living in a PMQ and they separate, he moves into the barracks [and] she must leave the base. ... The bottom line is that PMQs are not a family's rental accommodation. They are military housing.

An air officer adds:

> As soon as he's not married any more, he has no entitlement to live in married quarters. So he has to move out somewhere. He can throw her out the door. We don't really care, okay? Beyond a humanitarian level. Officially. She's *his* wife.

According to the military's Chief Social Worker, the informal policy has recently become "considerable latitude" for individual base commanders, especially in view of the military's new sensitivity to wife battering. But every wife who faces eviction still depends on an official's largesse.

When the wife leaves the military community — probably with few friends or work skills — she pays her own (and, if applicable, her children's) passage to where she is going, as if her only usefulness had been to her husband and relocating had been her own choice. A non-commissioned navy officer admonishes the departing wife's husband:

> It's up to you to take care of your family — it's your problem. You took on the spouse, okay? You weren't issued a spouse.

You were issued a uniform, boots, hat, rifle, and everything
else. It's not our problem!

On the topic of the wife's original relocation, a base surgeon shrugs:

It's a decision she made. She could have decided, "No, I'm not
going. I'm going to stay at home at the other place and make
money."

The military does pay the travel expenses of wives whose marriages
end overseas, rationalizing that it would have paid them anyway. An
NDHQ general explains:

Normally, what we will do for overseas, we'll bring her back
to Canada. I don't know the exact details of the regulation you
can act on. But, in principle, we will bring her back, because
we would be bringing her back anyway. That would be the
rationale.

The military procedure for overseas breakups is to fly the estranged wife (and, if applicable, her children) back to an air base at
Trenton or Ottawa. If her husband has signed a leave pass for her,
the wife may additionally be allowed a flip to the base that is closest
to where she is going. But the member does not have to sign a leave
pass, which means that wives who lack independent means may
remain stranded in Trenton or Ottawa.[5] Nor does the member have
to release his wife's half of their joint household goods, which are
stored in Canada under his name. Even if the member does release
these goods, the military does not pay to have them shipped to his
wife, and she often lacks the funds to send for them. According to a
former military social worker, since the lack of a Canadian court in
the foreign country gives the member such an enormous advantage
over his wife, the military is being shockingly remiss. He comments:

The military have put these people in a place where they can't
resolve their differences any other way. There is no court over
there to help them sort this out. If there was a court and some
sort of system where this could be adjudicated, the couple could
decide to split and they could share the costs of moving the
wife, the children, whatever, back to where they really wanted
to go or where it was best for them to be. The military has put

them into a place where they can't resolve it that way. And to say, "We will only take you back to Ottawa and dump you in Ottawa," I don't think it's fulfilling [their] commitment.

When she is still overseas, the estranged wife will have great difficulty finding a lawyer. The only Canadian lawyers overseas are military members, and the wife may be told that these lawyers are off-limits for her. In some circumstances, the wife may be assigned one military lawyer, while her husband is assigned another. Since both lawyers are employed by the military, this practice contravenes the conflict of interest provisions of most law societies.

During the years she was married, the military community comprised most of the wife's world. It provided one of the few stabilities in her existence, and it benefited considerably from her unpaid work. But the social invisibility of that work now enables the military to thrust the wife aside, as if she had always just been a burden to it. A non-commissioned navy officer summarizes the military's attitude:

We will actually try — if we know. We'll bend over backwards for you — for the wife. A guy's wife comes up and she's got a problem — her husband has to go to the Middle East — okay! We'll go out and shovel her sidewalks. We'll go and do all sorts of things — at least at my base. But if she was to be divorced, or separated, or leave, then she's left the mob. She's left the family. Boom! Bingo! That's the way it works. Because we look inward. I told you, we look inward.

From her perspective, a navy officer's wife who was turned away from her base's family support centre comments:

When I went to the military, to the Family Support Centre, to ask for information about a separation agreement, they didn't want to talk to me. And this is after feeling as though you have been part of the military community for 25 years. They didn't want anything to do with me. ... This is after years and years of being told, "You are part of the military community and we look after you." And when I needed help, it wasn't there. I was totally floored — just shocked.

At the moment of her separation, a long-time army wife felt that she had suddenly lost everything:

I had no identity. I wasn't me. I was somebody's something. Mrs. Chief Warrant Officer. You know? And I didn't realize. I thought that was what I was supposed to do. I really thought that was what I was supposed to do. Then suddenly I wasn't required any more. And I was wrapped up in the newspaper and put out like fish bones.

When the military wife's marriage ends, the vulnerability of her status becomes clear. The system that once monopolized her identity has now betrayed her and shut its doors. While the military still benefits from the sacrifices she made, she alone bears all their costs.

Pensions

The toll exacted by the invisibility of the wife's work is most apparent when we look at her future income. During her marriage, she spent so much time moving and doing other work for the military that she accumulated little — or no — equity in an employment pension plan. Since most of the paid work military wives do is part-time or temporary, it is ineligible for benefits. Generalizing from her experience of working in banks, a former navy wife summarizes:

The banks started quite a few years ago not hiring you as full-time staff. Like they called you part-time at 37 1/2 hours a week. ... So as long as they could call you part-time, they didn't have to involve you in the pension or any benefits. ... I worked all my life in military banking but never a long enough period that I could call myself a full-time employee. Because I'd be posted or I'd be part-time and then if I did happen to get on full-time, the first thing you know I'd get a posting. ... So I never had the opportunity. You were really disadvantaged as a military spouse as far as building up any security or any pension plan for yourself.

Wives who *do* manage to pay into pension plans are often unable to roll their contributions over when their husbands are transferred, because there is no reciprocal agreement between provinces or because they have not been in their jobs long enough to have their contributions vested. In the face of family pressures for recreational consumer goods — extra cars, furniture, computers, VCRs, and so on — these women usually accept returns of contributions in cash. Even wives who are eligible for leaves of absence from jobs because their husbands are being transferred are often unable to afford the lump sum contributions that their employers demand up front. They consequently resign and have their accumulated contributions returned. An army wife who was in this position when her husband was posted overseas allowed him to spend the money on a computer, VCR, and videocamera — which he took with him when he deserted her shortly afterwards for someone else.

The military wife who is still married knows she is economically vulnerable and often believes that she has little room to manoeuvre in her relationship. If for no other reason, she hopes her marriage will last so that she will one day be able to collect her share of the military pension. The wife of a former army officer observes:

> The only thing they can do is tote behind the husband like the General's wife does, and make sure they follow every need. Because that's what I say about looking after your future. I don't blame them. They have learned to deal with the situation they've got. And they're not dumb. They are going to make sure they get it [the pension].

An air officer's wife adds:

> It pays to get out young — you get your pension. And I don't want him to lose it. That's the only thing I've got for my 13 years is Harry's pension. ... I feel I gave up a lot. I gave up family, friends, job, for his life, his career. And I'd like something for it. I'd like to see something come of that. That I didn't do it all for nothing.

The wife's work for the military prevents her from accumulating her own pension. But because this work is socially invisible, the military associates *its* pension exclusively with her husband rather than treating it as a deferred family wage. The survivor benefit, or the half of the member's pension that is paid to his widow, is deemed to belong to his actual (present) widow, even if she is a second wife who was not married to him during his contributing years. Rather than being viewed as compensation for both marriage partners' work, the survivor benefit is treated as the member's bequest.

Members who are still working often speak of their earnings as *theirs* and of how they generously make these earnings available to their wives. An air element member says:

What she calls my salary, I call our money — I always have. It's our money. I have never been one of these kind of guys. You look in my wallet. I've got nothing in my wallet. I ask her for money. She looks after the cash, otherwise it'd be gone. ... And the little one was always well dressed. She always had everything she ever wanted as far as the baby went. Money! If she wanted to do something, she could do it. I never said no.

Wives tend to follow the same line. A navy wife whose husband was deployed during the Gulf War speaks disparagingly about wives who wanted their husbands' extra wartime pay sent directly to them. These women were wrong, in her view, because it was their husbands' money, and, consequently, the husbands had the right to spend it on gifts. She says:

We didn't know our husbands were getting a thousand dollars extra a month. So how can you say, "I need that thousand dollars to pay my bills and stuff"? I didn't agree with a lot of the wives going on about that. When [my husband] came home, he had a lot of money saved up. And he bought me gold, he bought me necklaces, gold chains, earrings, perfume, Persian carpets.

When members' marriages end, they usually continue to regard their deferred earnings as theirs and do not believe that their former wives deserve to share them. When asked to speculate, an air element member who is still married says:

I am of only one mind — when it's done it's done. I don't like to see alimony or support payments for the woman, to be perfectly honest. ... You do the 50-50 split, and then you say sayonara. And from that point on, you are on your own. That's the way I feel about it. I always have. I honestly can't change my mind about it. I try to rationalize and say, "God, you know, some of these girls [are] left in a hell of a scenario. They were 16 when they got married. They have no trade. They have no job. They have been looking after these kids." ... There's something wrong there. [But] at that point in time, when the marriage is over, when the divorce scenario is there, the fact that she has no academic — that's not his fault.

A former air member, who is divorced, agrees:

> Like I figure I worked for the pension, and I didn't think my ex-wife should have got any of [it]. But the law says different.

The current pension situation for a separated wife is that although provincial legislation considers pensions to be assets to be valued and divided equally between the spouses, there is no method of enforcing the payment. The problem is that the pension is often the only asset and is worth so much (usually between $200,000 and $800,000 for a 20-year relationship, depending on the rank of the member) that the husband does not have the means to pay his ex-wife in a lump sum. The ex-wife must therefore wait for her share until he retires. She can do this in one of two ways.

First, as part of her separation agreement, she can receive a portion of her ex-husband's pension as a support payment and receive a monthly cheque in her name directly from the plan. However, her ex-husband can apply to a court to have the payment lowered (or terminated) if his (or her) financial circumstances change. Alternatively, she can receive a portion of her ex-husband's pension as part of her property settlement. If so, she is not subject to court action to have it varied. However, the payment cannot be diverted directly to her from the plan, and she must rely on her ex-husband's goodwill to send her monthly cheques.[6]

In either case, the former wife often loses if her ex-husband dies and the authorities must decide who deserves the survivor benefit. If the couple was merely separated, Treasury Board may award the ex-wife the survivor benefit — if she is not living common-law. But if she is now living with another man, she has disentitled herself to the survivor benefit because she has presumably found herself another benefactor. The Director of Compensations and Benefits explains how a member's first wife is deemed legally dead by Treasury Board if she has established another relationship since her separation:

> The non-member spouse is living with somebody else, has established a common-law relationship, hence has a common-law marriage, a de facto marriage. The system sort of says, "Well, if there is a common-law marriage then we have a common-law divorce, and you're no longer the wife." That, I guess, was the thinking behind it. ... If the person basically meets the test of common-law status, then the person, by Treas-

ury Board, [is] deemed, for purposes of the Act, to have died before the pensioner.

If the former wife is actually divorced when her ex-husband dies, she is completely disentitled to the survivor benefit. In fact, if her ex-husband remarried or began to live common-law before his death, the survivor benefit is awarded to his new spouse.

Since its inception in 1984, the Organization of Spouses of Military Members (OSOMM) has been lobbying to change this situation. In 1987 OSOMM established a special new chapter comprised of ex-wives who had lost, or were in danger of losing, their earned share of pension benefits. In 1985, OSOMM sued the Department of National Defence under the Charter of Rights and Freedoms regarding the freedom of association of military wives. In 1990, OSOMM and four of its members filed a second Charter of Rights and Freedoms suit against the Department of National Defence, alleging that certain provisions of the Canadian Forces pension plans discriminated against spouses on the basis of sex and marital status.

OSOMM's lobbying is largely responsible for a new initiative, the Pension Benefits Division Act (PBDA), which applies to the federal public service, the military, the RCMP, and Members of Parliament. The PBDA, which received Royal Assent in 1992, will allow the former wife to enforce her pension entitlement by having her share paid in a lump sum directly from the Plan. Her pension entitlement will therefore not be jeopardized by the member's decision to cease monthly payments and will not be terminated by his death.

Nevertheless, the PBDA will have limited retroactivity. And, unlike the federal pension law (the Pension Benefits Standards Act) that was passed in 1985, it may not permit access for ex-wives until age 55 and will not permit them to receive more than 50 per cent of what Treasury Board determines is the value of the pension from the Plan, even in cases where both spouses contract for a larger share to the ex-wife. Most important, the new Act will not apply to divorced wives who are presently receiving their pension payments as support. OSOMM's lawsuit is consequently going forward.[7]

Nor will the new law be effective in situations where the ex-wife lacks the funds to procure a good lawyer, or has been traumatized by years of battering, alcoholism, or social isolation. Many battered wives are content to escape their marriages with their lives, and are unable to contemplate litigation until it is too late. One former such wife says:

Had I not divorced Hal, I guess after his death I would have
got the pension. But I felt that by getting the divorce, there
would be more people that would know about the battering and
then he wouldn't come after me. ... I felt it was the thing I had
to do, but I have regretted it. Because of the money. Because
it's later on down the line [that] you need the money.

Battered women are also known to sign away important economic
rights, in the hopes of avoiding battles over custody.

Many former military wives now live on social assistance, while
their ex-husbands (or their current widows) live comfortably. On
account of their severely disadvantaged financial situations, an ex-
ceptional percentage of former military wives lose custody of their
children. This is unspeakably hard to bear when the children's fathers
are abusive. Unfortunately, abusive fathers' charming personalities
often sway judges, especially if the judges are former military members.[8]

While acknowledging that the government's reluctance to treat
wives' contributions as work is unfair, the military shrugs the matter
off, saying that it cannot make changes in isolation from other departments and agencies. National Defence's Assistant Deputy Minister of Personnel says:

I mean, one of the disadvantages of comparability [is] we cannot lead the fleet. Because unless it's perfectly justifiable as
being unique to us — which it isn't because the same argument
can be made for people in External Affairs — we're not allowed to do it, unless it's also done in the Public Service.

His Director of Compensations and Benefits adds:

Any change here has to be done within the context of government. And government isn't just Treasury Board's personnel
policy group — it brings in the Department of Finance. And
the first thing the Department of Finance takes a look at, as I'm
sure you appreciate, is the deficit, government expenditures,
and so on. So it's done within that whole context.

More informally, many members of the military community assert
that the estranged wife "made her own bed" by not taking advantage

of the "numerous" work and educational opportunities that supporting her husband's career afforded her. An air element member says:

> If you are staying home looking after the kids by your choice, to me there's jobs out there. If you want to go to work, you can go to work.

An officer adds:

> The service has a whole number of programs. We have people on every base who are education officers. And if a spouse is in an isolated unit and wants to know what local resources there are in the community, and she doesn't want to go downtown, the education officer can tell her what universities in the area are offering programs that she can take. There are all those things in place. But ... a lot of people don't ever upgrade themselves — whether they're in or out of the service. ... It's the *domani* thing, I guess. I'll sign up and take an improvement course tomorrow.

Former wives view their past choices differently. Many of them struggled to maintain careers in what turned out to be impossible circumstances. All of them believe they are now in difficulty precisely for doing what the military demanded of them. A former army officer's wife says:

> I feel it's really unfair. I think it's very unfair. Because I really do think that if he hadn't been in the kind of job that he was in, that I would have had a career of my own. And I would have built up all of these assets, pension things, that he got. And I feel that I really sacrificed a lot of my own personal interests to support his career. And I was happy to do it because, of course, I thought I would benefit from the results.

At an age when their former husbands are starting to take things easy, most military ex-wives are working harder than ever before, just to keep bread on the table. A former navy officer's wife who has started a small business says:

> I shouldn't be working this hard at 55. I shouldn't be working for 15 hours a day. And I kid you not, it is 10:30 every night

when I leave there, 10 after 11 bus to here, and quarter to 12 or quarter to 1, depending on whether I do books at night. And if I don't do books at night, I do them at 6 a.m. ... He sailed off into the sunset six weeks ago. He's going to live permanently on the Med on his yacht.

Because they have no pensions, most former wives anticipate their old age with dread. A former air officer's wife confides:

It's scary. Sometimes it paralyzes me. It washes over me and goes away, then it will wash over me again if I'm tired or something. I just get paralyzed inside, and I think that, as much as anything, this business is what makes me so bad at working.

When asked how he feels about the former military wife who spent all those years helping her husband build his career and is now stranded with few assets, one prominent general is not bothered. He shrugs:

That's part of the game. If you don't want to join the game, don't join the game. Those are part of the risks of the game. I mean, it's a high-risk crap game.

The adult daughter of a former air officer's wife disagrees vehemently. She summarizes:

It's like they sap you — they milk you. And I see all these retired wives of military. It's like they've used your best years. They take you, and then they just blow you away when you're forty. And they use you. And they're suckers, going along with giving up their whole lives. I resent her for that — but I admire her.

The military uses its wives indeed. Without wives, the military would be unable to accomplish its moves, deployments, childrearing, social services, social life, or some of the most important parts of its public relations with civilians. But the military treats wives as if their work were incidental, as is patently clear when their marriages end.

Certainly poverty is a fate that awaits many elderly women. In April 1988, the National Council of Welfare reported that 71.7 per cent of the elderly poor were women, and 46.1 per cent of unattached women over sixty-five were existing below the poverty line. Despite working hard all their lives, most Canadian women — not just divorced military wives — retire with pensions that are appallingly inadequate.[9]

For reasons reviewed in the Introduction, most "women's work" is socially invisible.[10] When their marriages break up, women who have supported their husbands' careers have only very recently begun to be compensated for foregone earnings. Even now, few such women are compensated fairly.[11] What is special about the military wife's situation is the immensity of the military's control over her life. Military life makes it especially difficult for wives to do anything over and above raising children and supporting their husbands' careers. Divorced military wives thus especially deserve to be compensated for what they contributed.

Apart from the hardships of her lifestyle, the wife is positioned within certain military ideologies whose net effect is to trivialize the value of her work and to make her less assertive than she could be when she is trying to obtain a fair divorce settlement.

First, the ideology of combat readiness celebrates the principle of "national security" and its subsidiary imperatives of unit bonding, submission to military discipline, and suspension of civilian ties. These imperatives are facilitated by geographical mobility, away-from-home taskings, and member-only social events on the base. They are supported by an elaborate backdrop of uniforms, ceremonies, and parades. In this self-aggrandizing context, the military mission is all-important, and no price paid for it too high. The military wife's supportive role, in comparison, is regarded as menial.

Second, readiness imperatives are enacted within a culture of idealized male bonding in which any man who would rather be with his wife is a "wimp." This culture promotes the so-called "healthy" male aversion to marriage and the correctness of the traditional patriarchal family in which the head of the household asserts his "command." It legitimates depersonalizing wives, referring to them as "dependents," subjecting them to violence, and devaluing their work.

Third, the self-reliance mythology proclaims that military wives are especially stoic, more able than most women to cope solo while their husbands are preoccupied by readiness. While the member is keeping the world safe for democracy, his wife, by herself, is raising the children, organizing moves, managing stress, and breathing new life into an absentee marriage. Through its blatant flattery, this mythology keeps wives toeing the line. During special crises like the Gulf War, it is reinforced by the civilian press.

At first glance, the self-reliance mythology would seem to draw beneficial attention to wives. But, in practice, it accomplishes the opposite. Its universality, its prescriptive application to all wives, works to demean each individual wife. Elevating wives' work to the status of myth transforms it into wives' common currency. Instead of being an activity for which the wife should be compensated, her work becomes merely a personal attribute that she ought to have. The fact that all military wives are idealized as self-reliant trivializes the meaning of self-reliance. In a culture where "everyone" is supposedly X, the effort that goes into being X is viewed as insignificant.

Fourth, the combat-related "cover-up" principle structures the unit (and member) to keep their appearances smooth and make sure that the work — and suffering — that went into creating the appearances do not show. When the officer's wife entertains, she is likewise expected to conceal her behind-the-scenes work in the hope that her meal preparation, decorating, and wardrobe accomplishments will seem to have been executed with ease. If she is battered or her husband can't control his drinking, she is supposed to hide these realities too. Competition and the rank structure discourage the kind of openness amongst wives that might, in other circumstances, crack the deception. Confirmed in her isolation, each wife tries to convince herself that, like everyone else, she can manage her life with little effort. Her husband's climb up the ladder seals her silence.

Finally, the "military as happy family" ideology makes the wife's sacrifices less onerous by seeming to repay them. While the wife is married, this ideology provides her with a mythical permanent cushion — the idea that the military "takes care of its own" and will always be there to take care of her. The wife is thereby enabled to relax and settle into the predictable comforts afforded by the military community: fellowship, housing, built-in social life, and the sharing of a common world. She reckons that the risks involved in following her husband will be minimal because at every stop the military will provide continuity, familiarity, and a pre-selected circle of new friends. She feels that she can "go with the flow" because as a result of being free to do his job, her husband will be promoted, the family will benefit, she will be regarded as a career "asset," and the military will supply the rest. She is lulled into believing that what she is doing is not work or sacrifice but merely her "bit" for a community that is also doing its bit for her.

Many women are poor in old age for one powerful reason — the patriarchal or capitalist myth that each wife's domestic work is not work at all but a personal service she performs for love in the private sphere. Divorced women who have been long-time homemakers are especially vulnerable to ending up old and poor.

Military wives risk poverty for the same reason, and for additional reasons, too. They enjoy even fewer paid work opportunities than most civilian women and find their domestic work demeaned by an extra onslaught of damaging myths. Combat readiness and military machismo trivialize domestic work directly. The self-reliance mythology cheapens its social value. The cover-up principle provides incentives for concealing it. And the "happy military family" pretends that domestic work is a personal contribution to a stable and secure community. Being a military wife is not a high-risk crap game. It is a game that has been dangerously rigged.

8

Resistance

Wives — the military hopes — will develop the same loyalty to the organization as members, despite the fact that their relationship to the military is derived. When such "soft-sell" measures as family resource centres, wives' clubs, the regimental system, and volunteer work fail to secure wives' compliance, the military's tactics become more repressive.

Military life provides wives with few benefits for themselves. It uproots them, derails them from their careers, exploits their labour, and treats them like superfluous appendages. In spite of the social isolation of the military community, the impact on husbands' careers, and the military's sophisticated methods of intimidation and control, some wives find enough courage to resist.

Individual Resistance

We heard a number of stories of wives' resistance during our interviews. For example, the first time she attended a mixed dining-in, one army officer's wife was unprepared for the after-dinner custom of sending the women out of the room to allow the men to commingle with port and cigars. She left the room, called a taxi, and never attended a mess function again. An air element wife neglected to give her husband the telephone message when he was summoned for base fire brigade duty during the couple's first New Year's Eve party: instead, she plied him with alcohol so that he would be unfit to go. An army wife who was in the advanced stages of labour sent a military doctor away after he had refused her request for a natural childbirth.

Some wives challenge postings. Other wives begin privileging their own education and job prospects, realizing that if their marriages broke up they would be unable to support themselves and their children. An air element wife says:

I knew I could not get a job and support us. I knew that if by any chance I left my husband, I could not support my children. I knew that, no matter what I did, there was no way I could make it on my own. If I ever had to leave my husband, I'd have to leave my kids behind. ... So I looked at different areas of going back to school, seeing what I wanted to do.

Another air element wife, who was attempting to complete a university degree, decided to stop being involved in wives' organizations:

Geoff wanted me to head up a wives' club. He said that I should do it, you know, 'cause he is a warrant officer and I had experience with wives and all that. And I said, "No, I am not doing it. I don't care if you want me to or not. I don't want to get involved in other peoples' problems — I have enough on my plate."

Some officers' wives tire of the artificiality of the rank structure and opt out of military socializing. For example, an army officer's wife who was living on an overseas base found too unbearable the contrast between her daytime workplace, where the wives of all ranks mingled naturally, and the contrived nature of her evening social life. She says:

I had socialized with people all day long, and I liked working because it gave you a real cross-section of people. It was more normal. So then to have to go over into that superficial sort of rank-structured hierarchy again was difficult. I saw that. And I thought, "This is not genuine, this is not real, and I can't do it."

An air officer's wife who, against her husband's strenuous objections, maintained a close friendship with a non-commissioned member's wife recalls similar feelings:

I just felt like I didn't care. That I was going to do this anyway. I realized it was wrong, but I was going to do it anyway.

Other officers' wives tire of continually having to entertain strangers. One wife has decided that she will no longer fête American military personnel who visit Canada for their annual exercise:

I was told this year that it was Bring a Yank Home to Dinner on this one Wednesday night. Bring a Yank Home to Dinner. And John was going to bring four home. But I work Wednesdays. I get home at five. And I said, "Well, that's great — who's cooking?" ... 'Cause these guys would be here at six. I don't know them. I don't care to know them. I will never see them again as long as I live."

Other wives rebel against their "non-person" status — the military's longstanding (and cherished) categorization of them as "dependents." For example, until very recently the letters D/W ("dependent wife" or, in military slang, "Dumb Women") appeared after the name of every military wife on her base ID card.[1] Still other wives protest the military's trivialization of their work. The executive director of a Family Resource Centre remembers how she felt at a Change of Command Parade when she heard the Base Commander receive credit for the Centre's success:

I sulked for two days! The General mentioned the Family Support Services twice, and the Base Commander got a commendation for all his outstanding support and the good work done here. And I am saying, "My god, I didn't get invited to the damn thing — I had to go as my husband's guest!"

On a broader scale, some wives have determinedly struggled to establish their own lines of meaningful paid work. Against incredible odds, they have obtained good jobs and persuaded their husbands to leave the military or otherwise pay the career price. Other wives have resisted by crying for help through alcoholism, attempted suicide, depression, or a nervous breakdown. Or they have left a military batterer, knowing that in doing so they could risk their lives.

At a more public level, the wives of some of the members deployed to the Persian Gulf tried to get their husbands' extra wartime pay allotted to them, to help them keep their families functioning during a period of heightened stress. Despite fierce opposition from the military, wives on family resource centre boards have attempted to appoint independent-minded women to family support program staff positions. Wives who are family support staff have tried to carry out genuine community development, autonomous from military control. Largely through OSOMM, other wives have begun to make military problems public. They have risked arrest on bases by knowingly violating the military's "political activity" rules. They have also launched pathbreaking legal actions and, with very little money, have maintained an impressive national network of information and emotional support.

Wives who have behaved in such ways have been punished. The military's way of controlling "recalcitrant" wives is to put pressure on their husbands — a strategy that usually succeeds in an organization whose members have few rights. A non-commissioned navy officer explains:

> I don't deal with the spouses, okay? I don't have the tools available to deal with the spouse, from a disciplinary point of view or a support point of view. I just don't. But with a young sailor I do, and he understands the structure. He understands. It's all in place for me to deal with it. ... I've got CFAO, QR & O, Regulations, National Defence Act — I've got all that stuff there.

Anticipating just such a rejoinder, an air element wife who complained about hazardous conditions in a base's swimming pool pretended to be an irate civilian in the hopes that her complaint would be acted on. When it became evident during her presentation that her husband was a member (i.e., someone the military could control), her hopes appeared dashed:

> I said, "I don't want his section commander to get a copy of this report. I want a copy of the report, because I'm going to take it to my lawyer." And they said, "No, you can't get a copy of the report — your husband's commander has to get the copy of the report." So all of a sudden the table had turned. No longer was I a citizen or an individual. I was the wife of somebody in the military, and everything had to go through his commanding officer.

A wife who complained about military members shooting gophers near a schoolyard was silenced similarly. She recalls:

> I phoned all the RCMP in the area, and they all said that they would not allow any kind of shooting adjacent to any kind of residential area, and they couldn't believe the Armed Forces were doing that. And I phoned this person and that person.

There was nothing that they could do, so I wrote the CO. Chuck got a letter back telling him to shut me up.

The military also silences wives' inadvertent resistances. A francophone army member's wife, who became depressed as a result of the military lifestyle, attempted suicide. Despite reassurances to the contrary, her husband was denied a promotion. She recalls:

> Mon mari est allé voir le Colonel. Puis y a demandé, "Est-ce que je pourrais avoir un posting statique pendant deux ans?" Le Colonel y a dit, "Il n'y a pas de problème, on comprend ça." On ne fera aucun papier, mais on va t'en envoyer à l'école de combat. Fait que là mon mari était tout content, et a dit, "Bon — ça m'nuira pas." Y s'en va à l'école de combat. Un an après c'était le temps des PERs; il est rentré dans le bureau du Commandant. C'était un autre commandant y a dit, "Adjudant Bissonette, avant qu'on discute promotion vous savez pourquoi vous êtes ici?" Jean-Pierre y a dit, "Oui je lisais pourquoi je suis ici." [Le Commandant] a dit, "Ne pensez pas recevoir une promotion d'ici deux ans." Fait qu'c'est carrément c'qui est arrivé. Ses PERs ont été très bas pendant deux ans. Même y a jamais rien qui a paru nulle part. Ça était fait entre commandants.[2]

Punishing the member drives a wedge between the two marriage partners and serves as a warning to other wives. The threat of such punishment consequently intimidates most wives into self-censorship. An air element wife summarizes:

> When you marry a serviceman, you marry the military. You don't marry the guy. That comes after, because you have to follow the rules. You are his dependent. Everything you do goes on his record. If you are a medical problem, it's on his record. If you are a financial problem, it's on his record. You don't have anything that's yours — it's all him. So if you are not pleasant and nice and follow the golden rule, bang! It reflects back to him. The same with your children.

Organized Resistance

Organized resistance amongst military wives is rare. Wives are moved so often that strategic affiliations amongst them have little time to develop. The competitive structures of rank also incorporate wives and inhibit their potential alliances. Finally, most wives are so exhausted from the work of coping with the military lifestyle that they lack the energy that is required to become activists.

Despite these obstacles, two recent rebellions of Canadian wives can be considered social movements, in the sense that they were collective, organized, public, and sophisticated in their use of communications media.

The first such movement, at CFB Calgary in 1979, was prompted by the military's decision to stop charging members a flat rate for PMQ occupancy and tie PMQ rents to local economies. PMQ occupants in Calgary were hit especially hard because the city's oil boom was producing inflated prices. Wages did not keep up with the rent hikes. A number of Calgary military members were pushed below the poverty line, which was defined as needing to spend more than 61 per cent of one's income on basic necessities.[3] Some members became eligible for welfare.

Despite fear of reprisals from the military, many wives mustered enough courage to complain to the media, and over 95 per cent of the wives living in PMQs signed a petition that was sent to the Minister of National Defence. An army wife remembers her initial misgivings:

> I gave an interview. [The reporter] asked me to give one. I was a little leery at first, because I had heard all these stories: "If you talk to anybody watch what you say, because if it gets back through the military they get to the guys."

Wives who gave interviews to the media were expected to do so under military censorship. That is, they were expected not to say anything "political" against the Department of National Defence or the Clark Conservative government. The same wife remembers the conditions under which she was allowed to make a statement. She also remembers feeling grateful that she was permitted to do so without (she thought) her husband suffering repercussions:

> When the [Base Commander] called me, he told me that I could give any interview I wanted as long as everything I said was factual and that I didn't go saying the army's to blame for all my problems. Like he said, "If you've got facts, then fine — no problem." ... And it was written up in Standing Orders.

There was a list of names, and it said these people's wives are about to give interviews to various newspapers across the nation and that any one doing something ... I don't know how he worded it but, in other words, if he gets in any trouble for it, you know, "answer to me." And I thought that was really quite something. I mean, to me, I was really quite impressed with this man. That he would go to that length to allow it, because from all I'd been told the military wanted to squish everything.

As a result of the well-publicized protests against the Calgary rents, the military instituted an Accommodation Assistance Allowance in areas that had a high cost of living. But the military took care to post the wives who had spoken out (and their husbands) away from Calgary almost immediately and did not send any two of them to the same place. The military also took full credit for the Accommodation Assistance Allowance. It is rumoured that the Calgary Base Commander's career was derailed.

The national wives' social movement, the Organization of Spouses of Military Members (OSOMM), has existed for a decade. OSOMM originated in 1984 at CFB Penhold, where a group of wives began meeting informally to discuss how they might lobby for a family dental plan (until then, only members were covered), day care, pensions, and a safer traffic intersection. The women believed that these improvements would help every family on the base, and they assumed that the military would agree.

The Penhold wives were also motivated by a more general anger about the way the military had trivialized their work. Buried beneath a hill at CFB Penhold is the bunker where the western provincial premiers and senior cabinet ministers would be sheltered in the event of a war on Canadian territory. Many members stationed at Penhold would also be offered refuge in the bunker. Despite the fact that CFB Penhold is an obvious military target, the wives discovered that members' spouses and children would be left out in the cold. Additionally, despite wives' many contributions to the base community, the Penhold administration would not permit them to occupy leadership positions on its community council.

After the wives had distributed a newsletter to the community about dental care, traffic intersections, and school lunchrooms, the Base Commander invoked the "political activity" regulation and prohibited them from meeting on the base. His action was corroborated by a letter from the Minister of National Defence. The wives were amazed, especially when they realized that base facilities were being used for a retired members group lobbying for Ronald Reagan's Star Wars. These wives, who had always considered themselves part of the base "family," suddenly found themselves transformed into an "enemy." When they said they would continue distributing their newsletter without permission, military officials threatened to arrest them and evict them from their homes.

Contrary to its original intentions, the wives' group became a movement. Calling itself OSOMM, it responded to the letter from the Minister of Defence by obtaining a Secretary of State Women's Program grant to establish off-base headquarters. OSOMM subsequently mushroomed into a national organization, received considerable notoriety in Parliament and the national media, and, sponsored by LEAF (Women's Legal Education and Action Fund), sued the Department of National Defence under the Freedom of Association and Equality sections of the Charter of Rights and Freedoms. Considering the tremendous insularity of the military community, and wives' isolation from civilian feminists before that time, the Penhold wives' accomplishment was immense.

Quite accidentally, OSOMM had acquired the confrontational tactics that were to distinguish it from military wives' traditionally conciliatory ways of trying to change things. Indeed, familiarity with the military's normal repressive response to confrontation prompted many wives to refrain from joining OSOMM in the belief that its methods would never work. An army officer from another base claims:

> The women that came to join, many of them — about fifty of them — were crusaders. The other fifty were experienced people that understood the system. And the experienced people came to the conclusion that they didn't want to have anything to do with the crusaders, that they were much more capable of getting what they wanted, their mandate accomplished, by using the system, as opposed to confronting the system. And OSOMM on this base died on the vine.

A former military social worker disagrees. He believes that without the issues raised by OSOMM, the military would never have inaugurated anything like a national family support program:

Most of the changes that have come about in the last ten years with respect to issues that deal with families have come about not because the military has decided it's a priority. It's because a little bit of shit has been raised. And some heat has been put on, and some people have felt kind of embarrassed.

One of OSOMM's founders concurs. She says:

We were told that we should have gone through the system, through the proper channels. But we all know what happens when we go through the proper channels. The men get a hold of you, and you have to do as you are told. You don't end up doing what you want to do.

OSOMM's founders believe the military could have co-opted them if it had attempted to negotiate instead of moving so swiftly toward repression. As things stood, the Penhold wives felt that the only dignified option open to them — and the only way to achieve their goals — was to answer the military's challenge. One OSOMM founder observes:

It was such an insignificant thing. And had they handled us with dignity and with respect and appreciated what we were trying to do, there would have been no conflict at all. Because we were all quite amenable. We knew the rules. We wanted to go by the system. We wanted to help the girls. We were older, we'd had our children, we knew what the problems were, and we wanted to help. We were very surprised when we hit that wall, that "Sorry, you can't come in."

Another OSOMM founder adds:

It was no big deal. We didn't mean anything. We really weren't political. We were just a bunch of housewives, and actually very meek and mild for the most part. We didn't know any better. We thought, "Well, okay this would be fun to do, and let's do this. Let's see if we can get people working towards this." And we started it so innocently. It was never meant to be any big deal. We did have a lot of fun working out OSOMM, and the name and everything else. And then it just started.

The OSOMM founders' husbands and families suffered repercussions. Some OSOMM husbands were interrogated by their superiors; others were harangued by their co-workers. One of them was publicly insulted at his own retirement party. The promotion of another OSOMM husband was delayed for reasons that he accepts. Habituated to the "team" model of officer and wife, he believes that the officer responsible for delaying his promotion was right because his wife's efforts had undermined the military's effectiveness. He comments:

> He was right to do it because we're a team. And we're promoted on the basis of my performance and her performance as a subset of my performance. And so as a team we weren't ready to be promoted. ... It's important that the officers be examples of proper behaviour. And ... public expression of doubt about the military, lack of confidence in your boss or the organization, [is] not tolerated. ... It's very important that you have confidence in your superiors, because one day they may ask you to do something dangerous.

Many wives resigned from OSOMM because of pressure put on their husbands. Nevertheless, the civilian publicity OSOMM received brought results. The wives eventually obtained a dental plan for dependents, a safer traffic intersection near Penhold, and a slightly relaxed definition of political activity on bases.[4] The military also created the national Family Support Program.

This program, which was founded amidst a flurry of community development rhetoric, has itself been an occasion for wives' resistance. Built into community development philosophy are such civilian ideals as community autonomy and grassroots initiatives — which are totally at loggerheads with the military's imperative to maintain total control. Despite its stated intent to provide ownership to spouses, the MFSP set itself up in a way that was meant to retain the military's control. In other words, although it was forced to make concessions to civilianization, the military believed that it could contain the ensuing contradictions. But the wives on some bases have proved the military wrong. In their capacities as family resource centre board members and staffpersons, wives have taken the community development rhetoric seriously and tried to "run with it" toward genuine civilian control. And the military has done everything possible to undermine them.

The Future

It is important to understand why the military's response to wives' resistance is always repressive. We believe that the answer to this question is simple: The military is anxious to retain control over wives, and it is thoroughly cognizant of what might happen if it lost this control.

Enormous antagonisms exist between military imperatives and the legitimate aspirations of civilian wives and children. For example, the requirements of combat bonding catapult wives and the military into a conflict-of-interest standoff in which one side (usually the military) gains at the other's expense. Postings enhance the military and the member to the same extent that they strip the member's wife and children of friendships, schools, and jobs.

The military understands these — and other — antagonisms, and it understands how the women's movement has exacerbated them. Military family support programs in Canada and the United States have in fact been partly driven by military anxiety about the women's movement. The military may even understand how its culture creates alcoholism, battering, and sexual abuse and how military control imperatives intensify the impact of these problems on wives and children.

Much of the military's obsession with controlling wives is based on its fear of what would happen if wives faced — and acted on — the antagonisms between military culture and their own and their children's human needs. The military wishes to co-opt wives' work and loyalty partly because wives' contributions are useful and partly because controlling wives is an important way of controlling how wives view the military.

The military's ability to keep controlling wives is contrary to wives' best interests. At a gut level, wives know that bonding and postings work against them. They understand that alcoholism, battering, and sexual abuse somehow thrive in a military environment. They probably also know that until the military faces these antagonisms squarely, the research it sponsors into military families will proceed from misleading assumptions and there will be little essential change in military life. It is in wives' interests — but not the military's — for wives to begin "knowing what they know" and acting on this new basis.

For all these reasons, there is a pronounced conflict of interest between the military and wives. It follows that the best hope for change lies in the connections wives make — and the opportunities they seize — for themselves. Wives should not expect the military to take the initiative for them. From everything we have learned, it seems obvious that unless wives continue resisting and applying pressure from below, the military will make little effort to help them. And it is in the military's interest to prevent wives from helping themselves.

If we could make one three-part recommendation it would be this: the military should accept the fact that its priorities and forms of organization do significant harm to women and children, and should assume responsibility for the consequences and cost; future cost-benefit analyses of militarism should be expanded to include its social costs; and further civilian — not military — research should be done to spell these social costs out. Until we begin to assess militarism's everyday human costs, we will miss a crucial part of militarism's picture and lack a realistic basis from which to judge whether militarism's benefits exceed — or fall far short of — the enormous price taxpayers and human beings pay for them.

Although we could add to this general recommendation a number of specific recommendations for the improvement of conditions for Canada's military wives, we have decided that doing so would be presumptuous, counter to the spirit of our methodology, and counter to the generally negative tenor of our findings. Our purpose in this book was to provide an analysis that could serve as a backdrop for discussion, and we believe that this purpose has been fulfilled. We do know that a significant number of Canadian wives believe that they can no longer pursue meaningful lives on the military's traditional terms.[5] It is also our view that if lasting change is to occur, these women will have to start the process rolling themselves. As they do so, their efforts will help all military wives regain the power to direct their own lives.

Notes

Introduction

1. Minister of Finance, *Basic Facts on Federal Spending* (Ottawa: Department of Finance, 1994).
2. Howard Peter Langille, *Changing the Guard: Canada's Defence in a World in Transition* (Toronto: University of Toronto Press, 1990), pp. 152-53. Aid-to-the-civil-power operations are occasions when civilian authorities command the military to intervene in domestic crises, such as the FLQ (1970), Oka (1990), and natural disasters.
3. By such factors as fallout from nuclear testing, fallout from nuclear power plants, and occupational accidents in nuclear weapons facilities. See, for example, Rosalie Bertell, *No Immediate Danger: Prognosis for a Radioactive Earth* (Toronto: Women's Press, 1985); World Commission on Environment and Development, *Our Common Future* (Oxford: Oxford University Press, 1987); and Joni Seager, *Earth Follies: Coming to Feminist Terms with the Global Environmental Crisis* (New York: Routledge, 1993).
4. For us, "military wives" means primarily civilian women who are (or were) married to, engaged to, or living common-law with present or former military members. Although some military wives are also military members, this group of women is not our particular focus.
5. See Myna Trustram, *Women of the Regiment: Marriage and the Victorian Army* (Cambridge: Cambridge University Press, 1984), p. 10.
6. Ibid. See also Ruth Jolly, *Military Man, Family Man, Crown Property?* (London: Brassey's Defence Publishers, 1987), and Colonel Noel T. St. John Williams, *Judy O'Grady and the Colonel's Lady: The Army Wife and Camp Follower Since 1660* (London: Brassey's Defence Publishers, 1988).
7. See especially, Cynthia Enloe, *Does Khaki Become You? The Militarization of Women's Lives* (Boston: South End Press, 1983).
8. Trustram, *Women of the Regiment*, p. 30.
9. Ibid., Chapter Four.
10. Jolly, *Military Man, Family Man, Crown Property?* pp. 1-2.
11. Trustram, *Women of the Regiment*, p. 198.
12. Bonnie Domrose Stone et al., *Uncle Sam's Brides: The World of Military Wives* (New York: Walker, 1990), pp. 16-19. See also Nancy L. Goldman, "Trends in Family Patterns of U.S. Military Personnel during the 20th Century," in Nancy L. Goldman et al. (eds.), *The Social Psychology of Military Service* (Beverly Hills: Sage, 1976), pp. 119-20.
13. See Hector J. Massey (ed.), *The Canadian Military: A Profile* (Toronto: Copp Clark, 1972).
14. The Canadian military used to be made up of three separate entities — army, navy, and air force. Since unification in 1968, these entities have been combined, and each one is now known as an "element."

15. After receiving her transcript, one of our interviewees did in fact ask us not to use it.

16. See Dorothy E. Smith, *The Everyday World as Problematic: A Feminist Sociology* (Toronto: University of Toronto Press, 1987), p. 17.

17. Smith defines the "relations and apparatuses of ruling" as "that extraordinary complex of relations and organization mediated by texts that govern, manage, administer, direct, organize, regulate, and control contemporary capitalist societies." See "Feminist Reflections on Political Economy," in M. Patricia Connelly et al. (eds.), *Feminism in Action: Studies in Political Economy* (Toronto: Canadian Scholars' Press, 1992), pp. 1-21.

18. See, for example, Harold Garfinkel, *Studies in Ethnomethodology* (Englewood Cliffs, NJ: Prentice-Hall, 1967).

19. See Dorothy E. Smith, "Institutional Ethnography: A Feminist Method," *Resources for Feminist Research* 15:1 (1986): 6-13.

20. See "Biological Determinism" chapter in Pat Armstrong and Hugh Armstrong, *The Double Ghetto: Canadian Women and Their Segregated Work* (Revised Edition) (Toronto: McClelland and Stewart, 1984).

21. See Talcott Parsons and R.F. Bales, *Family Socialization and Interaction Process* (London: Routledge, 1956).

22. See especially, Margaret Benston, "The Political Economy of Women's Liberation," *Monthly Review* 21:4 (1969); Peggy Morton, "Women's Work Is Never Done," in *Women Unite* (Toronto: Canadian Women's Educational Press, 1972), pp. 46-48; Mariarosa Dalla Costa et al., *The Power of Women and the Subversion of the Community* (Bristol: Falling Wall Press, 1973); Wally Seccombe, "The Housewife and Her Labor under Capitalism," *New Left Review* 83 (January-February, 1974); Jean Gardiner, "Women's Domestic Labor," *New Left Review* 8:1 (1975); Armstrong and Armstrong, *The Double Ghetto*; Meg Luxton, *More Than a Labour of Love: Three Generations of Women's Work in the Home* (Toronto: Women's Press, 1980); and Bonnie Fox (ed.), *Hidden in the Household: Women's Domestic Labour under Capitalism* (Toronto: Women's Press, 1980).

23. See "Unpaid Housework Valued to $319-Billion, Statscan Say," *Globe and Mail,* 7 April 1994.

24. See especially, Armstrong and Armstrong, *The Double Ghetto.*

25. See Varda Burstyn, "Masculine Dominance and the State," *Socialist Register* (1983): 45-89.

26. See, for example, Zillah Eisenstein, "Developing a Theory of Capitalist Patriarchy," in Z. Eisenstein (ed.), *Capitalist Patriarchy and the Case for Socialist Feminism* (New York: Monthly Review Press, 1979), pp. 5-40; Heidi Hartmann, "The Unhappy Marriage of Marxism and Feminism: Towards a More Progressive Union," in Lydia Sargent (ed.), *Women and Revolution* (Boston: South End Press, 1981), pp. 1-41; Varda Burstyn, "Masculine Dominance and the State"; Christine Delphy, *Close to Home: A Materialist Analysis of Women's Oppression* (Amherst: University of Massachusetts Press, 1984); and Sylvia Walby, "From Public to Private Patriarchy," in *Theorizing Patriarchy* (Oxford: Basil Blackwell, 1990), pp. 173-201.

27. Walby, "From Public to Private Patriarchy," pp. 173-201.

28. See especially, Dorothy E. Smith, "Women, Class and Family," in Varda Burstyn et al., *Women, Class, Family and the State* (Toronto: Garamond, 1985), pp. 1-44.

29. See, for example, J.M. Pahl and R.E. Pahl, *Managers and Their Wives* (Harmondsworth: Penguin, 1971); Hanna Papanek, "Men, Women, and Work: Reflections on the Two-Person Career," in Joan Huber (ed.), *Changing Women in a Changing Society* (Chicago: University of Chicago Press, 1973), pp.

90-110; Rosabeth Kanter, *Men and Women of the Corporation* (New York: Basic Books, 1977); Janet Finch, *Married to the Job: Wives' Incorporation in Men's Work* (London: George Allen and Unwin, 1983); Leonard Sweet, *The Minister's Wife* (Philadelphia: Temple University Press, 1983); and Susan Riley, *Political Wives* (Toronto: Deneau and Wayne Publishers, 1987). An application of this perspective to Canadian military wives can be found in Judith MacBride-King, "Whose Job Is It Anyway? An Exploratory Study of the Relationship between the Military Organization and the Military Wife," M.A. thesis, Concordia University, 1986.

30. As of 31 December 1992; figures provided by Department of National Defence, Directorate of Recruiting and Selection.

31. See Cynthia Enloe, *The Morning After: Sexual Politics at the End of the Cold War* (Berkeley: University of California Press, 1993), p. 51.

32. See Gareth Morgan, *Images of Organization* (Newbury Park: Sage Publications, 1986), pp. 23-24.

33. See Meg Luxton, *More Than a Labour of Love*, and Dorothy E. Smith, "Women, Class and Family."

34. See especially, Walby, "From Public to Private Patriarchy."

35. Enloe, *Does Khaki Become You?* p. 13.

36. Burstyn, "Masculine Dominance and the State."

37. Enloe, *Does Khaki Become You?* pp. 12-15.

38. Enloe, *The Morning After* p. 57.

39. See especially, Enloe, *Does Khaki Become You?* and *The Morning After*.

Chapter One

1. CFB Cornwallis is scheduled to close in 1994–95. The training centre for francophone non-comissioned recruits is in St. Jean, Québec. Recruits (or existing members) achieve officer status through direct entry from university, enrolling in the Regular Officer Training Plan (ROTP) concurrently with university, receiving the ROTP by virtue of attending a university-level military college, being selected from the ranks to undergo the University Training Plan for Non-Commissioned Members (UTPNCM), or being directly commissioned from the ranks after long experience. All would-be officers must pass through a seven-week program called Basic Officer Training Course (BOTC).

2. The St. Jean training centre took in 265 new recruits, and 40 individuals bypassed basic training by virtue of having received the equivalent during Reserve service, making a grand total of 804 new non-commissioned entries to the Forces during that year.

3. Grade Ten is the minimum educational requirement for the Canadian Forces. When the demand for positions exceeds the supply, successful non-commissioned applicants usually have Grade Twelve.

4. See P.M. Hrabok, "The Pre-Adolescent in the Military Family," in *Proceedings of the Regional Social Work Conference on the Child in the Canadian Military Family* (CFB Trenton, 1978), pp. 20-31.

5. Information provided (1993) by the Department of National Defence, Directorate of Recruiting and Selection.

6. See Desmond Morton, *A Military History of Canada: From Champlain to the Gulf War* (Toronto: McClelland and Stewart, 1992).

7. Information provided (1993) by the Department of National Defence, Directorate of Recruiting and Selection. The Canadian Forces' most significant decline occurred between 1965 and 1975. See Charles A. Cotton et al., "Canada's Professional Military: The Limits of Civilianization," *Armed Forces and Society* 4:3 (May, 1978): 365-89.

8. Military documents stress this necessity continually. See especially, D.C. Loomis et al., "Taking into Account the Distinctiveness of the Military from the Mainstream of Society," *Canadian Defence Quarterly* (Autumn, 1980): 16-21.

9. See Erving Goffman, *Asylums: Essays on the Social Situation of Mental Patients and Other Inmates* (New York: Doubleday, 1961).

10. In the land and air elements, the lowest non-commissioned rank is private, which recruits may call themselves after successfully passing through basic training. The member then ascends the ranks in the following order: corporal, master corporal, sergeant, warrant officer, master warrant officer, and chief warrant officer. The last three of these are regarded as non-commissioned officer ranks. The comparable navy ranks are able seaman, leading seaman, master seaman, petty officer second class, petty officer first class, chief petty officer second class, and chief petty officer first class. The commissioned army and air officer ranks are, in ascending order, lieutenant, captain, major, lieutenant-colonel, colonel, brigadier-general, major-general, lieutenant-general, and general. In the navy, these are sub-lieutenant, lieutenant, lieutenant commander, commander, captain, commodore, rear admiral, vice admiral, and admiral.

11. Annual Personnel Evaluation Report, filled out by military supervisors.

12. See Captain Carol Barkalow, *In the Men's House: An Inside Account of Life in the Army by One of West Point's First Female Graduates* (New York: Poseidon Press, 1990), p. 52.

13. Until late 1992, admitted homosexuals were either denied career advancement or released.

14. The gas chamber drill consists of donning a gas mask quickly, entering a chamber full of tear gas, taking off the gas mask, inhaling the tear gas, putting on the mask quickly, and evacuating.

15. In the navy, the Officers' Mess is called the Wardroom.

16. Spouses are expected to attend other formal dinners at the Mess, which are usually referred to as "mixed dining-ins."

17. A flip is a military flight that is not quite full of members being flown on military business and that can therefore accommodate spouses and children. Sometimes a flip can only take civilians part-way to their destinations. On these occasions, civilians will get "bumped" in the middle of their trips, to make room for military members, and will have to wait at or near military airports, sometimes for several days, until another flip becomes available to take them the rest of the way.

18. See Franklin C. Pinch, "Military Manpower and Social Change: Assessing the Institutional Fit," *Armed Forces and Society* 8:4 (Summer, 1982): 575-600.

19. Ibid. See also John H. Faris, "The All-Volunteer Force: Recruitment from Military Families," *Armed Forces and Society* 7:4 (Summer, 1981): 545-59; and Charles A. Cotton et al., "Canada's Professional Military."

20. Queen's Regulations and Orders, Article 19:44.

21. Morris Janowitz, *The Professional Soldier: A Social and Political Portrait* (Glencoe: Free Press, 1960), p. 237.

22. Franklin D. Margiotta, "A Military Elite in Transition: Air Force Leaders in the 1980s," *Armed Forces and Society* 21:2 (February, 1976): 155-85.

23. Major J.C. Baril, "The Child in the Military Family," in *Proceedings of the Regional Social Work Conference on the Child in the Military Family*, pp. 1-7

24. *Globe and Mail*, 8, 11, 12, and 20 May 1993.

25. Canadian Forces Staff School, *Perspectives 1987* (Toronto).

26. Baril, "The Child in the Military Family."

27. Thank God It's Friday. TGIF celebrations occur at most military messes or wardrooms on Friday afternoons, sometimes lasting until Saturday mornings and until a few years ago being compulsory. In the navy, TGIFs are called "weepers."

28. See William Arkin et al., "Military Socialization and Masculinity," *Journal of Social Issues* 34:1 (1978): 151-68.

29. Barkalow, *In the Men's House.*

30. Ibid., p. 106.

31. Reported in the *Globe and Mail,* 6 May 1993.

32. See "Woman Pilot Recalls Terror of Running Naval Sex Gauntlet," *Toronto Star,* 25 June 1992.

33. See "Sex and the Military: Battling Harassment," *Globe and Mail,* 7 August 1993.

34. See P.M. Hrabok, "The Pre-Adolescent in the Military Family," in *Proceedings of the Regional Social Work Conference on the Child in the Canadian Military Family,* pp. 20-31.

35. See especially, D. Cahan and I.H. Cisin, "Navy Surveys Personnel Attitudes and Behavior Concerning Alcohol and Problem Drinking," *Journal of Alcohol and Drug Education* 22:1 (1976): 25-28; James Morrison, "Rethinking the Military Family Syndrome," *American Journal of Psychiatry* 138:3 (March, 1981): 354-57; Ronald Cosper and Florence Hughes, "So-Called Heavy Drinking Occupations: Two Empirical Tests," *Journal of Studies on Alcohol* 43:1 (1982): 110-18; Theodore G. Williams, "Substance Misuse and Alcoholism in the Military Family," in Florence Kaslow and Richard I. Ridenour (eds.), *The Military Family: Dynamics and Treatment* (New York: Guilford Press, 1984), pp. 73-97; and William A. Griffin and Allison R. Morgan, "Conflict in Maritally Distressed Military Couples," *American Journal of Family Therapy* 16:1 (1988): 14-22.

36. Hrabok, "The Pre-Adolescent."

37. Cahan and Cisin, "Navy Surveys."

38. Ibid.

39. Ibid.

40. Griffin and Morgan, "Conflict in Maritally Distressed Military Couples."

41. An officer who is an assistant to a commanding officer.

42. Canadian Panel on Violence against Women, *Changing the Landscape: Ending Violence Achieving Equality* (Ottawa: Supply and Services Canada, 1993).

43. See Larry Baron and Murray A. Straus, "Four Theories of Rape: A Macrosociological Analysis," *Social Problems* 34 (1987): 467-89; also Kimberly J. Cook, "Cultural Spillover Theory and Violence in the Family: The Case of the Military," paper presented at the American Society of Criminology meetings, 1990.

44. Paul D. Starr, "Military Socialization in the University: The Role of Subcultures in Navy-Marine ROTC," *Human Organization* 41:1 (Spring 1982): 64-69. See also Peter H. Neidig, "Domestic Violence in the Military Part II: The Impact of High Levels of Work-Related Stress on Family Functioning," *Military Family* (July-August, 1985): 3-5.

45. See Zahava Solomon, "The Effect of Combat-Related Posttraumatic Stress Disorder on the Family," *Psychiatry* 51 (August, 1988): 323-29; Linda Jean Maloney, "Post Traumatic Stresses on Women Partners of Vietnam Veterans," *Smith College Studies in Social Work* 58:2 (March, 1988): 122-43; and Edward W. Gondolf et al., "Wife Assault among VA Alcohol Rehabilitation Patients," *Hospital and Community Psychiatry* 42:1 (January, 1991): 74-79.

46. See especially, "Is Commando Unit Rotten to the Core?" *Globe and Mail,* 15 March 1994.

47. See Anson Shupe et al., *Violent Men, Violent Couples: The Dynamics of Domestic Violence* (Lexington, MA: Lexington Books, 1987). See also M.M. Brown et al., "Abusers of Clients of Women's Shelter: Their Socialization and Resources," *Journal of Sociology and Social Welfare* 8:3 (September, 1981): 462-70.

48. Gary Lee Bowen, "Spouse Abuse: Incidence and Dynamics," *Military Family* 3 (Nov-Dec, 1983): 4-6; Mario R. Schwabe et al., "Violence in the Military Family," in Florence W. Kaslow et al. (eds.), *The Military Family: Dynamics and Treatment,* pp. 125-46.

49. See S. Ward, "Suffer the Little Children and Their Family," *Medical Service Digest* (July, 1975): 4-20.

50. See Richard A. Dubanoski and Sally McIntosh, "Child Abuse and Neglect in Military and Civilian Families," *Child Abuse and Neglect* 8 (1984): 55-67; also John A. Shwed and Murray Straus, "The Military Environment and Child Abuse," unpublished paper, University of New Hampshire, 1979.

51. This discrepancy, of course, may partly reflect the fact that the reporting of suspected child abuse is mandatory by health professionals, whereas the reporting of suspected wife battering is not.

52. Dubanoski and McIntosh, "Child Abuse and Neglect in Military and Civilian Families"; Shwed and Straus, "The Military Environment and Child Abuse"; Francis J. Carmody et al., "Prevention of Child Abuse and Neglect in Military Families," *Children Today,* March-April, 1979; and A.N. Bennett et al., "A Study of Abused Children on the Gosport (Hampshire) Peninsula," *Journal of the Royal Society of Medicine* 72 (October, 1979): 743-47.

53. Dubanoski and McIntosh, "Child Abuse and Neglect."

54. Ibid. Also Schwabe et al., "Violence in the Military Family," and M.S. Plul, "Child Abuse and Neglect in the Military Family," in *Proceedings of the Regional Social Work Conference on the Child in the Canadian Military Family,* pp. 38-54.

55. See Women's Research Centre, *Recollecting Our Lives: Women's Experience of Childhood Sexual Abuse* (Vancouver: Press Gang, 1989).

56. Patricia W. Crigler, "Incest in the Military Family," in Kaslow et al., *The Military Family,* pp. 98-124.

57. For this insight we are indebted to Ron Ensom, Department of Psychiatry, Children's Hospital of Eastern Ontario, Ottawa.

58. Crigler, "Incest in the Military Family."

59. Conversation with Dr. David Palframan, Department of Psychiatry, Children's Hospital of Eastern Ontario, Ottawa.

Chapter Two

1. UN Transition Assistance Group.

2. Combat Engineers' Regiment.

3. See Jolly, *Military Man, Family Man, Crown Property?* Chapter Six, for a good account of how married life poses a threat to the bachelor context of military culture.

4. For salaries only. Funding for actual programs would be obtained through user fees and other community funding sources.

5. Director of Military Family Support, "The Military Family Support Program: Background, Structures, Principles, Funding," unpublished pamphlet, National Defence Headquarters, 1991.

6. Navy family resource centres are actually called family *support* centres. We have often used the two words interchangeably.

7. See, for example, Seth Spellman, "Utilization of Problem-Solving Resources Among Military Families," in H.I. McCubbin et al. (eds.), *Families in the*

Military System (Beverly Hills: Sage, 1976 [based on a 1965 doctoral dissertation], pp. 174-206; Frank Flores Montalvo, "Family Separation in the Army: A Study of the Problems Encountered and the Caretaking Resources Used by Career Army Families," in H.I. McCubbin et al. (eds.), *Families in the Military System*, pp. 147-73. [Based on a 1968 doctoral dissertation]; and Jerry L. McKain, "Alienation: A Function of Geographical Mobility among Families," in H.I. McCubbin et al. (eds.), *Families in the Military System*, pp. 69-91 [based on a 1969 doctoral dissertation].

8. See especially, Charles Moskos, "From Institution to Occupation: Trends in Military Organization," *Armed Forces and Society* 4:1 (Fall, 1977): 41-50.

9. Ruth Ann O'Keefe et al., "Military Family Service Centers," in Florence W. Kaslow et al. (eds.), *The Military Family: Dynamics and Treatment*, pp. 254-68. The American army had begun its family support efforts in 1965.

10. See "Military Family Services and Research on the Rise: Defense Department Looks for Ways to Help Its Families," *American Family* 8:3 (April, 1985): 2-7.

11. See Reuben Hill, *Families under Stress* (New York: Harper and Brothers, 1949); Reuben Hill, "Social Stresses on the Family," *Social Casework* 39 (1958): 139-50; and Frank A. Pedersen et al., "Relationships among Geographical Mobility, Parental Attitudes and Emotional Disturbances in Children," *American Journal of Orthopsychiatry* 34 (1964): 575-80.

12. For good formulations of this question, see M. Duncan Stanton, "The Military Family: Its Future in the All-Volunteer Context," in Nancy Goldman et al. (eds.), *The Social Psychology of Military Service* (Beverly Hills: Sage, 1976), pp. 135-49; H.I. McCubbin et al., "Family Policy in the Armed Forces: An Assessment," *Air University Review* 29:6 (September-October, 1978): 46-57; Janet A. Kohen, "The Military Career Is a Family Affair," *Journal of Family Issues* 5:3 (September, 1984): 401-18; and Mady Wechsler Segal, "The Military and the Family as Greedy Institutions," *Armed Forces and Society* 13:1 (Fall, 1986): 9-38.

13. See especially, Dennis K. Orthner, *Families in Blue: A Study of Married and Single Parent Families in the Air Force*, (Washington: Department of the Air Force, 1980); R. Szoc, *Family Factors Critical to Retention* (San Diego: Naval Personnel Research and Development Center, 1982); Dennis K. Orthner et al., "Family Contributions to Work Commitment," *Journal of Marriage and the Family* 48 (August, 1986): 573-81; Joe Pittman et al., "Predictors of Spousal Support for the Work Commitments of Husbands," *Journal of Marriage and the Family* 50 (May, 1988): 335-48; Gary Bowen at al., "Organizational Attitude toward Families and Satisfaction with the Military as a Way of Life: Perceptions of Civilian Spouses of U.S. Army Members," *Family Perspective* 23:1 (1989): 3-13; Dennis K. Orthner et al., *Building Strong Army Communities* (Research Note 90-110) (Alexandria, VA: United States Army Research Institute for the Behavioral and Social Sciences, 1990); and D. Bruce Bell et al., *The Army Family Research Program: Origin, Purpose and Accomplishments* (Army Project Number 2Q263731A792). (Alexandria, VA: United States Army Research Institute for the Behavioral and Social Sciences, 1991).

14. See Charlotte H. Campbell et al., *A Model of Family Factors and Individual and Unit Readiness: Literature Review* (Research Note 91-30). (Alexandria, VA: United States Army Research Institute for the Behavioral and Social Sciences, 1991).

15. Charles A. Cotton, "Institutional and Occupational Values in Canada's Army," *Armed Forces and Society* 8:1 (Fall, 1981): 99-110.

16. F.C. Pinch, "Statement on Socio-Demographic Research at CFPARU [Canadian Forces Personnel Applied Research Unit] and on Problems and Research Direction on the Military Family," in *Proceedings of the Regional Social Work*

Conference on the Canadian Military Family (CFB Trenton, 1977), pp. 58-60.

17. Ibid.

18. Pat Sullivan, "The Forces Family: A House in Disorder?" *Legion* (October, 1988): 19-21.

19. Advisory Group to the Minister of National Defence, "The Regulation of Political Activities in Canadian Forces Establishments," unpublished report, 1987.

20. Director of Military Family Support, "Family Support Services: A Statement of Organizational Philosophy, Purpose, Objective, and Goals" (Mississauga, 14 August 1987).

21. Canadian Forces, *Personnel Newsletter* 6 (1993).

22. On the importance attributed to professionalism, see Director of Military Family Support, "The Military Family Support Program: Background, Structures, Principles, Funding."

23. See, for example, Director of Military Family Support, "Investigation Report: Management Practices within the Military Family Resource Centre at 18 Wing Edmonton, Alberta," unpublished report, National Defence Headquarters, 1993.

24. A recent book whose point of view perpetuates self-reliance and other military myths is Dianne Collier's *Hurry Up and Wait: An Inside Look at Life as a Canadian Military Wife* (Carp: Creative Bound, Inc., 1994).

Chapter Three

1. The coalition members were Afghanistan, Argentina, Australia, Bahrain, Bangladesh, Belgium, Britain, Canada, Czechoslovakia, Denmark, Egypt, France, Germany, Greece, Italy, Kuwait, Morocco, the Netherlands, New Zealand, Niger, Norway, Oman, Pakistan, Poland, Qatar, Saudi Arabia, Senegal, South Korea, Spain, Syria, Turkey, United Arab Emirates, and the United States.

2. See Roger Cohen et al., *In the Eye of the Storm: The Life of General H. Norman Schwarzkopf* (New York: Farrar, Straus and Giroux, 1992), pp. 195 and 271.

3. See Michael T. Klare, "High-Death Weapons," in Mordecai Briemberg (ed.), *It Was, It Was Not: Essays and Art on the War against Iraq* (Vancouver: New Star Books, 1992), pp. 41-49.

4. See Louise Cainkar, "Desert Sin: A Post-War Journey through Iraq," in Michel Moushabeck et al. (eds.), *Beyond the Storm: A Gulf Crisis Reader* (New York: Olive Branch Press, 1991).

5. Suzanne Rose, "Ecological Implications of the War," in Mordecai Briemberg (ed.), *It Was, It Was Not*, pp. 88-105.

6. See Desmond Morton, *A Military History of Canada.*

7. A *company* is a sub-unit of a battalion.

Chapter Four

1. See Baril, "The Child in the Military Family," pp. 1-7.

2. See LCol. K.B. Jacobs, "Information on Family Services," in *Proceedings of the Regional Social Work Conference on the Canadian Military Family,* (CFB Trenton, 1977), pp. 1-8. On military social workers, Jacobs says: "Their common objective is to prevent and resolve social adjustment problems among serving members and their dependents, which could detract from the overall morale and efficiency of the Canadian Forces."

3. See Organization of Spouses of Military Members, "Brief to the Senate Finance Committee on Bill C-55, Respecting the Pension Benefits Division Act" (Ottawa: September, 1992).

4. "There are many women [posted] there from this region of Québec, and in this region one does not often have the occasion to speak English. There are many

women who arrive at that base who cannot speak English at all, and almost everyone there is English. And to work there, you must speak English. ... The people I worked with were completely English, and did not speak French at all. My work required that I speak French, but by working with them I learned English. In the beginning, I did not speak very much, but I listened all the time. And the films there, the videos, were all in English. So I rented those videos in order to learn."

5. "At Christmas time it's hard. That's why we took trips. We were in another country, and that made us less nostalgic. In Tunisia there was no snow and it didn't look like Christmas. But if you stay at home and listen to Christmas carols, you become sad."

6. "You can't talk about your problems to your family because they don't understand — they have never lived it. You talk to your sisters about it and it passes ten feet above their heads, because they always have their husbands with them, they always have someone to help them when they are in trouble. They don't understand what it is like to shoulder all the responsibilities, because they are always in a situation to share them."

7. "It's difficult. My youngest is in Grade Three. Every year he makes a friend. Every year the friend leaves, and my son starts again at zero at the beginning of the school year. I watch him go to school, and it breaks my heart. I say to myself, There he goes again starting at zero. In our neighbourhood, there are not many children his age. And, because it is a civilian area, the children are not all glued together, the way they are in the PMQs."

8. A term that used to be used to denote non-commissioned members.

Chapter Five

1. "It was practically a new life that had begun for me. When Jean-Paul started school, another horizon opened for me, something that was new and different. I realized that even I could achieve something. It slowly dawned on me that at thirty years old I was not just fit for the shelf, someone who was meant to stay at home and wait on anybody and everybody. I was still able to think, to react, and to write. I said to myself, 'My little girl, you are thirty years old. Today a new life begins for you.' My new life ended when I was 34, when we left [Canada] to come back here."

2. Information provided by Statistics Canada for the year 1991.

3. This point dovetails with what Rosabeth Moss Kanter has to say about the unpaid work of corporate wives whose husbands belong to total institutions. See her *Men and Women of the Corporation*, p. 124.

4. An elected committee of members and civilians, which oversees life in the PMQ community. The "mayor" and "vice-mayor" are appointed by the Base Commander.

5. Clella Reeves Collins, *Army Woman's Handbook* Revised Edition (New York: Whittlesey House, 1942), p. 181.

6. In their own way, appropriate to their own level, the senior non-commissioned members (warrant officers, master warrant officers, chief warrant officers) often internalize the military organization, too.

7. National Defence College is now slated to close.

8. See "No Wife No Promotion, Officer Tells Tribunal," *The Ottawa Citizen*, 9 September 1992.

9. See Cynthia Enloe, *Does Khaki Become You?* p. 49.

Chapter Six

1. See Hrabok, "The Pre-Adolescent in the Military Family," pp. 20-31.

2. See "Military Struggling to Stem an Increase in Family Violence," *New York Times*, 23 May 1994.
3. Mary Edwards Wertsch, *Military Brats: Legacies of Childhood inside the Fortress* (New York: Random House, 1991), p. 34.
4. Military slang for "career managers."
5. "He abused his daughter sexually and battered his wife. They returned her. She had said: 'I want to go back.' They didn't look after her. They returned her. It had no negative effect on him. He stayed here. He got a promotion. It was no big deal. The problem [had been] resolved."
6. A junior air officer recently alleged publicly that the former Base Commander at CFB Trenton flew a military plane a year earlier while under the influence of alcohol. See Air Command News Release, "Response to CTV Item," 30 November 1993.
7. Stone et al., *Uncle Sam's Brides*, p. 106.
8. "They have a tendency to believe the member. He's a good soldier, he's a good military man, he's a good worker. Therefore why would he beat his wife? So [the social worker] goes to see the member's sergeant: 'As you see it, do you think this is a violent guy?' 'No, he's a good guy.' And then they will do an inquiry to see whether it's true."
9. On this topic, see Laura Crites and Donna Coker, "What Therapists See That Judges May Miss: A Unique Guide to Custody Decisions When Spouse Abuse is Charged," *The Judges' Journal* 27:2 (Spring 1988), pp. 9-13, 40-43.

Chapter Seven

1. Jolly, *Military Man, Family Man, Crown Property?* p. 15.
2. Letter to wife of former attaché dated 15 December 1992, provided to the authors by Lieutenant-General Paul Addy, Assistant Deputy Minister (Personnel), Department of National Defence.
3. Earmarked "dependents' jobs" existed at the Canadian overseas bases, as a result of a military affirmative action program which was targeted at military dependents.
4. As a special privilege, she is sometimes permitted to remain until the end of the children's school year. As Myna Trustram has pointed out, military members who desert their families face considerably fewer financial obstacles than their civilian counterparts. See her *Women of the Regiment*, p. 199.
5. A well-kept secret in the military community is that a padre is also technically empowered to sign a leave pass for a departing wife.
6. Unless she can find some other way of enforcing the payment.
7. The PBDA is discussed in more detail in Organization of Spouses of Military Members, *Brief to the Senate Finance Committee on Bill C-55, Respecting the Pension Benefits Division Act* (Ottawa: September 1992).
8. See Crites and Coker, "What Therapists See That Judges May Miss."
9. See Ann Finlayson, *Whose Money Is It Anyway? The Showdown on Pensions* (Toronto: Penguin, 1988), for an excellent summary of the Canadian pension situation.
10. See, for example, Dorothy E. Smith, "Women, Class and Family," in Varda Burstyn et al., *Women, Class, Family and the State* (Toronto: Garamond, 1985), pp. 1-44. See also Mary Anne Burke and Aron Spector, "Falling through the Cracks: Women Aged 55-64 Living on Their Own," *Canadian Social Trends* 23 (Winter 1991): 14-17.
11. Homemakers' quest to be compensated for foregone earnings is proving to be an uphill struggle. The Ontario Court of Appeal recently overturned a decision by a lower court that had required a husband to pay his estranged wife a lump sum of $59,000, to compensate her for having stayed out of the labour market

to raise their two children. See "Court Rejects Motherhood Cost," *Globe and Mail,* 10 December 1993.

Chapter Eight

1. The custom was dropped only after the civilian husbands of female members began complaining.
2. "My husband went to see the Colonel and asked him, 'May I have a static posting for two years?' The Colonel told him that there was no problem, they understood these things, no paper work would be necessary, but they would send him to combat school. So my husband was very happy and said to himself, 'Good. This incident won't hurt me.' Then he went to combat school, and a year later it was time for PERs. He went back into the Commander's office. It was another commander, who said to him, 'Adjutant Bissonette, before we discuss your promotion, do you know why you are here?' Jean-Pierre told him that yes, he knew why he was there. [The Commander] told him, 'Don't even think about receiving a promotion for two years.' And that's exactly what happened. His PERs were very low for two years. Nothing was done in writing. It was a [verbal] agreement between the two commanders."
3. See "Troops on March to Welfare," *Calgary Herald,* 19 October 1979.
4. See *The Regulation of Political Activities in Canadian Forces Establishments* and "Political Curbs on Military Bases to End," *Globe and Mail,* 20 April 1988. Under the new rules, meetings that the base considers "political" may now be held inside individual PMQs, but not anywhere else on the base. The definition of "political activity" is still left to each individual base commander.
5. For example, an OSOMM presentation (authored by Leslie Taylor), "The Canadian Military Family: A Position Paper Defining Social and Family Problems in the Military Community" (May 1986), read in part: "While we understand the pivotal nature of military spouses and families in the functioning of military personnel and military communities, we take a determined stand against military patriarchy as the singular determinant of *how* we should function as the spouses of Armed Forces members in this pivotal role."

References

Advisory Group to the Minister of National Defence. *The Regulation of Political Activities in Canadian Forces Establishments. A Report by an Advisory Group to the Minister of National Defence.* Mississauga, 1987.

Air Command. "Response to CTV Item." News Release, 30 November 1993.

Arkin, William, et al. "Military Socialization and Masculinity," *Journal of Social Issues* 34:1 (1978): 151-68.

Armstrong, Pat and Hugh. *The Double Ghetto: Canadian Women and Their Segregated Work.* Toronto: McClelland and Stewart, 1984.

Baril, Major J.C. "The Child in the Military Family." *Proceedings of the Regional Social Work Conference on The Child in the Military Family.* CFB Trenton, 1978, pp. 1-7.

Barkalow, Captain Carol. *In the Men's House: An Inside Account of Life in the Army by One of West Point's First Female Graduates.* New York: Poseidon Press, 1990.

Baron, Larry, and Murray A. Straus. "Four Theories of Rape: A Macrosociological Analysis," *Social Problems* 34 (1987): 467-89.

Bell, D. Bruce, et al. *The Army Family Research Program: Origin, Purpose and Accomplishments.* Army Project Number 2Q263731A792. Alexandria, VA: United States Army Research Institute for the Behavioral and Social Sciences, 1991.

Bennett, A.N., et al. "A Study of Abused Children on the Gosport (Hampshire) Peninsula." *Journal of the Royal Society of Medicine* 72 (October, 1979): 743-47.

Benston, Margaret. "The Political Economy of Women's Liberation." *Monthly Review* 21:4 (1969).

Bertell, Rosalie. *No Immediate Danger: Prognosis for a Radioactive Earth.* Toronto: Women's Press, 1985.

Bowen, Gary Lee. "Spouse Abuse: Incidence and Dynamics." *Military Family* 3 (November-December, 1983): 4-6.

Bowen, Gary Lee. "Military Family Advocacy: A Status Report." *Armed Forces and Society* 10:4 (Summer, 1984): 583-96.

Bowen, Gary, et al. "Organizational Attitude Toward Families and Satisfaction With the Military as a Way of Life: Perceptions of Civilian Spouses of U.S. Army Members." *Family Perspective* 23:1 (1989): 3-13.

Brown, M.M., et al. "Abusers of Clients of Women's Shelter: Their Socialization and Resources." *Journal of Sociology and Social Welfare* 8:3 (September, 1981): 462-70.

Burke, Mary Anne, and Aron Spector. "Falling through The Cracks: Women Aged 55-64 Living on Their Own." *Canadian Social Trends* 23 (Winter, 1991): 14-17.

Burstyn, Varda. "Masculine Dominance and the State." *Socialist Register* (1983): 45-89.

Butler, Vorna. "The Military Family." *The Social Worker/Le Travailleur* 46:4 (Winter, 1978): 111-15.

Cahan, D., and I.H. Cisin. "Navy Surveys Personnel Attitudes and Behavior Concerning Alcohol and Problem Drinking." *Journal of Alcohol and Drug Education* 22:1 (1976): 25-8.

Cainkar, Louise. "Desert Sin: A Post-War Journey through Iraq." In Michel Moushabeck, et al. (eds.), *Beyond the Storm: A Gulf Crisis Reader*. New York: Olive Branch Press, 1991.

Calgary Herald. "Troops on March to Welfare." 19 October 1979.

Campbell, Charlotte H., et al. *A Model of Family Factors and Individual and Unit Readiness: Literature Review* (Research Note 91-30). Alexandria, VA: United States Army Research Institute for the Behavioral and Social Sciences, 1991.

Canadian Forces. *Personnel Newsletter* 6 (1993).

Canadian Forces Staff School. *Perspectives 1987*. Toronto, 1987.

Canadian Panel on Violence against Women. *Changing the Landscape: Ending Violence Achieving Equality*. Ottawa: Supply and Services Canada, 1993.

Carmody, Francis J., et al. "Prevention of Child Abuse and Neglect in Military Families." *Children Today*, March-April, 1979.

Cohen, Roger, et al. *In the Eye of the Storm: The Life of General H. Norman Schwarzkopf*. New York: Farrar, Straus and Giroux, 1992.

Collier, Dianne. *Hurry Up and Wait: An Inside Look at Life as a Canadian Military Wife*. Carp: Creative Bound Inc., 1994.

Collins, Clella Reeves. *Army Woman's Handbook* (Revised Edition). New York: Whittlesey House, 1942.

Cook, Kimberly J. "Cultural Spillover Theory and Violence in the Family: The Case of the Military." Paper presented at the American Society of Criminology meetings, 1990.

Cosper, Ronald, and Florence Hughes. "So-Called Heavy Drinking Occupations: Two Empirical Tests." *Journal of Studies on Alcohol* 43:1 (1982): 110-18.

Cotton, Charles A. "Institutional and Occupational Values in Canada's Army." *Armed Forces and Society* 8:1 (Fall, 1981): 99-110.

Cotton, Charles A., et al. "Canada's Professional Military: The Limits of Civilianization." *Armed Forces and Society* 4:3 (May, 1978): 365-89.

Crigler, Patricia W. "Incest in the Military Family." In Florence W. Kaslow, et al. (ed.), *The Military Family: Dynamics and Treatment*. New York: Guilford Press, 1984, pp. 98-124.

Crites, Laura, and Donna Coker. "What Therapists See That Judges May Miss: A Unique Guide to Custody Decisions When Spouse Abuse is Charged." *The Judges' Journal* 27:2 (Spring, 1988).

Dale, Stephen. "Guns n' Poses: The Myths of Canadian Peacekeeping." *This Magazine* 26:7 (March-April, 1993): 11-16.

Dalla Costa, Mariarosa, et al. *The Power of Women and the Subversion of the Community*. Bristol: Falling Wall Press, 1973.

Delphy, Christine. *Close to Home: A Materialist Analysis of Women's Oppression*. Amherst: University of Massachusetts Press, 1984.

Director of Military Family Support. "Family Support Services: A Statement of Organizational Philosophy, Purpose, Objective, and Goals." Unpublished pamphlet, National Defence Headquarters, 1991.

Director of Military Family Support. "The Military Family Support Program: Background, Structures, Principles, Funding." Unpublished pamphlet, National Defence Headquarters, 1991.

Director of Military Family Support. "Investigation Report: Management Practices within the Military Family Resource Centre at 18 Wing Edmonton, Alberta." Unpublished report, National Defence Headquarters, 1993.

Dubanoski, Richard A., and Sally McIntosh. "Child Abuse and Neglect in Military and Civilian Families." *Child Abuse and Neglect* 8 (1984): 55-67.

Eisenstein, Zillah. "Developing a Theory of Capitalist Patriarchy." In Z. Eisenstein (ed.), *Capitalist Patriarchy and the Case for Socialist Feminism*. New York: Monthly Review Press, 1979, pp. 5-40.

Enloe, Cynthia. *Does Khaki Become You? The Militarization of Women's Lives*. Boston: South End Press, 1983.

Enloe, Cynthia. *Bananas, Beaches, and Bases: Making Feminist Sense of International Politics*. London: Pandora, 1989.

Enloe, Cynthia. *The Morning After: Sexual Politics at the End of the Cold War*. Berkeley: University of California Press, 1993.

Faris, John H. "The All-Volunteer Force: Recruitment from Military Families." *Armed Forces and Society* 7:4 (Summer, 1981): 545-59.

Finch, Janet. *Married to the Job: Wives' Incorporation in Men's Work*. London: George Allen and Unwin, 1983.

Finlayson, Ann. *Whose Money Is It Anyway? The Showdown on Pensions*. Toronto: Penguin, 1988.

Fox, Bonnie (ed.). *Hidden in the Household: Women's Domestic Labour under Capitalism*. Toronto: Women's Press, 1980.

Friars, Gaila. *Military Wives*. Independent Inquiry Project, Carleton University Department of Social Work, 1987.

Gardiner, Jean. "Women's Domestic Labour." *New Left Review* 8:1 (1975).

Garfinkel, Harold. *Studies in Ethnomethodology*. Englewood Cliffs, NJ: Prentice-Hall, 1967.

Globe and Mail. "Political Curbs on Military Bases to End." 20 April 1988.

Globe and Mail. "Sex and the Military: Battling Harassment." 7 August 1993.

Globe and Mail. "Court Rejects Motherhood Cost." 10 December 1993.

Globe and Mail. "Is Commando Unit Rotten to the Core?" 15 March 1994.

Globe and Mail. "Unpaid Housework Valued to $319-Billion, Statscan Say." 7 April 1994.

Goffman, Erving. *Asylums: Essays on the Social Situation of Mental Patients and Other Inmates*. New York: Doubleday, 1961.

Goldman, Nancy L. "Trends in Family Patterns of U.S. Military Personnel during the 20th Century." In Nancy L. Goldman, et al. (eds.), *The Social Psychology of Military Service*. Beverly Hills: Sage, 1976, pp. 119-120.

Gondolf, Edward W., et al. "Wife Assault among VA Alcohol Rehabilitation Patients." *Hospital and Community Psychiatry* 42:1 (January, 1991): 74-79.

Griffin, William A., and Allison R. Morgan. "Conflict in Maritally Distressed Military Couples." *American Journal of Family Therapy* 16:1 (1988): 14-22.

Hartmann, Heidi. "The Unhappy Marriage of Marxism and Feminism: Towards a More Progressive Union." In Lydia Sargent (ed.), *Women and Revolution*. Boston: South End Press, 1981, pp. 1-41.

Hill, Reuben. *Families under Stress*. New York: Harper and Brothers, 1949.

Hill, Reuben. "Social Stresses on the Family." *Social Casework* 39 (1958): 139-50.

Hrabok, P.M. "The Pre-Adolescent in the Military Family." In *Proceedings of the Regional Social Work Conference on the Child in the Canadian Military Family*. CFB Trenton, 1978, pp. 20-31.

Isay, Richard A. "The Submariners' Wives Syndrome." *Psychiatric Quarterly* 42 (1968): 647-52.

Jacobs, LCol. K.B. "Information on Family Services." In *Proceedings of the Regional Social Work Conference on the Canadian Military Family*. Toronto: Canadian Forces Personnel Applied Research Unit, 1977, pp. 1-8.

Janowitz, Morris. *The Professional Soldier: A Social and Political Portrait*. Glencoe: Free Press, 1960.

Jolly, Ruth. *Military Man, Family Man, Crown Property?* London: Brassey's Defence Publishers, 1987.

Kanter, Rosabeth. *Men and Women of the Corporation*. New York: Basic Books, 1977.

Klare, Michael T. "High-Death Weapons." In Mordecai Briemberg (ed.), *It Was, It Was Not: Essays and Art on the War against Iraq*. Vancouver: New Star Books, 1992, pp. 41-49.

Kohen, Janet A. "The Military Career Is a Family Affair." *Journal of Family Issues* 5:3 (September, 1984): 401-18.

Lagrone, Don M. "The Military Family Syndrome." *American Journal of Psychiatry* 135:9 (September, 1978): 1040-43.

Langille, Howard Peter. *Changing the Guard: Canada's Defence in a World in Transition*. Toronto: University of Toronto Press, 1990.

Loomis, D.C., et al. "Taking into Account the Distinctiveness of the Military from the Mainstream of Society." *Canadian Defence Quarterly* (Autumn, 1980): 16-21.

Luxton, Meg. *More Than a Labour of Love: Three Generations of Women's Work in the Home*. Toronto: Women's Press, 1980.

MacBride-King, Judith. "Whose Job Is It Anyway? An Exploratory Study of the Relationship between the Military Organization and the Military Wife." Unpublished M.A. thesis, Concordia University, 1986.

Macintosh, Houston. "Separation Problems in Military Wives." *American Journal of Psychiatry* 125:2 (August, 1968): 156-61.

Maloney, Linda Jean. "Post Traumatic Stresses on Women Partners of Vietnam Veterans." *Smith College Studies in Social Work* 58:2 (March, 1988): 122-43.

Margiotta, Franklin D. "A Military Elite in Transition: Air Force Leaders in the 1980s." *Armed Forces and Society* 21:2 (February, 1976): 155-85.

Marshall, Katherine Tupper. *Together: Annals of an Army Wife*. New York: Tupper and Love, 1946.

Massey, Hector J. (ed.). *The Canadian Military: A Profile*. Toronto: Copp Clark, 1972.

McCubbin, H.I., et al. "Family Policy in the Armed Forces: An Assessment." *Air University Review* 29:6 (September-October, 1978): 46-57.

McKain, Jerry L. "Alienation: A Function of Geographical Mobility Among Families." In H.I. McCubbin, et al. (eds.), *Families in the Military System*. Beverly Hills: Sage, 1976, pp. 69-91.

"Military Family Services and Research on the Rise: Defense Department Looks for Ways to Help Its Families." *American Family* 8:3 (April, 1985): 2-7.

Minister of Finance. *Basic Facts on Federal Spending*. Ottawa: Department of Finance, 1994.

Montalvo, Frank Flores. "Family Separation in the Army: A Study of the Problems Encountered and the Caretaking Resources Used by Career Army Families." In H.I. McCubbin, et al. (eds.), *Families in the Military System*. Beverly Hills: Sage, 1976, pp. 147-73.

Morgan, Gareth. *Images of Organization*. Newbury Park: Sage Publications, 1986.

Morrison, James. "Rethinking the Military Family Syndrome." *American Journal of Psychiatry* 138:3 (March, 1981): 354-57.

Morton, Desmond. *A Military History of Canada: From Champlain to the Gulf War*. Toronto: McClelland and Stewart, 1992.

Morton, Peggy. "Women's Work Is Never Done." In *Women Unite*. Toronto: Canadian Women's Educational Press, 1972, pp. 46-48.

Moskos, Charles. "From Institution to Occupation: Trends in Military Organization." *Armed Forces and Society* 4:1 (Fall, 1977): 41-50.

Murphy, Mary Kay, et al. *Fitting In as a New Service Wife*. Harrisburg: Stackpole Books, 1966.

Neidig, Peter H. "Domestic Violence in the Military Part II: The Impact of High Levels of Work-Related Stress on Family Functioning." *Military Family* (July-August, 1985): 3-5.

New York Times. "Military Struggling to Stem an Increase in Family Violence." 23 May 1994.

O'Keefe, Ruth Ann, et al. "Military Family Service Centers." In Florence W. Kaslow, et al. (eds.), *The Military Family: Dynamics and Treatment*. New York: Guilford Press, 1984, pp. 254-68.

Organization of Spouses of Military Members (Leslie Taylor). "The Canadian Military Family: A Position Paper Defining Social and Family Problems in the Military Community." May 1986.

Organization of Spouses of Military Members. *Brief to the Senate Finance Committee on Bill C-55, Respecting the Pension Benefits Division Act.* Ottawa: September, 1992.

Orthner, Dennis K. *Families in Blue: A Study of Married and Single Parent Families in the Air Force.* Washington: Department of the Air Force, 1980.

Orthner, Dennis K., et al. "Attitudes toward Family Enrichment and Support Programs among Air Force Families." *Family Relations* 31 (July, 1982): 415-24.

Orthner, Dennis K., et al. "Family Contributions to Work Commitment." *Journal of Marriage and the Family* 48 (August, 1986): 573-81.

Orthner, Dennis K., et al. *Building Strong Army Communities* (Research Note 90-110). Alexandria, VA: United States Army Research Institute for the Behavioral and Social Sciences, 1990.

Ottawa Citizen. "No Wife No Promotion, Officer Tells Tribunal." 9 September 1992.

Pahl, J.M., and R.E. *Managers and Their Wives.* Harmondsworth: Penguin, 1971.

Papanek, Hanna. "Men, Women, and Work: Reflections on the Two-Person Career." In Joan Huber (ed.), *Changing Women in a Changing Society.* Chicago: University of Chicago Press, 1973, pp. 90-110.

Parsons, Talcott, and R.F. Bales. *Family Socialization and Interaction Process.* London: Routledge, 1956.

Pedersen, Frank A., et al. "Relationships among Geographical Mobility, Parental Attitudes and Emotional Disturbances in Children." *American Journal of Orthopsychiatry* 34 (1964): 575-80.

Pierson, Ruth Roach. *"They're Still Women after All": The Second World War and Canadian Womanhood.* Toronto: McClelland and Stewart, 1986.

Pinch, Franklin C. "Statement on Socio-Demographic Research at CFPARU [Canadian Forces Personnel Applied Research Unit] and on Problems and Research Direction on the Military Family." *Proceedings of the Regional Social Work Conference on the Canadian Military Family.* CFB Trenton, 1977, pp. 58-60.

Pinch, Franklin C. "Military Manpower and Social Change: Assessing the Institutional Fit." *Armed Forces and Society* 8:4 (Summer, 1982): 575-600.

Pittman, Joe, et al. "Predictors of Spousal Support for the Work Commitments of Husbands." *Journal of Marriage and the Family* 50 (May, 1988): 335-48.

Plul, M.S. "Child Abuse and Neglect in the Military Family." In *Proceedings of the Regional Social Work Conference on the Child in the Canadian Military Family.* CFB Trenton, 1978, pp. 38-54.

Popoff, Dr. T., et al. *The Military Family Study: Occupational Stress and Emotional Wellbeing Executive Summary.* Ottawa: Department of National Defence Operational Research and Analysis Establishment Directorate of Social and Economic Analysis, 1987.

Riley, Susan. *Political Wives.* Toronto: Deneau and Wayne Publishers, 1987.

Rose, Suzanne. "Ecological Implications of the War." In Mordecai Briemberg (ed.), *It Was, It Was Not: Essays and Art on the War against Iraq.* Vancouver: New Star Books, 1992, pp. 88-105.

Schlesinger, Benjamin. "The Military Family in Canada: Some Issues." *Le Travailleur/The Social Worker* 46:1-2 (Spring, 1978): 36-41.

Schwabe, Mario R., et al. "Violence in the Military Family." In Florence W. Kaslow, et al. (eds.), *The Military Family: Dynamics and Treatment.* New York: Guilford Press, 1984, pp. 125-46.

Seager, Joni. *Earth Follies: Coming to Feminist Terms with the Global Environmental Crisis.* New York: Routledge, 1993.

Seccombe, Wally. "The Housewife and Her Labor under Capitalism." *New Left Review* 83 (January-February, 1974).

Segal, Mady Wechsler. "The Military and the Family as Greedy Institutions." *Armed Forces and Society* 13:1 (Fall, 1986): 9-38.

Shupe, Anson, et al. *Violent Men, Violent Couples: The Dynamics of Domestic Violence.* Lexington, MA: Lexington Books, 1987.

Shwed, John A., and Murray Straus. "The Military Environment and Child Abuse." Unpublished paper, University of New Hampshire, 1979.

Smith, Dorothy E. "Women, Class and Family." In Varda Burstyn, et al., *Women, Class, Family and the State.* Toronto: Garamond, 1985, pp. 1-44.

Smith, Dorothy E. "Institutional Ethnography: A Feminist Method." *Resources for Feminist Research* 15:1 (1986): 6-13.

Smith, Dorothy E. *The Everyday World as Problematic: A Feminist Sociology.* Toronto: University of Toronto Press, 1987.

Smith, Dorothy E. "Feminist Reflections on Political Economy." In M. Patricia Connelly, et al. (eds.), *Feminism in Action: Studies in Political Economy.* Toronto: Canadian Scholars' Press, 1992, pp. 1-21.

Solomon, Zahava. "The Effect of Combat-Related Posttraumatic Stress Disorder on the Family." *Psychiatry* 51 (August, 1988): 323-29.

Spellman, Seth. "Utilization of Problem-Solving Resources among Military Families." In H.I. McCubbin, et al. (eds.), *Families in the Military System.* Beverly Hills: Sage, 1976, pp. 174-206.

Stanton, M. Duncan. "The Military Family: Its Future in the All-Volunteer Context." In Nancy Goldman, et al. (eds.), *The Social Psychology of Military Service.* Beverly Hills: Sage, 1976, pp. 135-49.

Starr, Paul D. "Military Socialization in the University: The Role of Subcultures in Navy-Marine ROTC." *Human Organization* 41:1 (Spring, 1982): 64-69.

Stoddard, Ellwyn R., et al. "The Army Officer's Wife: Social Stresses in a Complementary Role." In Nancy Goldman, et al. (eds.), *The Social Psychology of Military Service.* Beverly Hills: Sage, 1976, pp. 151-71.

Stone, Bonnie Domrose, et al. *Uncle Sam's Brides: The World of Military Wives.* New York: Walker and Company, 1990.

Sullivan, Pat. "The Forces Family: A House in Disorder?" *Legion* (October, 1988): 19-21.

Sweet, Leonard. *The Minister's Wife.* Philadelphia: Temple University Press, 1983.

Szoc, R. *Family Factors Critical to Retention*. San Diego: Naval Personnel Research and Development Center, 1982.

Taylor, Dianne J. *There's No Wife Like It*. Victoria: Braemar Books, 1985.

Toronto Star. "Woman Pilot Recalls Terror of Running Naval Sex Gantlet." 25 June 1992.

Trustram, Myna. *Women of the Regiment: Marriage and the Victorian Army*. Cambridge: Cambridge University Press, 1984.

Van Vranken, Edwin W., et al. "Family Awareness and Perceived Helpfulness of Community Supports." In Edna J. Hunter, et al. (eds.), *Military Families: Adaptation to Change*. New York: Praeger, 1978, pp. 209-21.

Walby, Sylvia. *Theorizing Patriarchy*. Oxford: Basil Blackwell, 1990.

Ward, S. "Suffer the Little Children and Their Family." *Medical Service Digest* (July, 1975): 4-20.

Waring, Marilyn. *If Women Counted: A New Feminist Economics*. New York: HarperCollins, 1988.

Wertsch, Mary Edwards. *Military Brats: Legacies of Childhood inside the Fortress*. New York: Random House, 1991.

Williams, Colonel Noel T. St. John. *Judy O'Grady and the Colonel's Lady: The Army Wife and Camp Follower Since 1660*. London: Brassey's Defence Publishers, 1988.

Williams, Theodore G. "Substance Misuse and Alcoholism in the Military Family." In Florence Kaslow and Richard I. Ridenour (eds.), *The Military Family: Dynamics and Treatment*. New York: Guilford Press, 1984, pp. 73-97.

Women's Research Centre. *Recollecting Our Lives: Women's Experience of Childhood Sexual Abuse*. Vancouver: Press Gang, 1989.

World Commission on Environment and Development. *Our Common Future*. Oxford: Oxford University Press, 1987.

Index

**AGMV
MARQUIS**

Québec, Canada
1999